FOR PERSONAL

Our Daily Bread

2023 ANNUAL GIFT EDITION

CONTENTS	PAGE
Introduction	2
Monthly Topics and Feature Articles	
JANUARY.... **Suffering and Hope:** *The Mystery of Suffering*	3
FEBRUARY... **Beatitudes:** *A Right-Side-Up Kingdom*	35
MARCH....... **Rest:** *Rest Is a Gift from God*	64
APRIL .... **Forgiveness:** *From Bitter Root to Flower of Forgiveness*	96
MAY.......... **Apologetics:** *No Need to Argue*	127
JUNE .... **Spiritual Growth:** *Growing in Christ*	159
JULY.......... **The Spirit's Leading:** *Led by the Spirit*	190
AUGUST ..... **Family of God:** *Fellow Citizens*	222
SEPTEMBER. **Biblical Theology of Mission:** *Hope Deeper than Death*	254
OCTOBER .... **Wisdom:** *Wisdom to Live Beautifully*	285
NOVEMBER.. **Making Disciples:** *Following Jesus Together*	317
DECEMBER .. **Living in a Multicultural World:** *Warm Hearts and Open Arms*	348
About the Publisher	380
Our Daily Bread Ministries Offices	381
Topic Index	382–384

INTRODUCTION

We're glad you've picked up a copy of the 2023 Annual Gift Edition of *Our Daily Bread*, which has been published to encourage believers in Jesus.

We hope the devotionals and feature articles will assist you in your walk with God. Several articles each month address a specific topic to help you grow in your understanding of it and in your faith in Christ.

Please share these devotionals with others who need to know more about the hope found in Jesus Christ.

If we can serve you, feel free to contact us.

The Our Daily Bread staff

COVER PHOTO: *Meadow with lupine flowers*
Yevhenii Chulovskyi © Shutterstock
EDITORIAL TEAM: Tom Felten, Tim Gustafson, Regie Keller, Alyson Kieda, Becky Knapp, Monica La Rose, Julie Schwab, and Peggy Willison
ACKNOWLEDGMENTS: Scripture taken from Holy Bible, New International Version®, NIV® Copyright © 1973, 1978, 1984, 2011 by Biblica, Inc.® Used by permission. All rights reserved worldwide.

© 2022 Our Daily Bread Ministries®, Grand Rapids, Michigan, USA

Internet address: ourdailybread.org • email: odb@odb.org

Printed in the United Kingdom.   ISBN: 978-1-913135-55-3

THE MYSTERY OF SUFFERING

L ife is marked by events of suffering, both great and small. Some are the by-product of a natural disaster impacting entire communities with loss, grief and sorrow. Others are the fruit of human evil that has a profound effect on the world. Still others are intensely private, affecting an individual person or a single family. In all these cases, a common thread is found—the struggle to understand suffering and why it happens.

The book of Job describes the intense suffering of Job. If you read up to chapter 38, when God finally speaks, you expect some kind of definitive answer to the problem of human suffering. Instead, the story takes a sharp turn. God doesn't give answers; He just asks questions—science questions, in fact, covering the fields of zoology, astronomy and meteorology, revealing His ultimate sovereignty over all creation.

Job stood before almighty God in dumbfounded silence. He wanted to know "Why?" but God responded with "Who?" The lesson for us is this: if God can run the universe in such a spectacular way, we can trust His love and wisdom with the inexplicable and puzzling mysteries of life. We don't know what God will do in the future for us or for our loved ones who are struggling, but we know we can trust Him.

When you're facing the mystery of suffering, read the final chapters of Job beginning with chapter 38. God, the ultimate Comforter, can be trusted.

Adapted from When You Don't Know What to Say *by Roy Clark.*

★ The topic of **SUFFERING AND HOPE** is addressed in the devotions for **January 1, 9, 16** and **23**. We trust these articles will bring you hope and encouragement.

When you pass through the waters,
I will be with you. [ISAIAH 43:2]

UNCHARTED WATERS

The crowd counts down to Big Ben chiming. The ball drops in New York's Times Square. Sydney Harbour erupts in fireworks. However your city marks it, there's something exciting about welcoming in a new year and the fresh start it brings. On New Year's Day we push out into new waters. What friendships and opportunities might we find?

For all its excitement, though, a new year can be unsettling. None of us knows the future or what storms it may hold. Many New Year's traditions reflect this: fireworks were invented in China to supposedly ward off evil spirits and make a new season prosperous. And New Year's resolutions date back to the Babylonians who made vows to appease their gods. Such acts were an attempt to make an unknown future secure.

When they weren't making vows, the Babylonians were busy conquering people—including Israel. In time, God sent the enslaved Jews this message: "Do not fear . . . . When you pass through the waters, I will be with you" (ISAIAH 43:1–2). Later, Jesus said something similar when He and the disciples were caught sailing in a violent storm. "Why are you so afraid?" He told them before commanding the waters to be still (MATTHEW 8:23–27).

Today we push out from the shore into new, uncharted waters. Whatever we face, He's with us—and He has the power to calm the waves.

SHERIDAN VOYSEY

**What possibilities excite you as you look forward
to a new year? What worries can you place in
God's hands?**

*God, thank You that whatever this new year brings,
You will be with me in it.*

The one who hears my words and does not
put them into practice is like a man who built
a house on the ground without a foundation.
[LUKE 6:49]

WHEN THE FLOODS COME

I live in Colorado, a state in the western US known for the Rocky
Mountains and our heavy annual snowfall. Yet the worst natural
disaster in my state had nothing to do with snow, but rain. A
flood occurred on 31 July, 1976. When the water finally receded,
the death toll was 144 lives, not including livestock. In the wake of
that disaster significant studies were done in the area, especially in
regard to the foundation of roads and motorways. The walls of the
roads that withstood the storm were those filled with concrete. In
other words, they had a sure and strong foundation.

In our lives the question is not *if* the floods will come, but *when*.
Sometimes we have advance notice, but usually not. Jesus stresses
a strong foundation for such times—one built by not just hearing His
words but also by living out the gospel (LUKE 6:47). That practice is
almost like pouring concrete into our lives. When the floods come,
and they will, we can withstand them because we've been "well
built" (V. 48). The absence of that practice leaves our lives vulnerable
to collapse and destruction (V. 49). It's the difference between being
wise and foolish.

It's good to pause occasionally and do a little foundation assess-
ment. Jesus will help us to fortify the weak places that we might
stand strong in His power when the floods come.   *JOHN BLASE*

What weak spots need attention in your life?
How might you work on them?

Jesus, I want to not just be a hearer but a doer as well.
Give me the vision to see weak places in my foundation
that need attention. And thank You for Your promised
presence when the floods do come.

"Lord," Martha said to Jesus, "if you had been here, my brother would not have died." [JOHN 11:21]

MOVING AT THE SPEED OF JESUS

Recently, my car needed work. The mechanic's shop was close, a mile from my home. So I decided to just walk home. But as I shuffled along next to a bustling thoroughfare, I noticed something: everyone else was moving *so* fast.

This isn't rocket science. Cars go faster than pedestrians. Zip, zip, zip! As I ambled home, I had a realisation: we're so used to moving fast. All the time. Then, another realisation: I often expect God to move just as quickly. I want His plans to fit my speedy timetable.

When Jesus lived on earth, His seemingly slow pace sometimes disappointed His friends. In John 11, Mary and Martha sent word that their brother, Lazarus, was sick. They knew Jesus could help (VV. 1–3). But He arrived some four days later (V. 17), after Lazarus had died. " 'Lord,' Martha said to Jesus, 'if you had been here, my brother would not have died' " (V. 21). Translation: Jesus didn't move fast enough. But He had bigger plans: raising Lazarus from the dead (VV. 38–44).

Can you relate to Martha's desperation? I can. Sometimes, I long for Jesus to move more quickly to answer a prayer. Sometimes, it seems like He's late. But Jesus' sovereign schedule is different from ours. He accomplishes His saving work on His timetable, not ours. And the ultimate outcome displays His glory and goodness in ways that are so much greater than our plans.   *ADAM R. HOLZ*

When have you been disappointed that Jesus seemingly didn't answer a prayer, only to realise that He was accomplishing something bigger? How did that realisation affect your perception of God and His sovereignty?

Father, sometimes I get so impatient. Help me to trust in Your perfect timing and to cling to Your goodness in faith.

Worship the LORD with gladness; come before him with joyful songs. [PSALM 100:2]

A LIFESTYLE OF WORSHIP

As I waited in the breakfast buffet line at a Christian conference centre, a group of women entered the dining hall. I smiled, saying hello to a woman who stepped into the line behind me. Returning my greeting, she said, "I know you." We scooped scrambled eggs onto our plates and tried to figure out where we'd met. But I was pretty sure she'd mistaken me for someone else.

When we returned for lunch, the woman approached me. "Do you drive a white car?"

I shrugged. "I used to. A few years ago."

She laughed. "We stopped at the same traffic light by the primary school almost every morning," she said. "You'd always be lifting your hands, singing joyfully. I thought you were worshipping God. That made me want to join in, even on tough days."

Praising God, we prayed together, hugged and enjoyed lunch.

My new friend affirmed that people notice how Jesus' followers behave, even when we think no one is watching. As we embrace a lifestyle of joyful worship, we can come before our Creator anytime and anywhere. Acknowledging His enduring love and faithfulness, we can enjoy intimate communion with Him and thank Him for His on-going care (PSALM 100). Whether we're singing praises in our cars, praying in public or spreading God's love through kind acts, we can inspire others to "praise his name" (V. 4). Worshipping God is more than a Sunday morning event.

XOCHITL DIXON

In what ways can you joyfully worship God throughout the day? When has someone else's worship led to your own?

Almighty God, please help me live to worship You with contagious joy and gratitude.

BIBLE IN A YEAR | GENESIS 10–12; MATTHEW 4

When your words came, I ate them;
they were my joy and my heart's delight.
[JEREMIAH 15:16]

A RIPENING PROCESS

Early in his fifty-year ministry in Cambridge, England, Charles Simeon (1759–1836) met a neighbouring pastor, Henry Venn, and his daughters. After the visit, the daughters remarked how harsh and self-assertive the young man seemed. In response, Venn asked his daughters to pick a peach from the trees. When they wondered why their father would want the unripe fruit, he responded, "Well, my dears, it is green now, and we must wait; but a little more sun, and a few more showers, and the peach will be ripe and sweet. So it is with Mr. Simeon."

Over the years Simeon did soften through God's transforming grace. One reason was his commitment to read the Bible and pray every day. A friend who stayed with him for a few months witnessed this practice and remarked, "Here was the secret of his great grace and spiritual strength."

Simeon in his daily time with God followed the practice of the prophet Jeremiah, who faithfully listened for God's words. Jeremiah depended on them so much that he said, "When your words came, I ate them." He mulled and chewed over God's words, which were his "joy" and "heart's delight" (JEREMIAH 15:16).

If we too resemble a sour green fruit, we can trust that God will help to soften us through His Spirit as we get to know Him through reading and obeying the Scriptures.   *AMY BOUCHER PYE*

> **How has reading the Bible changed you?**
> **Why might you sometimes not read it?**
>
> *God, the Scriptures feed me and protect me from sin.*
> *Help me to read them every day.*

See what great love the Father has lavished on
us, that we should be called children of God!
And that is what we are! [1 JOHN 3:1]

DEPTHS OF LOVE

Three-year-old Dylan McCoy had just learned to swim when
he fell through a rotted plywood covering into a forty-foot
deep, stone-walled well in his grandfather's back garden.
Dylan managed to stay afloat in ten feet of water until his father
went down to rescue him. Firefighters brought ropes to raise the
boy, but the father was so worried about his son that he'd already
climbed down the slippery rocks to make sure he was safe.

Oh, the love of a parent! Oh, the lengths (and depths) we will go
for our children!

When the apostle John wrote to believers in the early church
who were struggling to find footing for their faith as false teaching
swirled about them, he extended these words: "See what great love
the Father has lavished on us, that we should be called children of
God! And that is what we are!" (1 JOHN 3:1). Naming believers in Jesus
as "children" of God was an intimate and legal label that brought
validity to all who trust in Him.

Oh, the lengths and depths God will go for His children!

There are actions a parent will take only for their child—like Dylan's
dad descending into a well to save his son. And like the ultimate act
of our heavenly Father, who sent His only Son to gather us close to
His heart and restore us to life with Him (VV. 5–6).   *ELISA MORGAN*

> **When has God rescued you from a dark well of need?
> How have you seen Him bring you to a place of hope?**
>
> *Oh, heavenly Father, thank You for reaching into the well
> of my need to rescue me and bring me back to You!*

The earth is full of his unfailing love.
[PSALM 33:5]

CHOOSE JOY

I was taking yet another walk by myself on yet another day during the COVID-19 lockdown when words written on a driveway caught my attention. *Choose joy. Write down here what you're thankful for.* A container of chalk sat nearby. Among others, these answers had been scribbled down by passers-by: food, a home, my dad and mum, my dog, sweets, and God's love. The driveway was filled with words of gratitude.

Filled with words of gratitude. The unknown writer of Psalm 33 had a heart like that. In this psalm, he thanks God for His character and "unfailing love" (VV. 4–5), His majesty in creation (VV. 6–7), and His blessing on His people (V. 12). He praises God for His knowledge, His care and His power (VV. 13–19). The psalmist saw that the earth was full of God's goodness, and he reminded his fellow Israelites: "He is our help and our shield. In him our hearts rejoice, for we trust in his holy name" (VV. 20–21). Charles Spurgeon wrote about these verses: "Our soul, our life, must hang upon God; we are to trust him . . . with all we have and are."

God gives us many reasons to have a heart like the psalmist's that's filled with gratitude. May we trust Him, give Him the praise He deserves, and "shout for joy" (V. 3).   ANNE CETAS

What are you shouting for joy about today?
Read the psalm again to help get you started.

Heavenly Father, You are so good to me.
I thank You for . . .

God is not unjust; he will not forget your work
and the love you have shown him as you have
helped his people. [HEBREWS 6:10]

GOD OF THE INVISIBLE

"Sometimes I feel as if I'm invisible. But I so want God to
use me."

Ann was tidying up the gym room at the hotel I was
visiting when we struck up a conversation. As we talked, I discovered
she had an amazing story.

"I used to be a crack addict and prostitute living on the streets,"
she said. "But I knew God wanted me to put down my pipe and walk
with Him. One day years ago I knelt at Jesus' feet, and He set me free."

I thanked Ann for sharing what God had done for her and assured
her she wasn't invisible—He had used her in our conversation in a
beautiful way to remind *me* of His power to transform lives.

God loves to use people others might overlook. The apostle Andrew
isn't as well known as his brother Peter, but the Bible recounts that
"the first thing Andrew did was to find his brother Simon [Peter]
and tell him, 'We have found the Messiah'. . . . And he brought him
to Jesus" (JOHN 1:41–42).

Peter met Jesus through Andrew. When Andrew, one of John the
Baptist's disciples, learned about Jesus from John, he followed Jesus
and believed—and immediately told his brother. Andrew's quiet
faithfulness had an impact that would shake the world.

God values faithful service over fame. He can use us powerfully
wherever we are—even when no one is looking.   *JAMES BANKS*

Whose quiet faithfulness made a difference in your life?
How can you serve God by serving someone else today?

*Thank You for never overlooking me, Father! I'm thankful
You can use me to make a difference wherever I am.*

Get rid of all bitterness. [EPHESIANS 4:31]

DIG IT UP

When Rebecca's brother and sister-in-law started having marriage problems, Rebecca prayed earnestly for their reconciliation. But they divorced. Then her sister-in-law took the children to live with her and their dad didn't protest. Rebecca never again saw the nieces she dearly loved. Years later she said, "Because of trying to handle this sadness on my own, I let a root of bitterness start in my heart, and it began to spread to my family and friends."

The book of Ruth tells about a woman named Naomi who struggled with a heart of grief that grew into bitterness. Her husband died in a foreign land, and ten years later both her sons died. She was left destitute with her daughters-in-law, Ruth and Orpah (1:3–5). When Naomi and Ruth returned to Naomi's home country, the whole town was excited to see them. But Naomi told her friends: "The Almighty has made my life very bitter. . . . The LORD has afflicted me" (VV. 20–21). She even asked them to call her "Mara," meaning bitter.

Who hasn't faced disappointment and been tempted towards bitterness? Someone says something hurtful, an expectation isn't met or demands from others make us resentful. When we acknowledge to ourselves and God what's happening deep in our hearts, our tender Gardener can help us dig up any roots of bitterness—whether they're still small or have been growing for years—and can replace them with a sweet, joyful spirit.   *ANNE CETAS*

> **What areas of life do you tend to become bitter about? What's growing inside your heart that needs God's loving care?**
>
> *God, help me to see the goodness in life You're always displaying. And dig up any root of bitterness in my heart that dishonours You.*

🐟 **1 CORINTHIANS 6:1–6**   TUESDAY | **10 JANUARY**

The Lord's people will judge the world.
[1 CORINTHIANS 6:2]

PAPER CROWNS

After a birthday meal at my house, everyone opened party favours filled with sweets, small toys and confetti. But there was something else in the favours—a paper crown for each of us. We couldn't resist trying them on, and we smiled at each other as we sat around the table. For just a moment, we were kings and queens, even if our kingdom was a dining room littered with the remnants of our dinner.

This sparked a memory of a Bible promise I don't often think about. In the next life, all believers will share ruling authority with Jesus. Paul mentions this in 1 Corinthians 6 where he asks, "Do you not know that the Lord's people will judge the world?" (V. 2). Paul referenced this future privilege because he wanted to inspire believers to settle disputes peacefully on earth. They had been suing each other and consequently harming the reputation of other believers in their community.

We become better at resolving conflict as the Holy Spirit produces self-control, gentleness and patience within us. By the time Jesus returns and completes the Spirit's work in our lives (1 JOHN 3:2–3), we'll be ready for our eventual role as "a kingdom and priests to serve our God, and . . . reign on the earth" (REVELATION 5:10). Let's hold on to this promise that glitters in Scripture like a diamond set in a crown of gold.   *JENNIFER BENSON SCHULDT*

How does the Holy Spirit influence your words and actions when you experience conflict? How does this affect those around you?

Almighty God, thank You for the wonderful future I have with You. Help me to look to You when it's hard to cooperate with others.

BIBLE IN A YEAR | GENESIS 25–26; MATTHEW 8:1–17   13

My help comes from the LORD, the Maker of
heaven and earth. [PSALM 121:2]

LIFT UP YOUR EYES

The clouds hung low, blocking the horizon and limiting visibility
to only a few hundred yards. The minutes dragged on. The
effect on my mood was noticeable. But then, as afternoon
approached, the clouds began to break, and I saw it: beautiful Pikes
Peak, the most recognisable landmark of my city, flanked on each side
by the mountain range. A smile broke over my face. I considered that
even our physical perspective—our literal line of sight—can affect
our spiritual vision. And I was reminded of the psalmist singing, "I lift
up my eyes to the mountains" (PSALM 121:1). Sometimes we simply
need to lift our eyes a bit higher!

The psalmist pondered where his help came from, maybe because the hilltops around Israel were dotted with altars to pagan
gods and often contained robbers. Or it could have been because
the psalmist looked up beyond the hills to Mount Zion where the
temple stood, and remembered that the Maker of heaven and earth
was his covenant God (V. 2). Either way, to worship we must *look up*.
We have to lift our eyes higher than our circumstances, higher than
our troubles and trials, higher than the empty promises of the false
gods of our day. Then we can see the Creator and Redeemer, the
One who calls us by name. He's the One who will "watch over your
coming and going" today and forevermore (V. 8).   *GLENN PACKIAM*

> **How can you 'look up' today—beyond your
> circumstances—to see God? What would it look
> like to call upon Him for the help you really need?**
>
> *Dear Father, thank You that You're the Creator and
> Keeper—the One who made the heavens and the
> earth and watches over me. Help me to lift my eyes
> higher to see You and to put my trust in You.*

If anyone is in Christ, the new creation has
come: The old has gone, the new is here!
[2 CORINTHIANS 5:17]

BREAKING THE CYCLE

David's first beating came at the hands of his father on his
seventh birthday, after he accidentally broke a window. "He
kicked me and punched me," David said. "Afterwards, he
apologised. He was an abusive alcoholic, and it's a cycle I'm doing
my best to end now."

But it took a long time for David to get to this point. Most of his
teen years and twenties were spent in jail or on probation, and in
and out of addiction treatment centres. When it felt like his dreams
were entirely dashed, he found hope in a Christ-centred treatment
centre through a relationship with Jesus.

"I used to be filled with nothing but despair," David says. "Now I'm
pushing myself in the other direction. When I get up in the morning,
the first thing I tell God is that I'm surrendering my will over to Him."

When we come to God with lives shattered, whether by others'
wrongdoing or by our own, God takes our broken hearts and makes
us new: "If anyone is in Christ, . . . the old has gone, the new is here!"
(2 CORINTHIANS 5:17). Christ's love and life breaks into the cycles of
our past, giving us a new future (VV. 14–15). And it doesn't end there!
Throughout our lives, we can find hope and strength in what God
has done and continues to do in us—each and every moment.

ALYSON KIEDA

***Where were you headed when you received Jesus as your
Saviour? How does it help to know that God continues to
shape your life to increasingly resemble His?***

*Dear God, thank You for interrupting the downward
trajectory of my life and making me a new creation!
Make me ever more like You.*

But as for me, it is good to be near God.
[PSALM 73:28]

WHEN DISTANCE ISN'T GOOD

In just a matter of weeks, the dreaded COVID-19 virus turned the world upside down. "Everyone's walking around not talking to each other. There's no eye contact. It's a very eerie feeling. The tension is really high. It feels like doom." These were one person's comments in our local newspaper describing life at the beginning of lockdown. People were told to keep safe distances from each other for their own protection and for the protection of others.

Physical social distance is a good thing when it's necessary for human safety. However, this "distancing" principle doesn't apply in our relationships; especially in our relationship with God. Spiritual distance isn't good. The writer of Psalm 73 wisely concluded, "But as for me, it is good to be near God" (V. 28). But aren't there days and seasons when God seems far off? Things don't add up; life doesn't make sense. The 'wrong teams' are winning (VV. 2–15). Confusion reigns in our lives and we cry out, "God, where are you? Have you forgotten about me?"

Then we come to our senses. Sometimes it's in the context of worship (VV. 16–17) or through reading Scripture or through the encouragement of friends. Our hearts become sensitive again; prayers begin to rise from within (VV. 23–25). Our sight becomes clear and once again we recognise that "God is the strength of my heart and my portion forever" (V. 26). Even in the difficulties of life, we can be assured of God's presence and draw close to Him.   *ARTHUR JACKSON*

> **When have you felt far from God? What led to the
> renewal of your faith and a closer relationship with Him?**
>
> *God, grant me clear vision to see You even when it's
> difficult because of my circumstances.*

You stretch out your hand against the anger of
my foes. [PSALM 138:7]

OUR COMPASSIONATE GOD

The winter night was cold when someone threw a large stone
through a Jewish child's bedroom window. A star of David
had been displayed in the window, along with a menorah to
celebrate Hanukkah, the Jewish Festival of Lights. In the child's town
of Billings, Montana, thousands of people—many of them believers
in Jesus—responded to the hateful act with compassion. Choosing
to identify with the hurt and fear of their Jewish neighbours, they
pasted pictures of menorahs in their own windows.

As believers in Jesus, we too receive great compassion. Our Saviour humbled Himself to live among us (JOHN 1:14), identifying with
us. On our behalf, He, "being in very nature God . . . made himself
nothing by taking the very nature of a servant" (PHILIPPIANS 2:6–7).
Then, feeling as we feel and weeping as we weep, He died on a
cross, sacrificing His life to save ours.

Nothing we struggle with is beyond our Saviour's concern. If
someone 'throws rocks' at our lives, He comforts us. If life brings
disappointments, He walks with us through despair. "Though
the LORD is exalted, he looks kindly on the lowly; though lofty, he
sees them from afar" (PSALM 138:6). In our troubles, He preserves us,
stretching out His hand against both "the anger of [our] foes" (V. 7)
and our own deepest fears. Thank You, God, for Your compassionate
love.

PATRICIA RAYBON

In what areas of your life do you need God's compassion?
How can you show His care and love to others?

O God, I thank You for understanding my struggles and
comforting me with loving care. Remind me always to
share Your compassion with others.

Jesus answered, "I am the way and the truth and the life." [JOHN 14:6]

ALL ROADS?

"Don't get on the motorway!" That text came from my daughter one day as I was leaving work. The route home had become a virtual car park. I began trying alternate routes, but after experiencing gridlock on other roads, I gave up. The trip home would have to wait till later in the day, so I drove in the opposite direction to an athletic event my granddaughter was involved in.

Discovering that no roads would lead me home made me think about people who say that all roads lead to an eternal relationship with God. Some believe the road of kindness and good behaviour will get you there. Others choose the road of doing religious things.

Relying on those roads, however, leads to a dead end. There's only one road to take to God's eternal presence. Jesus clarified this when He said, "I am the way and the truth and the life. No one comes to the Father except through me" (JOHN 14:6). He was revealing that He was going to die to open the way for us to enter His Father's house—to His presence and the real life He provides for today and eternity.

Skip the blocked roads that don't lead to God's presence. Instead, trust Jesus as Saviour, for "whoever believes in the Son has eternal life" (3:36). And for those who already believe in Him, rest in the way He's provided.

DAVE BRANON

Why is it vital to know that only Jesus can save us?
Why are we prone to try to add to what it takes to
be welcomed into His family?

Dear God, I want to trust You for eternity.
Thank You for the salvation found in Jesus alone.

[Goliath] looked David over and saw that he was little more than a boy. [1 SAMUEL 17:42]

MIGHTY

Baby Saybie, born as a "micro-preemie" at 23 weeks, weighed only 8.6 ounces. Doctors doubted Saybie would live and told her parents they'd probably only have an hour with their daughter. However, Saybie kept fighting. A pink card near her crib declared "Tiny but Mighty." After five months in the hospital, Saybie miraculously went home as a healthy five-pound baby. And she took a world record with her: the world's tiniest surviving baby.

It's powerful to hear stories of those who beat the odds. The Bible tells us one of these stories. David, a shepherd boy, volunteered to fight Goliath—a mammoth warrior who defamed God and threatened Israel. King Saul thought David was ridiculous: "You are not able to go out against this Philistine and fight him; you are only a young man, and he has been a warrior from his youth" (1 SAMUEL 17:33). And when the boy David stepped onto the battlefield, Goliath "looked David over and saw that he was little more than a boy" (V. 42). However, David didn't step into battle alone. He came "in the name of the LORD Almighty, the God of the armies of Israel" (V. 45). And when the day was done, a victorious David stood above a dead Goliath.

No matter how enormous the problem, when God is with us there's nothing that we need to fear. With His strength, we're also mighty.   *WINN COLLIER*

When do you feel small and insignificant?
How can you see God present with you and
strengthening you despite insurmountable odds?

God, I feel tiny today. Left to myself, there's no way
forward. But I trust You to be with me and guide
me. I'm trusting in Your strength.

There before me was a throne in heaven with
someone sitting on it. [REVELATION 4:2]

WONDERFUL ONE

I n *The Wonderful Wizard of Oz,* Dorothy, the Scarecrow, the Tin
Man and the Cowardly Lion return to Oz with the broomstick
that empowered the Wicked Witch of the West. The Wizard
had promised, in return for the broomstick, that he would give the
four their deepest desires: a ride home for Dorothy, a brain for the
Scarecrow, a heart for the Tin Man and courage for the Cowardly
Lion. But the Wizard stalls and tells them to come back the next day.

While they plead with the Wizard, Dorothy's dog Toto pulls back
the curtain, behind which the Wizard spoke, to reveal that the Wizard
isn't a wizard at all. He's just a fearful, fidgety man.

It's said that the author, L. Frank Baum, had a serious problem
with God, so he wanted to send the message that only we have the
power to solve our problems.

In contrast, the apostle John pulls back the veil to reveal the
truly Wonderful One behind the 'curtain'. Words fail John (note the
repeated use of the preposition *like* in the passage), but the point
is well made: God is seated on His throne, surrounded by a sea of
glass (REVELATION 4:2, 6). Despite the troubles that plague us here
on earth (chs. 2–3), God isn't pacing the floor and biting His nails.
He's actively at work for our good, so we can experience His peace.

DAVID H. ROPER

> **What do you fear today? How does it help you to
> know that God controls the troubles that surround
> you? How can you better trust and surrender to Him?**
>
> *I'm grateful, God, that I can count on You to walk with
> me through everything. Thank You for Your peace.*

Accept one another, then, just as Christ
accepted you, in order to bring praise to God.
[ROMANS 15:7]

A LEGACY OF ACCEPTANCE

n his book *Breaking Down Walls,* Glen Kehrein writes about
climbing to the roof of his university dorm in Chicago after the
assassination of civil rights activist Dr. Martin Luther King Jr. in
1968. "The sound of gunfire bounced eerily back and forth off the
large buildings, and soon my rooftop perch provided a near pano-
ramic, yet horrific, view. . . . How in the world did I [find myself in]
a war zone in the inner city of Chicago?" Compelled by his love for
Jesus and people whose backgrounds were different from his, Glen
led a ministry in Chicago that provided food, clothing, shelter and
other services until his death in 2011.

Glen's life mirrors the efforts of believers in Jesus who've come
to grips with the need to embrace those who are different from
themselves. Paul's teaching and example helped Roman believers
see that God's plan to rescue wayward humanity included Jews *and*
gentiles (ROMANS 15:8–12). Believers are called to follow His example
of acceptance of others (V. 7); prejudice and discord have no place
among those called to glorify God with "one mind and one voice"
(V. 6). Ask God to help you cross barriers and break down walls and
to warmly embrace everyone, regardless of their differences. Let's
strive to leave behind a legacy of acceptance.   *ARTHUR JACKSON*

> **How can you be more intentional with people who are
> different from you? What steps do you need to take to
> be more in line with Jesus' embrace of all people?**
>
> *Father in heaven, help me to represent You and make
> adjustments in my thinking and actions today as I strive
> to love others well.*

You will keep in perfect peace those whose
minds are steadfast, because they trust in you.
[ISAIAH 26:3]

UNBREAKABLE FAITH

After doctors diagnosed their first-born son with autism, Diane Dokko Kim and her husband grieved facing a lifetime of caring for a cognitively disabled child. In her book *Unbroken Faith,* she admits to struggling with adjusting their dreams and expectations for their beloved son's future. Yet through this painful process, they learned that God can handle their anger, doubts and fears. Now, with their son reaching adulthood, Diane uses her experiences to encourage parents of children with special needs. She tells others about God's unbreakable promises, limitless power and loving faithfulness. She assures people that He gives us permission to grieve when we experience the death of a dream, an expectation, a way or a season of life.

In Isaiah 26, the prophet declares that God's people can trust in the Lord forever, "for the LORD . . . is the Rock eternal" (v. 4). He's able to sustain us with supernatural peace in every situation (v. 12). Focusing on His unchanging character and crying out to Him during troublesome times revitalises our hope (v. 15).

When we face any loss, disappointment or difficult circumstance, God invites us to be honest with Him. He can handle our ever-changing emotions and our questions. He remains with us and refreshes our spirits with enduring hope. Even when we feel like our lives are falling apart, God can make our faith unbreakable.   *XOCHITL DIXON*

> *Have you ever struggled with being honest with God*
> *when life feels overwhelming? How has God helped you*
> *deal with the death of a dream or expectation?*

> *Loving God, please help me believe You can always be*
> *trusted with my honest emotions.*

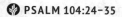

How many are your works, Lᴏʀᴅ!
[PSALM 104:24]

GOD'S FOOTPRINTS

"I know where God lives," our four-year-old grandson told my wife, Cari. "Where is that?" she asked, her curiosity piqued. "He lives in the woods beside your house," he answered.

When Cari told me about their conversation, she wondered what prompted his thinking. "I know," I responded. "When we went for a walk in the woods during his last visit, I told him that even though we can't see God, we can see the things He's done." "Do you see the footprints I'm making?" I had asked my grandson as we stepped through a sandy place by a river. "The animals and the trees and the river are like God's footprints. We know that He's been here because we can see the things He's made."

The writer of Psalm 104 also pointed to the evidence for God in creation, exclaiming "How many are your works, Lᴏʀᴅ! In wisdom you made them all; the earth is full of your creatures" (ᴠ. 24). The Hebrew word for wisdom found here is often used in the Bible to describe skilful craftsmanship. God's handiwork in nature proclaims His presence and makes us want to praise Him.

Psalm 104 begins and ends with the words: "Praise the Lᴏʀᴅ" (ᴠᴠ. 1, 35). From a baby's hand to an eagle's eye, our Creator's artistry all around us speaks of His consummate skill. May we take it all in with wonder today—and praise Him for it!   *JAMES BANKS*

Where do you see God's handiwork in creation?
How might you point someone to it—and to Him—today?

I praise You for all You've made, God! Help me to live in wonder at Your wisdom and goodness today.

Come, follow me.
[MATTHEW 19:21]

SMALL FISH

Over several years, a British couple living in West Africa developed a strong friendship with a man in their town and many times shared the love of Jesus and the story of salvation with him. Their friend, however, was reluctant to relinquish the lifetime of allegiance he had to another religion, even though he came to recognise that faith in Christ was "the greater truth". His concern was partly financial, since he was a leader in his faith and depended on the compensation he received. He also feared losing his reputation among the people in his community.

With sadness, he explained, "I'm like a man fishing with my hands in a stream. I have caught a small fish in one, but a bigger fish is swimming by. To catch the bigger fish, I have to let go of the smaller one!"

The rich young ruler in Matthew 19 had a similar problem. When he approached Jesus, he asked, "What good thing must I do to get eternal life?" (V. 16). He seemed sincere, but he didn't want to fully surrender his life to Jesus. He was rich, not only in money, but also in his pride of being a rule-follower. Although he desired eternal life, he loved something else more and rejected Christ's words.

When we humbly surrender our life to Jesus and accept His free gift of salvation, He invites us, "Come, follow me" (V. 21).

CINDY HESS KASPER

What one thing does Jesus require of us to receive salvation and the promise of eternal life with Him? What's keeping you from fully surrendering to Him?

Dear Father, thank You for offering Your Son as payment for my sin. Help me to surrender wholly to You.

So the women . . . ran to tell his disciples.
[MATTHEW 28:8]

RUNNING TO TELL

The modern-day marathon is based on the story of a Greek messenger, Pheidippides. According to legend, in 490 BC he ran approximately twenty-five miles (forty kilometres) from Marathon to Athens to announce the Greeks' victory against their formidable foe, the invading Persians. Today, people run marathons for the personal satisfaction of an athletic achievement, but Pheidippides had a greater purpose behind his effort: each of his steps was run for the sheer joy of delivering good news to his kinsmen!

Some five hundred years later, two women also ran to deliver good news—the most pivotal news in all of history. When Mary and Mary Magdalene arrived at the tomb where Jesus had been placed after His crucifixion, they found it empty. An angel told them that Jesus had "risen from the dead" and to "go quickly and tell his disciples" (MATTHEW 28:7). The women, "afraid yet filled with joy," ran to tell the disciples what they'd discovered (V. 8).

May we have the same joyful exuberance at the resurrection of Jesus, and may it invigorate us to share the good news with others. We may not even need to 'run' further than next door to find someone who needs to know about our Saviour. He won the battle against death so we might live victoriously with Him forever!

KIRSTEN HOLMBERG

Who shared the good news of Christ's resurrection with you? How will you share it with others today?

God, I rejoice because of Your victory over death. Thank You for allowing me the privilege of sharing this good news with those You've put in my life.

I am worn out from my groaning. [PSALM 6:6]

THE DEEPEST PLACES

Victor Hugo (1802–1885), a poet and novelist during the social and political upheavals of nineteenth-century France, is perhaps best known for his classic *Les Miserables.* Over a century later, a musical adaptation of his novel has become one of our generation's most popular productions. This shouldn't surprise us. As Hugo once said, "Music expresses that which cannot be said and on which it is impossible to be silent."

The psalmists would have agreed. Their songs and prayers provide us with honest reflections on life and its inevitable pain. They touch us in places we find difficult to access. For example, in Psalm 6:6 David cries out, "I am worn out from my groaning. All night long I flood my bed with weeping and drench my couch with tears."

The fact that such raw honesty is included in the inspired songs of the Scriptures gives us great encouragement. It invites us to bring our fears to God, who welcomes us into His presence for comfort and help. He embraces us in our heartfelt honesty.

Music can give us the ability to express our feelings when words are hard to come by, but whether that expression is sung, prayed or silently cried, our God reaches into the deepest places in our hearts and gives us His peace.

BILL CROWDER

How would you characterise your prayer life?
How does it make you feel to realise that God
Himself allows you to come into His presence
just as you are?

Thank You, loving God, for welcoming me with
all my pain, fear, struggles and disappointments.
Thank You that You don't want 'correct' or
'sanitised' prayers, but my honest heart instead.

Peter spoke up, "We have left everything to follow you!" [MARK 10:28]

SURRENDERING ALL

Two men remembered for serving others for Jesus left careers in the arts to commit themselves to where they believed God had called them. James O. Fraser (1886–1938) decided not to pursue being a concert pianist in England to serve the Lisu people in China, while the American Judson Van DeVenter (1855–1939) chose to become an evangelist instead of pursuing a career in art. He later wrote the hymn "I Surrender All."

While having a vocation in the arts is the perfect calling for many, these men believed God called them to relinquish one career for another. Perhaps they found inspiration from Jesus counselling the rich, young ruler to give up his possessions to follow Him (MARK 10:17–25). Witnessing the exchange, Peter exclaimed, "We have left everything to follow you!" (V. 28). Jesus assured him that God would give those who follow Him "a hundred times as much in this present age" and eternal life (V. 30). But He would give according to His wisdom: "Many who are first will be last, and the last first" (V. 31).

No matter where God has placed us, we're called to daily surrender our lives to Christ, obeying His gentle call to follow Him and serve Him with our talents and resources—whether in the home, office, community or far from home. As we do, He'll inspire us to love others, putting their needs above our own.   *AMY BOUCHER PYE*

> **Who comes to mind when you think of someone who's sacrificed for Jesus? How is God calling you to surrender?**
>
> *Jesus, help me to surrender my all for You today as I serve You and those around me for Your honour.*

Because the hand of the LORD my God was on me, I took courage and gathered leaders from Israel to go up with me. [EZRA 7:28]

RIPPLE EFFECT

The little Bible college in northern Ghana didn't look impressive—just a tin-roofed cinder-block building and a handful of students. Yet Bob Hayes poured his life into those students. He gave them leadership roles and encouraged them to preach and teach, despite their occasional reluctance. Bob passed away years ago, but dozens of thriving churches, schools and two additional Bible institutes have sprung up across Ghana—all started by graduates of that small school.

During the reign of King Artaxerxes (465–424 BC), Ezra the scribe assembled a band of Jewish exiles to return to Jerusalem. But Ezra found no Levites among them (EZRA 8:15). He needed Levites to serve as priests. So he commissioned leaders to "bring attendants to us for the house of our God" (V. 17). They did so (VV. 18–20), and Ezra led them all in fasting and prayer (V. 21).

Ezra's name means "helper", a characteristic that resides at the heart of good leadership. Under Ezra's prayerful guidance, he and his protégés would lead a spiritual awakening in Jerusalem (see chapters 9–10). All they had needed was a little encouragement and wise direction.

That's how God's church works too. As good mentors encourage and build us up, we learn to do the same for others. Such an influence will reach far beyond our lifetime. Work done faithfully for God stretches into eternity.   *TIM GUSTAFSON*

Who is your primary spiritual mentor? (If you don't have one, who might you ask to mentor you?) Why is mentoring in Christ something vital for you to receive and extend to others?

Father, show me someone I can mentor.

Hosanna to the Son of David! Blessed is he who comes in the name of the Lord! Hosanna in the highest heaven! [MATTHEW 21:9]

THE PROBLEM WITHIN

A few years ago, a woodpecker began tapping on the wall of our home. We thought the problem was only external. Then one day, my son and I climbed up a ladder into the attic only to have a bird fly past our startled faces. The problem was worse than we'd suspected: it was *inside* our house.

When Jesus arrived in Jerusalem, the crowd was hoping He would be the one to fix their external problem—their oppression by the Romans. They went wild, shouting, "Hosanna to the Son of David! Blessed is he who comes in the name of the Lord! Hosanna in the highest heaven!" (MATTHEW 21:9). This was the moment they'd been waiting for; God's appointed King had come. If God's chosen Deliverer was going to begin reforming things, wouldn't He start with all the wrong *out there*? But, in most gospel accounts, the "triumphal entry" is followed by Jesus driving out exploitative moneychangers . . . from the *temple* (VV. 12–13). He was cleaning up, and from the inside out.

That's what happens when we welcome Jesus as King; He comes to set things right—and He starts with us. He makes us confront the evil inside. Jesus on the donkey is like the warriors in the Trojan horse. The horse was welcomed as a symbol of peace, but its ultimate aim was unconditional surrender. Jesus our King requires the same from us.   *GLENN PACKIAM*

> **What does it mean for Jesus to be your King?**
> **Why is it vital for you to surrender your all to Him?**

Dear Jesus, You're the true King. Forgive me for wanting You to only fix the problems in the world around me and not to confront the sin in my heart. Show me where I'm prone to wander and expose the ways I want to run my own life.

If the Son sets you free, you will be free
indeed. [JOHN 8:36]

FREE AT LAST

Twenty long years passed before British journalist John Mc-
Carthy—a five-year hostage during Lebanon's gruelling civil
war—met the man who negotiated his release. When McCarthy
finally met U.N. envoy Giandomenico Picco, McCarthy simply said,
"Thank you for my freedom!" His heartfelt words carried great weight
because Picco had risked his own life during dangerous negotiations
to secure freedom for McCarthy and others.

We as believers can relate to such hard-won freedom. Jesus gave
up His life—enduring death on a Roman cross—to secure spiritual
freedom for all people, including each of us. Now as His children,
we know "it is for freedom that Christ has set us free," the apostle
Paul boldly declared (GALATIANS 5:1).

The gospel of John also teaches of freedom in Christ, noting, "If
the Son sets you free, you will be free indeed" (JOHN 8:36).

But free in what ways? In Jesus, we experience freedom not
only from sin and its hold on us but also from guilt, shame, worry,
Satan's lies, superstitions, false teaching and eternal death. No
longer hostages, we have freedom to show love to enemies, walk
in kindness, live with hope and love our neighbours. As we follow
the Holy Spirit's leading, we can forgive as we've been forgiven.

For all of this, let's thank God today. Then let's love so others will
know the power of His freedom too.　　　　　　*PATRICIA RAYBON*

What spiritual chains still hold you hostage?
As you release those chains to the Lord, what words
can you use to thank God for setting you free?

Dear liberating God, thank You for my freedom—
for setting me free from spiritual death and
releasing me to love.

Whoever refreshes others will be refreshed.
[PROVERBS 11:25]

IT PAYS TO GIVE

The rent was due, but the landlord's tenants couldn't pay. The husband had lost his job and his wife couldn't find extra work. Then the COVID-19 pandemic struck, with everyone in their area ordered to stay home. Thus, they all—including the landlord—faced bills. But no one could leave home to earn money.

After praying, however, the landlord waived his tenants' rent payment. As he said, "Sure, I had bills to pay, too. But I'd hate to see my tenants get sick trying to go out and make money to pay me." Grateful to God for providing for his own family, the landlord passed on practical love to his tenants.

The result? "Total peace and joy," the landlord said. "Helping my tenants gave me great contentment." Even more, "my faith in God has grown," he said. "When it comes to this year's bills, I'm no longer worried. The Lord will provide."

The Bible promises such refreshing faith for those who give loving, compassionate help to others. "One person gives freely, yet gains even more," says Proverbs 11:24. The contrast? "Another withholds unduly, but comes to poverty." This life lesson goes against logic. But simply helping others always benefits the giver.

"Whoever refreshes others will be refreshed" (V. 25). It's such a simple Bible principle. But when we reach out to help those in need, as with the landlord, we can find that God provides the faith and provision we truly need.   *PATRICIA RAYBON*

Who in your life needs your practical, loving help?
How would your faith in God grow if you offered
your loving help to others?

Compassionate God, You own everything, so encourage
me to open my hands and give practical help to others—
sharing the loving bounty You provide to me.

Six days you shall labour and do all your work,
but the seventh day is a sabbath to the LORD
your God. [DEUTERONOMY 5:13–14]

OUT OF BREATH

There's a home-improvement shop near me that has a big green button in one of its departments. If no assistant is present, you push the button, which starts a timer. If you're not served within a minute, you get a discount on your purchase.

We like being the customer in this scenario who enjoys the speedy service. But the demand for fast service often takes a toll when we're the one expected to deliver it. So many of us today feel rushed doing our jobs, working long hours, checking emails multiple times a day and feeling pressured to meet tighter and tighter deadlines. The customer service tactics of the home-improvement shop have seeped into all our lives, creating a culture of rush.

When God told the Israelites to keep a Sabbath, He added an important reason: "Remember that you were slaves in Egypt" (DEUTERONOMY 5:15). There they'd been forced to work ceaselessly under Pharaoh's excessive time constraints (EXODUS 5:6–9). Now freed, they were to give themselves a whole day each week to ensure they and those who served them could rest (DEUTERONOMY 5:14). Under God's rule, there were to be no flush-faced, out-of-breath people.

How often do you work to the point of exhaustion or get impatient with people who keep you waiting? Let's give ourselves and each other a break. A culture of rush is Pharaoh's doing, not God's.

SHERIDAN VOYSEY

***How can you resist the urge to overwork? How will you
be patient this week with people who keep you waiting?***

*Lord of the Sabbath, thank You for commanding me
to rest so I can be whole.*

If I am a man of God, may fire come down
from heaven. [2 KINGS 1:10]

WEARING OUR COURAGE

Andrew lives in a country that's closed to the gospel. When I
asked how he keeps his faith a secret, he said he doesn't. He
wears a button that advertises his church, and whenever he's
arrested he tells the police that "they need Jesus too". Andrew has
courage because he knows who's on his side.

Elijah refused to be intimidated, even when the king of Israel
sent fifty soldiers to arrest him (2 KINGS 1:9). The prophet knew God
was with him, and he called down fire that consumed the platoon.
The king sent more soldiers, and Elijah did it again (V. 12). The king
sent more, but the third platoon had heard about the others. The
captain begged Elijah to spare his soldiers' lives. They were more
afraid of him than he'd ever been of them, so the angel of the Lord
told Elijah it was safe to go with them (VV. 13–15).

Jesus doesn't want us to call down fire on our enemies. When the
disciples asked if they could call down fire on a Samaritan village,
Jesus rebuked them (LUKE 9:51–55). We're living in a different time.
But Jesus does want us to have Elijah's boldness—to be ready to
tell everyone about the Saviour who died for them. It may seem
like we're one person taking on fifty, but it's actually One against
fifty. Jesus provides what we need to courageously love and reach
out to others.   *MIKE WITTMER*

How does Jesus provide what you need to be courageous?
What does God want you to know and do?

Holy Spirit, thank You for living in me.
Fill me with courage as I tell others about Jesus.

Do not be overcome by evil, but overcome evil
with good. [ROMANS 12:21]

A FUTURE WITH FORGIVENESS

In 1994, when South Africa made the transition from government
by apartheid (imposed racial segregation) to a democracy, it faced
the difficult question of how to address the crimes committed
under apartheid. The country's leaders couldn't ignore the past, but
merely imposing harsh punishments on the guilty risked deepening
the country's wounds. As Desmond Tutu, the first black Anglican
Archbishop of South Africa, explained in his book *No Future Without
Forgiveness*, "We could very well have had justice, retributive justice,
and had a South Africa lying in ashes."

Through establishing the Truth and Reconciliation Committee, the
new democracy chose the difficult path of pursuing truth, justice
and mercy. Those guilty of crimes were offered a path to restoration—if they were willing to confess their crimes and seek to make
restitution. Only by courageously facing the truth could the country
begin to find healing.

In a way, South Africa's dilemma mirrors the struggle we all face.
We're called to pursue both justice *and* mercy (MICAH 6:8), but mercy
is often misunderstood to be a lack of accountability, while pursuing
justice can become distorted into pursuing revenge.

Our only path forward is a love that not only "hates what is evil"
(ROMANS 12:9) but also longs for the transformation and good of our
"neighbour" (13:10). Through the power of Christ's Spirit, we can learn
what it means to have a future of overcoming evil with good (12:21).

MONICA LA ROSE

> ***When have you witnessed times when the goal of mercy
> and grace seemed distorted to enable injustice? When have
> you seen both justice and mercy working in harmony?***
> *Loving God, when the pain and injustice around me breaks my heart,
> help me to still believe in Your love and power to transform and heal.
> Help me to point with my life to Your justice, mercy and love.*

A RIGHT-SIDE-UP KINGDOM

I n the Sermon on the Mount, Jesus presents the foundational ideas that describe life in His kingdom. Because these ideas are so counter-cultural to the way life is pursued in our world, scholars have referred to His teaching as the presentation of an upside-down King for an upside-down kingdom.

However, it's our world that's upside-down. We need a serious corrective to our upside-down perspective, and Jesus provides it. His opening statements of blessing—known as the Beatitudes (MATTHEW 5:3–12)—are shocking in the way they challenge our thinking. Who would describe the poor, grieving or persecuted as *blessed*? Well, Jesus would.

Jesus' statements of blessing don't constitute a path into relationship with the King or citizenship in His kingdom. They describe the person already living under the influence of the one true King. Mourners aren't blessed because they mourn; they're blessed because God will respond to their mourning with comfort (V. 4). It's not a statement of transaction but of hope and expectation. In the midst of their grief, they know that God is the God of all comfort.

In the right-side-up kingdom of Jesus, He assures us that His response to whatever we encounter will always be more than enough to carry us through. When we see that our state of blessedness comes not from life's circumstances but rather by the faithfulness of the King who cares for His people, we can begin to live life right-side-up.

Bill Crowder, Our Daily Bread *author*

★ The **BEATITUDES** and living in God's kingdom are the focus of the devotions for **February 1, 9, 16** and **23**. We trust these articles will encourage you in your walk with Christ.

Every branch that does bear fruit he prunes so
that it will be even more fruitful. [JOHN 15:2]

PRUNED TO THRIVE

A s I watched a bumblebee land lightly on the Russian sage, I
marvelled at the bush's lush branches exploding with colour.
Its brilliant blue blossoms attracted eyes and bees alike. Yet
only last Autumn, I'd wondered if it would ever blossom again. When
my wife's parents trimmed the periwinkle plant down to a stub, I'd
assumed they'd decided to get rid of it. But now I was witnessing
the radiant result of pruning that had seemed brutal to me.

The surprising beauty that results from harsh cuts may be one
of the reasons Jesus chose pruning imagery to describe God's work
among believers. In John 15, He says, "I am the true vine, and my
Father is the gardener. . . . Every branch that does bear fruit he
prunes so that it will be even more fruitful" (VV. 1–2).

Jesus' words remind us that in the good times and bad, God is
always working in us towards spiritual renewal and fruitfulness (V. 5).
During 'pruning' seasons of suffering or emotional barrenness, we
may wonder if we'll ever thrive again. But Christ encourages us to
continue to stick close to Him: "No branch can bear fruit by itself;
it must remain in the vine. Neither can you bear fruit unless you
remain in me" (V. 4).

As we continually draw spiritual nourishment from Jesus, the
resulting beauty and fruitfulness in our lives (V. 8) will show the world
God's goodness.   *ADAM R. HOLZ*

**How have you seen God use struggle in your life to produce
growth and fruitfulness? How do you think time gives us the
perspective to see God's hand at work in our lives?**

*Father, help me to trust You during difficult seasons
in my life, knowing that You are at work to bring
beauty and change.*

Everyone who [practises] these words of mine . . .
is like a wise man who built his house on the rock.
[MATTHEW 7:24]

A HOUSE ON A ROCK

As many as 34,000 homes in one state in America are at risk of collapsing due to faulty foundations. Without realising it, a concrete company pulled stone from a quarry laced with a mineral that, over time, causes concrete to crack and disintegrate. The foundations of nearly six hundred homes have already crumbled, and that number will probably skyrocket over time.

Jesus used the image of building a home atop a faulty foundation to explain the far riskier danger of building our lives on unsteady ground. He explained how some of us construct our lives on sturdy rock, ensuring that we hold steady when we face fierce storms. Others of us, however, erect our lives on sand; and when the tempests rage, our lives tumble "with a great crash" (MATTHEW 7:27). The one distinction between building on an unshakable foundation and a crumbling one is whether or not we put Christ's words "into practise" (V. 26). The question isn't whether or not we *hear* His words, but whether we *practise* them as He enables us.

There's much wisdom offered to us in this world—plus lots of advice and help—and much of it is good and beneficial. If we base our life on any foundation other than humble obedience to God's truth, however, we invite trouble. In His strength, doing what God says is the only way to have a house, a *life,* built on rock.   *WINN COLLIER*

> ***Whose wisdom, insights or opinions do you listen to the
> most? How can you better build your life's foundation by
> putting Jesus' words into practise?***
>
> *God, so much of what I experience feels unsteady and
> temporary, a life built on sand. I want to live a solid life.
> Help me to obey You.*

Though it linger, wait for it. [HABAKKUK 2:3]

WAITING FOR A BLESSING

A popular restaurant in Bangkok serves soup from a broth that has been cooking for forty-five years and is replenished a bit each day. The practice, called "perpetual stew", dates back to medieval times. Just as some leftovers taste better a few days later, the extended cooking time blends and creates unique flavours. The restaurant has won multiple awards for the most delicious broth in Thailand.

Good things often take time, but our human nature struggles with patience. The question "How long?" occurs throughout the Bible. One poignant example is from the prophet Habakkuk, who begins his book by asking, "How long, LORD, must I call for help, but you do not listen?" (HABAKKUK 1:2). Habakkuk (whose name means "grappler") prophesied God's judgement on his country (Judah) through the invasion of the ruthless Babylonian Empire, and he wrestled with how God could allow corrupt people to prosper as they exploited others. But God promised hope and restoration in His own time: "For the revelation [of God's help] awaits an appointed time . . . . Though it linger, wait for it; it will certainly come and will not delay" (2:3).

The Babylonian captivity lasted seventy years. By human reckoning that's a long time, but God is always faithful and true to His Word.

Some of God's best blessings may be long in coming. Though they linger, keep looking to Him! He prepares every blessing with perfect wisdom and care—and He's always worth waiting for. *JAMES BANKS*

What blessings are you waiting for from God?
How do you plan to worship Him regardless of
when blessings come?

Abba, Father, thank You for Your kindness and
faithfulness in every season and blessing of life.
Help me to look forward to You most of all.

Teach [these words of mine] to your children.
[DEUTERONOMY 11:19]

FAITH INVESTMENTS

On his twelfth Christmas, the boy eagerly awaited the opening of the gifts under the tree. He was yearning for a new bike, but his hopes were dashed—the last present he received was a *dictionary*. On the first page, he read: "To Charles from Mother and Daddy, 1958. With love and high hopes for your best work in school."

In the next decade, Charles did do well in school. He graduated from university and later, aviation training. He became a pilot working overseas, fulfilling his passion to help people in need and to share Jesus with them. Now some sixty years after receiving this gift, he shared the well-worn dictionary with his grandchildren. It had become for him a symbol of his parents' loving investment in his future, and Charles still treasures it. But he's even more grateful for the daily investment his parents made in building his faith by teaching him about God and the Scriptures.

Deuteronomy 11 talks about the importance of taking every opportunity to share the words of Scripture with children: "Teach them to your children, talking about them when you sit at home and when you walk along the road, when you lie down and when you get up" (V. 19).

For Charles, the eternal values planted when he was a boy bloomed into a lifetime of service for his Saviour. With God's enablement, who knows how much our investment in someone's spiritual growth will yield.

CINDY HESS KASPER

Who invested in your spiritual life as you were growing up? How can you direct children's hearts to the wisdom found in Scripture?

Loving Father, help me to invest more of my time reading the wisdom found in the Bible so that I may grow in my knowledge of You and share it with others—including children.

When did we see you sick . . . and go to visit you?
[MATTHEW 25:39]

A PEOPLE OF HEALING

Believers in Jesus, though a meagre minority, enacted a bold witness as the plagues overwhelmed the Roman Empire. According to Rodney Stark in *The Rise of Christianity*, while the wealthy managed private medical care and fled the city, believers cared for their sick neighbours, nursing them to health or caring for them until death. In the fourth century, Basil of Caesarea continued this practice by organising the first major hospital, caring for lepers.

From the church's founding through the Middle Ages and into the COVID-19 crisis, one of the sure signals of its faithfulness has been sacrificial care for the sick. Likewise, when we ignore those who suffer, we can be certain we've abandoned our calling. Scripture warns that at the end of our life when we must give account for our actions, one of the questions we'll answer is how we cared for those who were ill (MATTHEW 25:37–39). We even hear a stunning reality: to care for the sick is to care for Jesus. "Truly I tell you," He said, "whatever you did for one of the least of these . . . you did for me" (V. 40).

While this doesn't mean we're to abandon all safety and take risks with our own health, we're called to be a people of healing. As we move towards those who suffer, we enact the sacrificial life God has given us, and we directly touch and serve Jesus.　　*WINN COLLIER*

> ***Where do you see suffering or sickness?***
> ***How, with your resources and capacity,***
> ***might God call you to be a person of healing?***
>
> *God, there's suffering everywhere. And I don't*
> *know what to do about it. Would You show me?*
> *Would You make me a person of healing?*

Now you are light in the Lord. Live as children
of light. [EPHESIANS 5:8]

WHAT'S YOUR REPUTATION?

A t local high school sporting events, Ted was the largest and
loudest fan in the stands. Before a degenerative condition took
its toll on him, he stood six feet six inches tall and weighed
290 pounds. Ted's crowd-stirring chants of "Blue!" (the university's
colour) at events and games were legendary, earning him the name
"Big Blue".

But Ted's reputation in his community wasn't just for being a
great supporter of his university teams. Neither was it for the alcohol addiction he experienced as a younger man. No, he will be
remembered for his love for God and family, for his generosity and
kindness. At a four-hour service that celebrated his life, person after
person came forward to testify about the vibrant Christ-like ways
of a man who'd been rescued from darkness by the power of Jesus
through the gospel.

In Ephesians 5:8, Paul reminded believers that they "were once
darkness" but quickly noted, "but now you are light in the Lord.
Live as children of light." Such is the call for every believer in Jesus.
Children of light, like Ted, have much to offer those engulfed in this
world's darkness. "Fruitless deeds of darkness" are to be avoided
(SEE VV. 3–4, 11). Those in our communities and throughout the
world need the brilliant, distinctive witness of those upon whom
Jesus has shined (V. 14). How distinctive? As different as light is from
darkness.   *ARTHUR JACKSON*

*What are some reasons you hesitate to more intentionally
spread Christ's light in this world? Where are the places
around you that need His light?*

*Father, forgive me for my passivity about being light.
Lead me and use me as light in the dark spaces of this world.*

But David found strength in the LORD his God.
[1 SAMUEL 30:6]

RECOVERING WHAT'S LOST

At the phone shop, the young pastor steeled himself for bad news. His smart phone, accidentally dropped during our Bible class, was a total loss, right? Actually, no. The shop assistant recovered all of the pastor's data, including his Bible videos and photos. She also recovered "every photo I'd ever deleted," he said. The shop also "replaced my broken phone with a brand-new phone." As he said, "I recovered all I had lost and *more.*"

David once led his own recovery mission after an attack by the vicious Amalekites. Spurned by Philistine rulers, David and his army discovered the Amalekites had raided and burned down their town of Ziklag—taking captive "the women and everyone else in it," including all their wives and children (1 SAMUEL 30:2–3). "So David and his men wept aloud until they had no strength left to weep" (V. 4). The soldiers were so bitter with their leader David that they talked of "stoning him" (V. 6).

"But David found strength in the LORD his God" (V. 6). As God promised, David pursued the Amalekites and "recovered everything the Amalekites had taken . . . . Nothing was missing: young or old, boy or girl, plunder or anything else they had taken. David brought everything back" (VV. 18–19). As we face spiritual attacks that rob us even of hope, may we find renewed strength in God. He will be with us in every challenge of life.   *PATRICIA RAYBON*

*What spiritual attacks or life loss are you experiencing?
Turning from your despair to God, how will you find
renewed strength in Him?*

*God, help me to find hope in You even as I face
life's challenges.*

Believe in the light . . . so that you
may become children of light. [JOHN 12:36]

TRUST THE LIGHT

The weather forecast said *bomb cyclone*. That's what happens when a winter storm rapidly intensifies as the atmospheric pressure drops. By the time night fell, the blizzard conditions made the road to the airport almost impossible to see. Almost. But when it's your daughter who's flying home to visit, you do what you have to do. You pack extra clothes and water (just in case you get stranded on the motorway), drive very slowly, pray without ceasing and last but not least, trust your headlights. And sometimes you can achieve the almost impossible.

Jesus foretold of a storm on the horizon, one that would involve His death (JOHN 12:31–33), and one that would challenge His followers to stay faithful and serve (V. 26). It was going to get dark and be almost impossible to see. Almost. So what did Jesus tell them to do? Believe, or trust, the Light (V. 36). That was the only way they could keep going forward and stay faithful.

Jesus would only be with them a little while longer. But believers have His Spirit as our constant guide to light the way. We too will face dark times when it's almost impossible to see the way ahead. *Almost.* But by believing, or trusting in the Light, we can press on.

JOHN BLASE

What dark season have you been through lately?
How did Jesus, the Light, help you keep going?

Jesus, thank You for being the light in my darkness.
Help me to trust and keep going.

Set your minds on things above, not on
earthly things. [COLOSSIANS 3:2]

LOOKING UP

The cockeyed squid lives in the ocean's 'twilight zone' where sunlight barely filters through the deep waters. The squid's nickname is a reference to its two extremely different eyes: the left eye develops over time to become considerably larger than the right—almost twice as big. Scientists studying the mollusc have deduced that the squid uses its right eye, the smaller one, to look down into the darker depths. The larger, left eye, gazes upwards, towards the sunlight.

The squid is an unlikely depiction of what it means to live in our present world and also in the future certainty we await as people who "have been raised with Christ" (COLOSSIANS 3:1). In Paul's letter to the Colossians, he insists we ought to "set [our] minds on things above" because our lives are "hidden with Christ in God" (VV. 2–3).

As earth-dwellers awaiting our lives in heaven, we keep an eye trained on what's happening around us in our present reality. But just as the squid's left eye develops over time into one that's larger and more sensitive to what's happening overhead, we, too, can grow in our awareness of the ways God works in the spiritual realm. We may not have yet fully grasped what it means to be alive in Jesus, but as we look 'up', our eyes will begin to see it more and more.

KIRSTEN HOLMBERG

How can you develop your 'upwards' vision?
How can you set your mind on heavenly things?

*Loving God, help me to set my mind and heart on
those things that are of You!*

Simeon . . . was righteous and devout. He was
waiting for the consolation of Israel, and the
Holy Spirit was on him. [LUKE 2:25]

WAITING IN HOPE

n the movie *Hachi: A Dog's Tale,* a university professor befriended
a stray Akita puppy named Hachi. The dog expressed his loyalty
by waiting at the train station each day for the professor to
return from work. One day, the professor suffered a fatal stroke.
Hachi waited hours at the train station, and for the next ten years
he returned each day—awaiting His loving master.

Luke tells the story of a man named Simeon who patiently waited
for the coming of his Master (LUKE 2:25). The Holy Spirit revealed to
Simeon that he would not see death until he saw the Messiah (V. 26).
As a result, Simeon kept waiting for the One who would provide
"salvation" for God's people (V. 30). When Mary and Joseph entered
the temple with Jesus, the Holy Spirit whispered to Simeon that He
was the One! The wait was finally over! Simeon held Christ in his
arms—the hope, salvation and comfort for all people (VV. 28–32).

If we find ourselves in a season of waiting, may we hear the
words of the prophet Isaiah with fresh ears: "Those who hope in
the LORD will renew their strength. They will soar on wings like
eagles; they will run and not grow weary, they will walk and not be
faint" (ISAIAH 40:31). As we await Jesus' return, He provides the hope
and strength we need for each new day.   *MARVIN WILLIAMS*

> **When have you become weary as you waited for God? What**
> **encouraged you to endure during that challenging season?**
>
> *Jesus, I will wait for You. Through pain, tears and uncertainty,*
> *help me to not become weary but to rest in Your provision.*

Be still before the LORD and wait patiently for him.
[PSALM 37:7]

THE TICKING WATCH

A group of workers were cutting ice out of a frozen lake and storing it in an icehouse when one of them realised he'd lost his watch in the windowless building. He and his friends searched for it in vain.

After they gave up, a young boy who'd seen them exit went into the building. Soon, he emerged with the watch. Asked how he'd found it, he replied: "I just sat down and kept quiet, and soon I could hear it ticking."

The Bible talks much about the value of being still. And no wonder, for God sometimes speaks in a whisper (1 KINGS 19:12). In the busyness of life, it can be hard to hear Him. But if we stop rushing about and spend some quiet time with Him and the Scriptures, we may hear His gentle voice in our thoughts.

Psalm 37:1–7 assures us that we can trust God to rescue us from the "wicked schemes" of evil people, give us refuge and help us stay faithful. But how can we do this when turmoil is all around us?

Verse 7 suggests: "Be still before the LORD and wait patiently for him." We could start by learning to keep silent for a few minutes after prayer. Or by quietly reading the Bible and letting the words soak into our hearts. And then, perhaps, we'll hear His wisdom speaking to us, quiet and steady as a ticking watch.　　*LESLIE KOH*

How can you be still before God each day?
What will help you stay silent and listen?

Loving God, grant me the patience and discipline
to stay still for a while each day, that I might hear
Your gentle whisper in my life.

The wedding of the Lamb has come.
[REVELATION 19:7]

A JOYFUL CELEBRATION

My friend Sharon passed away one year prior to the death of my friend Dave's teenage daughter Melissa. They both had been tragically killed in car accidents. One night both Sharon and Melissa were in my dream. They giggled and talked as they hung streamers in a large banquet hall and ignored me when I stepped into the room. A long table with white tablecloths had been set with golden plates and goblets. I asked if I could help decorate, but they didn't seem to hear me and kept working.

But then Sharon said, "This party is Melissa's wedding reception."

"Who's the groom?" I asked.

Neither responded but smiled and looked at each other knowingly. Finally, it dawned on me—it's Jesus!

"Jesus is the groom," I whispered as I woke up.

My dream brings to mind the joyful celebration believers in Jesus will share together when He returns. It's portrayed in Revelation as a lavish feast called "the wedding supper of the Lamb" (19:9). John the Baptist, who prepared people for the first coming of Christ, had called Him "the Lamb of God, who takes away the sin of the world" (JOHN 1:29). He also referred to Jesus as "the bridegroom" and to himself as the "friend" (like the best man) who waited for Him (3:29).

On that banquet day and for all eternity we will enjoy unbroken fellowship with Jesus, our groom, and with Sharon and Melissa and all of God's people.   *ANNE CETAS*

***What does Jesus' invitation to come to Him for forgiveness and
eternal life mean to you? Who could you tell your story to?***

*I look forward to that day of celebration and seeing You,
Jesus. Come quickly.*

See, I am doing a new thing! . . . I am making
. . . streams in the wasteland. [ISAIAH 43:19]

SOMETHING NEW

Farming is difficult in areas that lack fresh water. To help solve this problem, the Seawater Greenhouse company has created something new: "cooling houses" in Somaliland, Africa, and other countries with similar climates. Cooling houses use solar pumps to drizzle saltwater over walls made of corrugated cardboard. As the water moves down each panel, it leaves its salt behind. Much of the remaining fresh water evaporates inside the structure, which becomes a humid place where fruit and vegetable crops can flourish.

Through the prophet Isaiah, God promised to do a "new thing" as He provided "streams in the wasteland" for ancient Israel (ISAIAH 43:19). This new thing contrasted with the old thing He had done to rescue His people from the Egyptian army. Remember the Red Sea account? God wanted His people to recall the past but not let it overshadow His current involvement in their lives (V. 18). He said, "See, I am doing a new thing! Now it springs up; do you not perceive it? I am making a way in the wilderness" (V. 19).

While *looking* to the past can bolster our faith in God's provision, *living* in the past can blind us to all the fresh work of God's Spirit today. We can ask God to show us how He's currently moving—helping, remaking and sustaining His people. May this awareness prompt us to partner with Him to meet the needs of others, both near and far.　　　　　　　　　　　*JENNIFER BENSON SCHULDT*

What new thing is God doing in your life?
How is He using you to touch others' lives
and help make the world a better place?

Dear God, I praise You as the living One who
constantly does new things. Help me to trust
You to meet my changing needs.

I sought the LORD, and he answered me.
[PSALM 34:4]

SENDING OUT AN SOS

When the hut of a settler in a mountainous region of Alaska caught fire, the settler was left without adequate shelter and with few provisions—in the middle of a frigid winter. Three weeks later, the man was finally rescued when an aircraft flew over and spied the large SOS he had stamped out in the snow and darkened with soot.

The psalmist David was certainly in dire straits. He was being pursued by jealous King Saul who sought to kill him. And so he fled to the city of Gath, where he pretended to be insane in order to preserve his life (SEE 1 SAMUEL 21). Out of those events emerged Psalm 34, where David cried out in prayer to God and found peace (VV. 4, 6). God heard his pleas and delivered him.

Are you in a desperate situation and crying out for help? Be assured that God still hears and responds to our desperate prayers today. As with David, He's attentive to our distress calls and takes away our fears (V. 4)—and sometimes even saves us "out of [our] troubles" (V. 6).

Scripture invites us to "cast [our] cares on the LORD and he will sustain [us]" (PSALM 55:22). When we turn our difficult circumstances over to God, we can trust that He'll provide the help we need. We're secure in His capable hands.   *ALYSON KIEDA*

When have you felt peace after crying out to God?
When has He rescued you from a desperate situation?

Loving Father, thank You for hearing my prayers and bringing comfort, peace—whatever I need most. And thank You especially for rescuing me from my sin.

The Son is the image of the invisible God, the firstborn over all creation. [COLOSSIANS 1:15]

SPITTING IMAGE

During an outing, we met a woman who had known my husband's family since he was a child. She looked from Alan to our son, Xavier. "He's the spitting image of his daddy," she said. "Those eyes. That smile. Yep. Looks just like him." As the woman delighted in acknowledging such a strong resemblance between father and son, she even noted similarities in their personalities. Still, though they are alike in many ways, my son doesn't reflect his father perfectly.

There's only one Son—Jesus—who reflects His Father completely. Christ is the "image of the invisible God, the firstborn over all creation" (COLOSSIANS 1:15). In Him and through Him and for Him all things were created (V. 16). "He is before all things, and in him all things hold together" (V. 17).

We can spend time in prayer and Bible study, discovering the Father's character by looking at Jesus—God in the flesh. He invites us to witness His love in action by examining how He interacts with others in Scripture and in our day-to-day living. After surrendering our lives to Christ and receiving the gift of the Holy Spirit, we can grow in knowing and trusting our loving Father. He transforms us to reflect His character, so we can live for Him.

What a joy it would be if others could say we look just like Jesus!

XOCHITL DIXON

What character trait of Jesus have you seen cultivated in your life over the last year? What trait would you like to cultivate in the coming year?

Lord Jesus, please help me know You more as You make me more like You!

Do not conform to the pattern of this world.
[ROMANS 12:2]

THINKING DIFFERENTLY

During university, I spent a good chunk of a summer in Venezuela. The food was astounding, the people delightful, the weather and hospitality beautiful. Within the first day or two, however, I recognised that my views on time management weren't shared by my new friends. If we planned to have lunch at noon, this meant anywhere between 12:00 and 1:00 p.m. The same for meetings or travel: timeframes were approximations without rigid punctuality. I learned that my idea of 'being on time' was far more culturally formed than I'd realised.

All of us are shaped by the cultural values that surround us, usually without us even noticing. Paul calls this cultural force the "world" (ROMANS 12:2). Here, "world" doesn't mean the physical universe, but rather refers to the ways of thinking pervading our existence. It refers to the unquestioned assumptions and guiding ideals handed to us simply because we live in a particular place and time.

Paul warns us to be vigilant to "*not* conform to the pattern of this world." Instead, we must be "transformed by the renewing of [our] mind" (V. 2). Rather than passively taking on the ways of thinking and believing that engulf us, we're called to actively pursue God's way of thinking and to learn how to understand His "good, pleasing and perfect will" (V. 2). May we learn to follow God rather than every other voice.   *WINN COLLIER*

> *How would you describe the values and assumptions*
> *that surround you? What would it look like for you*
> *to not conform to the world's ways and to instead*
> *follow Jesus' ways?*
>
> *God, I don't even recognise my assumptions and*
> *values most of the time. Help me to live out Your*
> *truth and Your mind in it all.*

You did not . . . have regard for the One who
planned it long ago. [ISAIAH 22:11]

DESPERATE SOLUTIONS

I n the late sixteenth century, William of Orange intentionally
flooded much of his nation's land. The Dutch monarch resorted
to such a drastic measure in an attempt to drive out the invading
Spaniards. It didn't work, and a vast swath of prime farmland was lost
to the sea. "Desperate times call for desperate measures," they say.

In Isaiah's day, Jerusalem turned to desperate measures when the
Assyrian army threatened them. Creating a water storage system to
endure the siege, the people also tore down houses to shore up the
city walls. Such tactics may have been prudent, but they neglected
the most important step. "You built a reservoir between the two
walls for the water of the Old Pool," God said, "but you did not look
to the One who made it, or have regard for the One who planned
it long ago" (ISAIAH 22:11).

We aren't likely to encounter a literal army outside our homes
today. "The batterings always come in commonplace ways and
through commonplace people," said Oswald Chambers. Yet, such
"batterings" are genuine threats. Thankfully, they also bring with
them God's invitation to turn to Him *first* for what we need.

When life's irritations and interruptions come, will we see them
as opportunities to turn to God? Or will we seek our own desperate
solutions?　　　　　　　　　　　　　　　　　　*TIM GUSTAFSON*

What ordinary threats do you face today?
What do you need to face them?

Today, loving God, I turn to You first with all of my
challenges, large and small.

How good it is to sing praises to our God.
[PSALM 147:1]

REMEMBER TO SING

Nancy Gustafson, a retired opera singer, was devastated when she visited her mother and observed her decline from dementia. Her mum no longer recognised her and barely spoke. After several monthly visits, Nancy had an idea. She started singing to her. Her mother's eyes lit up at the musical sounds, and she began singing too—for twenty minutes! Then Nancy's mum laughed, joking they were "The Gustafson Family Singers!" The dramatic turnaround suggested the power of music, as some therapists conclude, to evoke lost memories. Singing old favourites has also been shown to boost mood, reduce falls, lessen visits to the emergency room and decrease the need for sedative drugs.

More research is underway on a music-memory link. Yet, as the Bible reveals, the joy that comes from singing is a gift from God—and it's real. "How good it is to sing praises to our God, how pleasant and fitting to praise him!" (PSALM 147:1).

Throughout the Scriptures, in fact, God's people are urged to lift their voices in songs of praise to Him. "Sing to the LORD, for he has done glorious things" (ISAIAH 12:5). "He put a new song in my mouth, a hymn of praise to our God. Many will see and fear the LORD and put their trust in him" (PSALM 40:3). Our singing inspires us but also those who hear it. May we all remember: our God is great and worthy of praise. *PATRICIA RAYBON*

What role does singing play in your life? How can you make more time for singing songs of praise with those who are experiencing memory problems?

May I sing praises to You, God. Thank You for so often unlocking minds through the beauty and power of song.

BIBLE IN A YEAR | LEVITICUS 23-24; MARK 1:1-22   53

In the pride of your heart you say, "I am a god."
[EZEKIEL 28:2]

WE'RE NOT GOD

In *Mere Christianity,* C. S. Lewis recommended asking ourselves some questions to find out if we're proud: "How much do I dislike it when other people snub me, or refuse to take any notice of me, . . . or patronise me, or show off?" Lewis saw pride as a vice of the "utmost evil" and the chief cause of misery in homes and nations. He called it a "spiritual cancer" that eats up the very possibility of love, contentment and even common sense.

Pride has been a problem throughout the ages. Through the prophet Ezekiel, God warned the leader of the powerful coastal city of Tyre against his pride. He said the king's pride would result in his downfall: "Because you think you are . . . as wise as a god, I am going to bring foreigners against you" (EZEKIEL 28:6–7). Then he would know he wasn't a god, but a mortal (V. 9).

In contrast to pride is humility, which Lewis named as a virtue we receive through knowing God. Lewis said that as we get in touch with Him, we become "delightedly humble," feeling relieved to be rid of the silly nonsense about our own dignity that previously made us restless and unhappy.

The more we worship God, the more we'll know Him and the more we can humble ourselves before Him. May we be those who love and serve with joy and humility.   *AMY BOUCHER PYE*

How did you answer Lewis' questions about whether or not you're proud? Did that surprise you? Why or why not?

Almighty God, help me to revel in my identity as one You created, knowing You are great and mighty and yet You love me.

Though [we] may stumble, [we] will not fall.
[PSALM 37:24]

WE WILL NOT BREAK

In the early, harrowing days of the global coronavirus pandemic, Dr. Craig Smith posted a note to his hospital colleagues every day. In one memo, after outlining their dire reality (the skyrocketing cases, the impending need for ventilators and ICU rooms), he closed with this powerful image: "A forest of bamboo bends to the ground in a typhoon but rarely breaks. We are that forest and we must not break."

There are critical moments—tragedy, heartache, sickness, financial loss, family disintegration, national catastrophe—when we must gather our wits, steady our courage and refuse to surrender. We face the impossible challenge, and we know that we must not break.

And yet, we also know that if we're left only to our own strength and resources, we're doomed. If we're to hold fast, we need God to help us. Thankfully, as we surrender our future to God and fix our hope in Him, we discover how "the LORD makes firm [our] steps" (PSALM 37:23). We discover that even though we "may stumble, [we] will not fall, for the LORD upholds [us] with his hand" (V. 24).

Our resilience rests not on our vigour, effectiveness or tenacity but in knowing that our God is with us. He upholds us. And we trust that in Him we will not break.   *WINN COLLIER*

> **What causes you to stumble and threaten to break? How can you lean into God when you face those challenges?**

*God, I'm wavering. I'm bending in the storm.
But I trust that You're with me. I trust that
You're all I need in this treacherous place.*

He has given us his very great and precious
promises. [2 PETER 1:4]

UNIMAGINABLE PROMISES

n our moments of greatest failure, it can be easy to believe it's
too late for us, that we've lost our chance at a life of purpose and
worth. That's how Elias, a former inmate at a maximum-security
prison, described feeling as a prisoner. "I had broken . . . promises,
the promise of my own future, the promise of what I could be."

It was the university degree programme he took in prison that began
to transform Elias' life. While on the programme, he participated
on a debate team, which in 2015 debated a team from Harvard—and
won. For Elias, being "part of the team . . . [was] a way of proving
that these promises weren't completely lost."

A similar transformation happens in our hearts when we begin to
understand that the good news of God's love in Jesus is good news
for us too. *It's not too late,* we begin to realise with wonder. *God
still has a future for me.*

And it's a future that can neither be earned nor forfeited, dependent only on God's extravagant grace and power (2 PETER 1:2–3).
A future where we're set free from the despair in the world and
in our hearts into one filled with His "glory and goodness" (V. 3). A
future secure in Christ's unimaginable promises (V. 4); and a future
transformed into the "freedom and glory of the children of God"
(ROMANS 8:21).　　　　　　　　　　　　　　　　*MONICA LA ROSE*

> *Why can it be difficult for us to accept unearned grace and
> love? How does it touch your heart to consider that in God's
> eyes you have a future filled with unimaginable beauty?*
>
> *Jesus, some days all I can see is the ways I've disappointed
> myself and others, the ways I've broken the future I've
> dreamed of. Help me to see the unchanging beauty of the
> future I find in You.*

For those God foreknew he also predestined
to be conformed to the image of his Son.
[ROMANS 8:29]

LIKE JESUS

As a boy, theologian Bruce Ware was frustrated that 1 Peter 2:21–23 calls us to be like Jesus. Ware wrote of his youthful exasperation in his book *The Man Christ Jesus*. "Not fair, I determined. Especially when the passage says to follow in the steps of one 'who did no sin.' This was totally outlandish. . . . I just couldn't see how God could really mean for us to take it seriously."

I understand why Ware would find such a biblical challenge so daunting! An old chorus says, "To be like Jesus, to be like Jesus. My desire, to be like Him." But as Ware rightly noted, we are incapable of doing that. Left to ourselves, we could never become like Jesus.

However, we're *not* left to ourselves. The Holy Spirit has been given to the child of God, in part so that Christ *can* be formed in us (GALATIANS 4:19). So it should come as no surprise that in Paul's great chapter on the Spirit we read, "For those God foreknew he also predestined to be conformed to the image of his Son" (ROMANS 8:29). God will see His work completed in us. And He does it through the Spirit of Jesus living in us.

As we yield to the Spirit's work in us, we truly become more like Jesus. How comforting to know that's God's great desire for us!

BILL CROWDER

What attribute of the fruit of the Spirit would you like
to live out to a greater degree? (see Galatians 5:22–23).
What will help you do so?

Father, I long to be more like Your Son but so often fall short in
word, thought, or deed. Forgive me, and help me to yield to the
work of Your Spirit so that Jesus might be formed in me.

Let your light shine before others, that they
may see your good deeds and glorify your
Father in heaven. [MATTHEW 5:16]

TURN ON THE LIGHT

As my husband and I prepared to move far away, I wanted to ensure that we kept in touch with our grown sons. I found a unique gift, friendship lamps connected by wireless internet, which can be turned on remotely. When I gave the lamps to my sons, I explained that their lamps will turn on when I touch my lamp—to provide a shining reminder of my love and on-going prayers. No matter how great the distance between us, a tap on their lamps would trigger a light in our home too. Though we knew nothing could replace our more personal moments of connection, we could be encouraged by knowing we're loved and prayed for every time we turned on those lights.

All God's children have the privilege of being light-sharers powered by the Holy Spirit. We're designed to live as radiant beacons of God's everlasting hope and unconditional love. When we're sharing the gospel and serving others in the name of Jesus, we become brilliant spotlights and living testimonies. Every good deed, kind smile, gentle word of encouragement and heartfelt prayer produces a beaming reminder of God's faithfulness and His unconditional and life-transforming love (MATTHEW 5:14–16).

Wherever God leads us, and however we serve Him, we can be used by Him to help others shine His light. As God, by His Spirit, provides the true illumination, we can reflect the light and love of His presence.

XOCHITL DIXON

How can you be a light for Christ, intentionally expressing His love to those in your sphere of influence this week? How can you shine a light on God's love as you serve people who don't know Him?

Loving Father, please fuel me with Your perfect truth and love so I can shine a spotlight on You by loving You and others wherever I go.

Two are better than one . . . If either of
them falls down, one can help the other up.
[ECCLESIASTES 4:9–10]

NEVER ALONE

"I t can be an affliction more harrowing than homelessness,
hunger or disease," wrote Maggie Fergusson in *The Economist's 1843* magazine. Her subject? Loneliness. Fergusson
chronicled the increasing rates of loneliness, irrespective of one's
social or economic status, using heart-wrenching examples of what
it feels like to be lonely.

The hurt of feeling alone isn't new to our day. Indeed, the pain of
isolation echoes off the pages of the ancient book of Ecclesiastes.
Often attributed to King Solomon, the book captures the sorrow of
those who seem to lack any meaningful relationships (4:7–8). The
speaker lamented that it's possible to acquire significant wealth and
yet experience no value from it because there's no one to share it with.

But the speaker also recognised the beauty of companionship,
writing that friends help you accomplish more than you could
achieve on your own (V. 9); companions help in times of need (V. 10);
partners bring comfort (V. 11); and friends can provide protection in
difficult situations (V. 12).

Loneliness is a significant struggle—God created us to offer and
receive the benefits of friendship and community. If you're feeling
alone, pray that God would help you form meaningful connections
with others. In the meantime, find encouragement in the reality
that the believer is never truly alone because Jesus' Spirit is always
with us (MATTHEW 28:20).   *LISA M. SAMRA*

> ***How might you reach out to someone who's lonely?***
> ***How have you experienced the blessing of God's Spirit***
> ***with you when you've felt alone?***
>
> *Heavenly Father, when I feel lonely, give me courage to*
> *reach out to others with an offer of friendship.*

Jerusalem, Jerusalem . . . how often I have
longed to gather your children together, as
a hen gathers her chicks under her wings.
[MATTHEW 23:37]

TO BE HUMAN

"**M**r. Singerman, why are you crying?" asked twelve-year-old
Albert as he watched the master craftsman construct
a wooden box.

"I cry," he said, "because my father cried, and because my grandfather cried." The woodworker's answer to his young apprentice
provides a tender moment in an episode of *Little House on the
Prairie.* "Tears," explained Mr. Singerman, "come with the making
of a coffin."

"Some men don't cry because they fear it is a sign of weakness,"
he said. "I was taught that a man is a man because he *can* cry."

Emotion must have welled up in the eyes of Jesus as He compared
His concern for Jerusalem to the care of a mother hen for her chicks
(MATTHEW 23:37). His disciples were often confused by what they saw
in His eyes or heard in His stories. His idea of what it meant to be
strong was different. It happened again as they walked with Him
from the temple. Calling His attention to the massive stone walls
and magnificent decor of their place of worship (24:1), the disciples
noted the strength of human accomplishment. Jesus saw a temple
that would be levelled in AD 70.

Christ shows us that healthy people know when to cry and why.
He cried because His Father cares and His Spirit groans for children
who couldn't yet see what breaks His heart.   *MART DEHAAN*

*In what situations in your life might you be avoiding grief?
How can your faith in a Saviour who cries (John 11:35) help
you express your grief in a healthy way?*

*Father, please replace any cold illusions of strength I cling to
with a growing understanding of the cares and concerns that
break Your heart for children like me.*

When I am afraid, I put my trust in you.
[PSALM 56:3]

FACING FEAR

Warren moved to a small town to pastor a church. After his ministry had some initial success, one of the locals turned on him. Concocting a story accusing Warren of horrendous acts, the man took the story to the local newspaper and even printed his accusations on pamphlets to post through the letterboxes of the local residents. Warren and his wife started praying hard. If the lie was believed, their lives would be upended.

King David once experienced something similar. He faced an attack of slander by an enemy. "All day long they twist my words," he said, "all their schemes are for my ruin" (PSALM 56:5). This sustained assault left him fearful and tearful (V. 8). But in the midst of the battle, he prayed this powerful prayer: "When I am afraid, I put my trust in you. . . . What can mere mortals do to me?" (VV. 3–4).

David's prayer can be a model for us today. *When I am afraid*—in times of fear or accusation, we turn to God. *I put my trust in you*—we place our battle in God's powerful hands. *What can mere mortals do to me?*—facing the situation with Him, we remember how limited the powers against us really are.

The newspaper ignored the story about Warren. For some reason, the pamphlets were never distributed. What battle do you fear today? Talk to God. He's willing to fight it with you. *SHERIDAN VOYSEY*

What real fears do you face?
How can David's prayer help you deal with them?

Loving God, I'm afraid—and so today I put my trust in You.
What can mere mortals do to me when You're fighting for
me? Thank You for the coming victory.

I have been crucified with Christ and I no
longer live, but Christ lives in me. The life I now
live in the body, I live by faith in the Son of
God, who loved me and gave himself for me.
[GALATIANS 2:20]

NO LONGER YOURSELF

I n the summer of 1859, Monsieur Charles Blondin became the first
person to cross Niagara Falls on a tightrope—something he would
go on to do hundreds of times. Once he did it with his manager
Harry Colcord on his back. Blondin gave Colcord these instructions:
"Look up, Harry . . . you are no longer Colcord, you are Blondin. . . . If
I sway, sway with me. Do not attempt to do any balancing yourself.
If you do, we will both go to our death."

Paul, in essence, said to the Galatian believers: *You can't walk
the line of living a life that is pleasing to God apart from faith in
Christ. But here's the good news—you don't have to!* No amount of
attempting to earn our way to God will ever cut it. So are we passive
in our salvation? No! Our invitation is to cling to Christ. Clinging to
Jesus means putting to death an old, independent way of living; it's
as if we ourselves have died. Yet, we go on living. But "the life [we]
now live in the body, [we] live by faith in the Son of God, who loved
[us] and gave himself for [us]" (GALATIANS 2:20).

Where are we trying to walk the tightrope today? God hasn't
called us to walk out on the rope to Him; He's called us to cling to
Him and walk this life with Him. *GLENN PACKIAM*

> **How can you stop trying to please God on your own?**
> **Where do you need to cling to Jesus today, trusting His**
> **righteousness?**

> *Dear Jesus, thank You for doing for me what I could never do*
> *for myself. I turn away from trying to please You on my own.*
> *I'm so glad I don't need to earn Your love.*

[God's] compassions never fail. They are new
every morning. [LAMENTATIONS 3:22–23]

NEW EVERY MORNING

My brother Paul grew up battling severe epilepsy, and when
he entered his teenage years it became even worse. Night-
time became excruciating for him and my parents, as he'd
experience continuous seizures for often more than six hours at a
time. Doctors couldn't find a treatment that would alleviate the
symptoms while also keeping him conscious for at least part of the
day. My parents cried out in prayer: "God, oh God, help us!"

Although their emotions were battered and their bodies exhausted,
Paul and my parents received enough strength from God for each
new day. In addition, my parents found comfort in the words of the
Bible, including the book of Lamentations. Here Jeremiah voiced his
grief over the destruction of Jerusalem by the Babylonians, remembering "the bitterness and the gall" (3:19). Yet Jeremiah didn't lose
hope. He called to mind the mercies of God, that His compassions
"are new every morning" (v. 23). So too did my parents.

Whatever you're facing, know that God is faithful every morning.
He renews our strength day by day and gives us hope. And sometimes,
as with my family, He brings relief. After several years, a new medi-
cation became available that stopped Paul's continuous night-time
seizures, giving my family restorative sleep and hope for the future.

When our souls are downcast (v. 20), may we call to mind that
God's mercies are new every morning.   *AMY BOUCHER PYE*

**How has God sustained you through the trials you've
faced? How could you support someone who's
enduring a challenging time?**

*God, Your love will never leave me. When I feel spent and
without hope, remind me of Your mercies and compassion.*

REST IS A GIFT FROM GOD

Tossing and turning in bed, I fretted over my list of weekly tasks. Family, friends and even people I barely knew depended on me. For the fourth night in a row, I watched the clock change to three a.m. before I fell asleep. The alarm I'd set for six a.m. shocked me into starting my day. I snapped at my husband. Barking orders at my son, I rushed him into the car. I don't remember driving to his school. But I'll never forget watching his teacher close the classroom door before I collapsed from exhaustion onto the playground.

A friend drove me home and promised to care for my son until my husband returned from work. My neighbour prayed over me and stayed close by until I woke up . . . eight hours later.

God knows His children worry, fear and sometimes try to do too much. He also knows how desperately we need down time to rejuvenate physically, emotionally, mentally and spiritually.

In Psalm 62, David says his "soul finds rest *in* God" (V. 1). For this holistic revitalisation, David needed to be silent and still as he leaned into God's proven trustworthiness as all-sufficient hope-giver, deliverer and protector (VV. 5–7). Urging others to trust in God "at all times" by approaching Him with honest prayers, David demonstrates bold dependence on God and His power (VV. 8, 12).

God didn't design us to be weighed down by worry or the need to meet everyone's needs. He does, however, prove His dependability. When we trust His constant presence and His power, we can worship Him by resting. What a priceless gift from God!

Xochitl Dixon, Our Daily Bread *author*

★ The devotions for **March 1, 9, 16** and **23** address the topic of **REST**. We trust these articles will encourage you to rest in God's care.

Whoever dwells in the shelter of the Most
High will rest in the shadow of the Almighty.
[PSALM 91:1]

SAFE AND STILL

As a full-of-energy pre-schooler, my son Xavier avoided afternoon quiet time. Being still often resulted in an unwanted, though much-needed, nap. So, he'd wiggle in his seat, slide off the sofa, scoot across the hardwood floor and even roll across the room to evade the quiet. "Mum, I'm hungry . . . I'm thirsty . . . I have to go to the bathroom . . . I want a hug."

Understanding the benefits of stillness, I'd help Xavier settle down by inviting him to snuggle. Leaning into my side, he'd give in to sleep.

Early in my spiritual life, I mirrored my son's desire to remain active. Busyness made me feel accepted, important and in control, while noise distracted me from fretting over my shortcomings and trials. Surrendering to rest only affirmed my frail humanity. So I avoided stillness and silence, doubting God could handle things without my help.

But He's our refuge, no matter how many troubles or uncertainties surround us. The path ahead may seem long, scary or overwhelming, but His love envelops us. He hears us, answers us and stays with us . . . now and forever into eternity (PSALM 91).

We can embrace the quiet and lean into God's unfailing love and constant presence. We can be still and rest in Him because we're safe under the shelter of His unchanging faithfulness (V. 4). *XOCHITL DIXON*

> **In what ways have you seen God's protection in your life?
> How can you face difficulties knowing that God has you
> under His wings?**

> *Heavenly Father, thank You for providing a safe haven
> of unfailing love.*

Keep this Book of the Law always on your lips.
[JOSHUA 1:8]

NEVER GIVE UP

"Time went by. War came in." That's how Bishop Semi Nigo of the Keliko people of South Sudan described delays in his church's long struggle to get the Bible in their own language. Not one word, in fact, had ever been printed in the Keliko language. Decades earlier, Bishop Nigo's grandfather had courageously started a Bible translation project, but war and unrest kept halting the effort. Yet, despite repeated attacks on their refugee camps in northern Uganda and the Democratic Republic of the Congo, the bishop and fellow believers kept the project alive.

Their persistence paid off. After nearly three decades, the New Testament Bible in Keliko was delivered to the refugees in a rousing celebration. "The motivation of the Keliko is beyond words," said one project consultant.

The commitment of the Keliko reflects the perseverance God asked of Joshua. As God told him, "Keep this Book of the Law always on your lips; meditate on it day and night, so that you may be careful to do everything written in it. Then you will be prosperous and successful" (JOSHUA 1:8). With equal persistence, the Keliko pursued the translation of Scripture. Now, "when you see them in the camps, they are smiling," said one translator. Hearing and understanding the Bible "gives them hope." Like the Keliko people, may we never give up seeking the power and wisdom of Scripture.   *PATRICIA RAYBON*

> *How persistent are you in seeking to read and study Scripture? In what way do you need help in understanding it and who could you ask to help you grow deeper in it?*
>
> *Loving God, the Bible is vital to my life. Stir up in me a greater hunger to seek, study and know it, never giving up my quest to understand Your wisdom.*

The LORD himself goes before you.
[DEUTERONOMY 31:8]

PRESERVED

While I was clearing out the garden in preparation for spring planting, I pulled up a large clump of winter weeds . . . and leapt into the air! A venomous snake lay hidden in the undergrowth just below my hand—an inch lower and I would have grabbed it by mistake. I saw its colourful markings as soon as I lifted the clump; the rest of it was coiled in the weeds between my feet.

When my feet hit the ground a few feet away, I thanked God I hadn't been bitten. And I wondered how many other times He had kept me from dangers I never knew were there.

God watches over His people. Moses told the Israelites before they entered the Promised Land, "The LORD himself goes before you and will be with you; he will never leave you nor forsake you. Do not be afraid; do not be discouraged" (DEUTERONOMY 31:8). They couldn't see God, but He was with them nonetheless.

Sometimes difficult things happen that we may not understand, but we can also reflect on the number of times God has preserved us without our ever being aware!

Scripture reminds us that His perfect, providential care remains over His people every day. He's always with us (MATTHEW 28:20).

JAMES BANKS

***How does the biblical truth that God watches over
His people comfort you? Who can you tell about
His faithfulness today?***

*Faithful Father, thank You for watching over me
every day. Please give me grace to walk closely with
You in everything I do today.*

Jesus answered: "Don't you know me, Philip, even
after I have been among you such a long time?
Anyone who has seen me has seen the Father."
[JOHN 14:9]

KNOWING THE FATHER

According to legend, British conductor Sir Thomas Beecham
once saw a distinguished-looking woman in a hotel foyer.
Believing he knew her but unable to remember her name, he
paused to talk with her. As the two chatted, he vaguely recollected
that she had a brother. Hoping for a clue, he asked how her brother
was doing and whether he was still working at the same job. "Oh,
he's very well," she said, "And still *king*."

A case of mistaken identity can be embarrassing, as it was for Sir
Beecham. But at other times it may be more serious, as it was for
Jesus' disciple Philip. The disciple knew Jesus, of course, but he hadn't
fully appreciated who He was. He wanted Jesus to "show [them] the
Father," and Jesus responded, "Anyone who has seen me has seen
the Father" (JOHN 14:8-9). As God's unique Son, Jesus reveals the
Father so perfectly that to know one is to know the other (VV. 10-11).

If we ever wonder what God is like in His character, personality
or concern for others, we only need to look to Jesus to find out.
Jesus' character, kindness, love and mercy reveal God's character.
And although our amazing, awesome God is beyond our complete
comprehension and understanding, we have a tremendous gift in
what He's revealed of Himself in Jesus.　　　　*CON CAMPBELL*

How well do you know God's character?
How does it match your perception of who Jesus is?

Dear God, help me to grow in my knowledge and
appreciation of who You are.

When times are good, be happy; but when times are bad, consider this: God has made the one as well as the other. [ECCLESIASTES 7:14]

WHO KNOWS?

According to Chinese legend, when Sai Weng lost one of his prized horses, his neighbour expressed sorrow for his loss. But Sai Weng was unconcerned. He said, "Who knows if it may be a good thing for me?" Surprisingly, the lost horse returned home with another horse. As the neighbour congratulated him, Sai Weng said, "Who knows if it may be a bad thing for me?" As it turned out, his son broke his leg when he rode on the new horse. This seemed like a misfortune, until the army arrived at the village to recruit all able-bodied men to fight in the war. Because of the son's injury, he wasn't recruited, which ultimately could have spared him from death.

This is the story behind a Chinese proverb which teaches that a difficulty can be a blessing in disguise and vice versa. This ancient wisdom has a close parallel in Ecclesiastes 6:12, where the author observes: "Who knows what is good for a person in life?" Indeed, none of us know what the future holds. An adversity might have positive benefits and prosperity might have ill effects.

Each day offers new opportunities, joys, struggles and suffering. As God's beloved children, we can rest in His sovereignty and trust Him through the good and bad times alike. God has "made the one as well as the other" (7:14). He's with us in all the events in our lives and promises His loving care.   *POH FANG CHIA*

Can you think of an example where a misfortune turned out to be a blessing? How can you keep your focus on God in good times as well as in bad times?

Sovereign God, thank You for ordering my life. Help me to praise You in both good and bad times, believing that You work all things for the ultimate good of those who love You.

Mind your own business and work with
your hands. [1 THESSALONIANS 4:11]

MINDING MY OWN BUSINESS

Years ago, my son Josh and I were making our way up a mountain
trail when we spied a cloud of dust rising in the air. We crept
forwards and discovered a badger busy making a den in a dirt
bank. He had his head and shoulders in the hole and was vigorously
digging with his front paws and kicking the dirt out of the hole with
his hind feet. He was so invested in his work he didn't hear us.

I couldn't resist and prodded him from behind with a long stick
lying nearby. I didn't hurt the badger, but he leaped straight up in
the air and turned towards us. Josh and I set new world records for
the hundred-metre sprint!

I learned something from my brashness: sometimes it's best not
to poke around in other people's business. That's especially true
in relationships with fellow believers in Jesus. The apostle Paul
encouraged the Thessalonians to "make it your ambition to lead a
quiet life: You should mind your own business and work with your
hands" (1 THESSALONIANS 4:11). We're to pray for others and seek,
by God's grace, to share the Scriptures and occasionally we may
be called to offer a gentle word of correction. But learning to live a
quiet life and not meddling in others' lives is important. It becomes
an example to those who are now outside God's family (V. 12). Our
calling is to "love each other" (V. 9).   *DAVID H. ROPER*

> **What happens when you meddle in other people's
> business? What's the first thing you should do
> instead for others?**
>
> *God, teach me to know what it means to love
> others better.*

I, Daniel, understood from the Scriptures. . . .
So I turned to the Lord God and pleaded with
him in prayer and petition. [DANIEL 9:2–3]

PLEADING WITH GOD

A family's prayer time ended with a surprising announcement one morning. As soon as Dad said, "Amen," five-year-old Kaitlyn proclaimed, "And I prayed for Logan, because he had his eyes open during prayer."

I'm pretty sure praying for your ten-year-old brother's prayer protocol isn't what Scripture has in mind when it calls us to intercessory prayer, but at least Kaitlyn realised that we can pray for others.

Bible teacher Oswald Chambers emphasised the importance of praying for someone else. He said that intercession is "having [God's] mind and perspective." It's praying for others in light of what we know about God and His love for us.

We find a great example of intercessory prayer in Daniel 9. The prophet understood God's troubling promise that the Jews would have seventy years of captivity in Babylon (JEREMIAH 25:11–12). Realising that those years were nearing their completion, Daniel went into prayer mode. He referenced God's commands (DANIEL 9:4–6), humbled himself (V. 8), honoured God's character (V. 9), confessed sin (V. 15) and depended on His mercy as he prayed for His people (V. 18). And he got an immediate answer from God (V. 21).

Not all prayer ends with such a dramatic response, but be encouraged that we can go to God on behalf of others with an attitude of trust and dependence on Him.   *DAVE BRANON*

> **When you pray for others, how are you seeking the
> mind of God? How do you seek His perspective?**
>
> *Dear heavenly Father, help me to know You better so
> that when I pray for others, I can filter my requests
> through my knowledge of Your will.*

But these are written that you may believe.
[JOHN 20:31]

THE REASON FOR WRITING

"The Lord is my high tower . . . . We left the camp singing."
On 7 September, 1943, Etty Hillesum wrote those words
on a postcard and threw it from a train. Those were the
final recorded words we would hear from her. On 30 November,
1943, she was murdered at Auschwitz. Later, Hillesum's diaries
of her experiences in a concentration camp were translated and
published. They chronicled her perspectives on the horrors of Nazi
occupation along with the beauty of God's world. Her diaries have
been translated into sixty-seven languages—a gift to all who would
read and believe the good as well as the bad.

The apostle John didn't sidestep the harsh realities of Jesus' life
on earth; he wrote of both the good Jesus did and the challenges He
faced. The final words from his gospel give insight into the purpose
behind the book that bears his name. Jesus performed "many other
signs . . . which are not recorded" (20:30) by John. But these, he says,
were "written that you may believe" (v. 31). John's 'diary' ends on
the note of triumph: "Jesus is the Messiah, the Son of God." The
gift of those gospel words allows us the opportunity to believe and
"have life in his name."

The gospels are diary accounts of God's love for us. They're words
to read and believe and share, for they lead us to life. They lead us
to Christ.   *JOHN BLASE*

> *How might it change the way you read the gospels if you
> thought of them as diaries? How are you being led to the
> heart of Christ through them?*
>
> *Gracious God, thank You for the gift of the Scriptures, written
> down by faithful hands so that I might believe and have life.*

He says to the snow, "Fall on the earth," and
to the rain shower, "Be a mighty downpour."
[JOB 37:6]

SNOW MUSE

The grassroots musical group Over the Rhine sings about
a transformation that takes place each year in their city.
"Whenever we'd get our first real snowfall of the year, it felt
like something sacred was happening," explains band co-founder
Linford Detweiler. "Like a little bit of a fresh start. The city would
slow down and grow quiet."

If you've experienced a heavy snowfall, you understand how it
can inspire a song. A magical quietness drapes the world as snow
conceals grime and greyness. For a few moments, winter's bleakness
brightens, inviting our reflection and delight.

Elihu, the one friend of Job's who may have had a helpful view
of God, noted how creation commands our attention. "God's voice
thunders in marvellous ways," he said (JOB 37:5). "He says to the snow,
'Fall on the earth,' and to the rain shower, 'Be a mighty downpour.' "
Such splendour can interrupt our lives, demanding a sacred pause.
"So that everyone he has made may know his work, he stops all
people from their labour," Elihu observed (VV. 6–7).

Nature sometimes seizes our attention in ways we don't like.
Regardless of what happens to us or what we observe around us,
each moment—magnificent, menacing or mundane—can inspire
our worship. The poet's heart within us craves the holy hush.

TIM GUSTAFSON

> ***What events or things motivate you to ponder God's
> greatness and creativity? How can you experience His
> wonder in your ordinary moments today?***
>
> *Father, help me to see Your hand in everything today.
> Give me a heart to appreciate Your amazing works.*

BIBLE IN A YEAR | DEUTERONOMY 8–10; MARK 11:19–33   73

Whatever you have learned or received or heard from me, or seen in me—put it into practice. [PHILIPPIANS 4:9]

PRACTISE THESE THINGS

As I helped my son with his maths homework, it became apparent he was less than enthusiastic about doing multiple problems related to the same concept. "I've got it, Dad!" he insisted, hoping I would let him out of doing all of his assignment. I then gently explained to him that a concept is just a concept until we learn how to work it out in *practice*.

Paul wrote about practice to his friends in Philippi. "Whatever you have learned or received or heard from me, or seen in me—put it into practice" (PHILIPPIANS 4:9). He mentions five things: *reconciliation*—as he urged Euodia and Syntyche to do (VV. 2–3); *joy*—as he reminded his readers to cultivate (V. 4); *gentleness*—as he urged them to employ in their relation to the world (V. 5); *prayer*—as he had modelled for them in person and in writing (VV. 6–7); and *focus*—as he had shown even in prison (V. 8). Reconciliation, joy, gentleness, prayer and focus—things we're called to live out as believers in Jesus. Like any habit, these virtues must be practised in order to be cultivated.

But the good news of the gospel, as Paul had already told the Philippians, is that "it is God who works in you to will and to act in order to fulfil his good purpose" (2:13). We're never practising in our own power. God will provide what we need (4:19).   *GLENN PACKIAM*

> ***What things do you need to practise as you seek to imitate Jesus? How can you practise in the power of the Holy Spirit?***
>
> *Jesus, may You give me the grace to practise Your ways by the power of the Holy Spirit. Empower me to cultivate the soil of my life by repeated actions—even my weak and feeble ones that fail so often—so that the fruit of the Spirit may appear.*

They all gave out of their wealth; but she, out
of her poverty, put in everything—all she had
to live on. [MARK 12:44]

OUT OF OUR POVERTY

Warren Buffett and Bill and Melinda Gates made history
when they launched the Giving Pledge, promising to donate
half of their money. As of 2018, this meant giving away 74
billion pounds. The pledge made psychologist Paul Piff curious to
study giving patterns. Through a research test, he discovered that
the poor were inclined to give 44 percent more of what they had
than wealthy people. Those who've felt their own poverty are often
moved to greater generosity.

Jesus knew this. Visiting the temple, He watched the crowds
drop gifts into the treasury (MARK 12:41). The rich tossed in wads of
cash, but a poor widow pulled out her last two copper coins, worth
maybe a penny, and placed them into the basket. I picture Jesus
standing up, delighted and astounded. Immediately, He gathered His
disciples, making sure they didn't miss this dazzling act. "This poor
widow has put more into the treasury than all the others," Jesus
exclaimed (V. 43). The disciples looked at each other, bewildered,
hoping someone could explain what Jesus was talking about. So, He
made it plain: those bringing huge gifts "gave out of their wealth;
but she, out of her poverty, put in everything" (V. 44).

We may have little to give, but Jesus invites us to give out of our
poverty. Though it may seem meagre to others, we give what we
have, and God finds great joy in our lavish gifts.   *WINN COLLIER*

**What does it mean for you to give out of your poverty?
How can you give everything for Jesus today?**

*God, I don't feel like I have much to offer. My gifts feel
puny and worthless. But I'm here. All of me. Will You
receive me in my poverty?*

I will put breath in you. [EZEKIEL 37:6]

EVERY BREATH

When Tee Unn came down with a rare autoimmune disease that weakened all his muscles and nearly killed him, he realised that being able to breathe was a gift. For more than a week, a machine had to pump air into his lungs every few seconds, which was a painful part of his treatment.

Tee Unn made a miraculous recovery, and today he reminds himself not to complain about life's challenges. "I'll just take a deep breath," he says, "and thank God I can."

How easy it is to focus on things we need or want, and forget that sometimes the smallest things in life can be the greatest miracles. In Ezekiel's vision (EZEKIEL 37:1–14), God showed the prophet that only He could give life to dry bones. Even after tendons, flesh and skin had appeared, "there was no breath in them" (V. 8). It was only when God gave them breath that they could live again (V. 10).

This vision illustrated God's promise to restore Israel from devastation. It also reminds me that anything I have, big or small, is useless unless God gives me breath.

How about thanking God for the simplest blessings in life today? Amid the daily struggle, let's stop occasionally to take a deep breath, and "let everything that has breath praise the LORD" (PSALM 150:6)

LESLIE KOH

***What will you thank God for right now? How can you
remind yourself to thank Him more often today?***

*Thank You, God, for every breath You've given me.
Thank You for the smallest things in life and the
greatest miracles of life.*

God blessed them. . . . God saw all that
he had made, and it was very good.
[GENESIS 1:28, 31]

GOD'S STORYBOOK

Wanting to enjoy the beautiful day, I headed out for a walk
and soon met a new neighbour. He stopped me and introduced himself: "My name is Genesis, and I'm six and
a half years old."

"Genesis is a great name! It's a book in the Bible," I replied.

"What's the Bible?" he asked.

"It's God's storybook about how He made the world and people
and how He loves us."

His inquisitive response made me smile: "Why did He make the
world and people and cars and houses? And is my picture in His book?"

While there isn't a literal picture of my new friend Genesis or the
rest of us in the Scriptures, we're a big part of God's storybook. We
see in Genesis 1 that "God created mankind in his own image, in
the image of God He created them" (v. 27). God walked with them
in the garden, and then warned about giving in to the temptation
to be their own god (CH. 3). Later in His book, God explained how, in
love, His Son, Jesus, came to walk with us again and brought about
a plan for our forgiveness and the restoration of His creation.

As we look at the Bible, we learn that our Creator wants us to
know Him, talk with Him and even ask Him our questions. He cares
for us more than we can imagine.   *ANNE CETAS*

Where do you see yourself in God's story?
In what ways are you experiencing His fellowship?

Loving God, thank You for making me a part of Your story.
May I love You and others as You love me.

[Jesus] said to his disciples, "Why are you
so afraid? Do you still have no faith?"
[MARK 4:40]

STORMS OF FEAR

n a TV commercial I saw recently, a woman casually asks someone
in a group watching TV, "What are you searching for, Mark?" "A
version of myself that doesn't make decisions based on fear," he
responds soberly—not realising that she was just asking what he
liked to watch on TV!

Whoa, I thought. I wasn't expecting a TV commercial to hit me
so profoundly! But I related to poor Mark: sometimes I too feel
embarrassed by the way fear sometimes seems to direct my life.

Jesus' disciples also experienced the profound power of fear. Once,
as they headed across the Sea of Galilee (MARK 4:35), "a furious squall
came up" (V. 37). Terror gripped them, and they suggested that Jesus
(who'd been sleeping!) might not care about them: "Teacher, don't
you care if we drown?" (V. 38).

Fear *distorted* the disciples' vision, blinding them to Jesus' good
intentions for them. After He rebuked the wind and waves (V. 39),
Christ confronted the disciples with two penetrating questions: "Why
are you so afraid? Do you still have no faith?" (V. 40).

Storms rage in our lives as well, don't they? But Jesus' questions
can help us put our fears in perspective. His first question invites us
to *name* our fears. The second invites us to *entrust* those distorted
feelings to Him—asking Him for eyes to see how He guides us even
through life's most raging storms.   *ADAM R. HOLZ*

**What storms are you facing right now? How can you entrust
your fears and emotions to Jesus when the winds blow and
the waters rise?**

*Loving Saviour, thank You that You're always present in the
storm. As I move through life's scary moments, help me each
day to talk to You and entrust You with my fears.*

You are a chosen people, a royal priesthood,
a holy nation, God's special possession.
[1 PETER 2:9]

CARING LETTERS

Decades ago, Dr. Jerry Motto discovered the power of a 'caring letter'. His research found that simply sending a letter expressing care to discharged patients who had previously attempted suicide reduced the rate of recurrence by half. Recently, health care providers have rediscovered this power when sending 'caring' texts, postcards and even social media memes as follow-up treatment for the severely depressed.

Twenty-one books in the Bible are actually letters—epistles—caringly written to first-century believers who struggled for a variety of reasons. Paul, James and John wrote letters to explain the basics of faith and worship, and how to resolve conflict and build unity.

The apostle Peter, however, specifically wrote to believers who were being persecuted by the Roman emperor, Nero. Peter reminded them of their intrinsic value to God, describing them this way in 1 Peter 2:9, "You are a chosen people, a royal priesthood, a holy nation, God's special possession." This lifted their gaze to God's great purpose for them in their world: "that you may declare the praises of him who called you out of darkness into his wonderful light."

Our great God Himself wrote a book filled with caring letters to us—inspired Scripture—that we might always have a record of the value He assigns us as His own. May we read His letters daily and share them with others who need the hope Jesus offers.

ELISA MORGAN

*How does reading the epistles as caring letters help you
receive God's encouragement? How will you share the hope
of God's caring letters today?*

Loving God, thank You for the caring letters in the Bible!

My flesh and my heart may fail, but God is the strength of my heart and my portion forever.
[PSALM 73:26]

A STRONG HEART

In his book *Fearfully and Wonderfully Made,* co-authored with Philip Yancey, Dr. Paul Brand observed, "A hummingbird heart weighs a fraction of an ounce and beats eight hundred times a minute; a blue whale's heart weighs half a tonne, beats only ten times per minute and can be heard two miles away. In contrast to either, the human heart seems dully functional, yet it does its job, beating 100,000 times a day [65–70 times a minute] with no time off for rest, to get most of us through seventy years or more."

The amazing heart so thoroughly powers us through life that it has become a metaphor for our overall inner wellbeing. Yet, both our literal and metaphorical hearts are prone to failure. What can we do?

The psalmist Asaph, a worship leader of Israel, acknowledged in Psalm 73 that true strength comes from somewhere—Someone—else. He wrote, "My flesh and my heart may fail, but God is the strength of my heart and my portion forever" (V. 26). Asaph was right. The living God is our ultimate and eternal strength. As the Maker of heaven and earth, He knows no such limitations to His perfect power.

In our times of difficulty and challenge, may we discover what Asaph learned through his own struggles: God is the true strength of our hearts. We can rest in that strength every day. *BILL CROWDER*

How is your metaphorical heart like your spiritual heart?
When you feel like you're 'losing heart', how can you find
strength in your loving, caring Father?

Heavenly Father, I thank You that when I'm weak You're strong. That when I'm overwhelmed, You're enough. That when I'm confused, You have perfect clarity.

God has chosen to make known . . . the
glorious riches of this mystery, which is Christ
in you, the hope of glory. [COLOSSIANS 1:27]

IT'S JESUS!

During an episode of the popular American television talent
competition *America's Got Talent*, a five-year-old girl sang
with such exuberance that a judge compared her to a famous
child singer and dancer in the 1930s. He remarked, "I think Shirley
Temple is living somewhere inside of you." Her unexpected response:
"Not Shirley Temple. Jesus!"

I marvelled at the young girl's deep awareness that her joy came
from Jesus living in her. Scripture assures us of the amazing reality
that all who trust in Him not only receive the promise of eternal life
with God but also Jesus' presence living in them through His Spirit—our hearts become Jesus' home (COLOSSIANS 1:27; EPHESIANS 3:17).

Jesus' presence in our hearts fills us with countless reasons for
gratitude (COLOSSIANS 2:6–7). He brings the ability to live with purpose
and energy (1:28–29). He cultivates joy in our hearts in the midst of
all circumstances, in both times of celebration and times of struggle
(PHILIPPIANS 4:12–13). Christ's Spirit provides hope to our hearts that
God is working all things together for good, even when we can't see
it (ROMANS 8:28). And the Spirit gives a peace that persists regardless
of the chaos swirling around us (COLOSSIANS 3:15).

With the confidence that comes from Jesus living in our hearts,
we can allow His presence to shine through so that others can't help
but notice.   *LISA M. SAMRA*

*What blessing of Jesus' presence in your life
encourages you today? How might you share Him
as the reason for your hope and joy?*

*Jesus, thank You for making my heart Your home.
Please help my life to reflect Your presence.*

We are God's handiwork, created in Christ
Jesus to do good works. [EPHESIANS 2:10]

SMALL YET MIGHTY

There are times late at night in North America's harsh Sonoran Desert where one can hear a faint, high-pitched howl. But you probably wouldn't suspect the source of the sound—the small yet mighty grasshopper mouse, howling at the moon to establish its territory.

This unique rodent (dubbed the "werewolf mouse") is also carnivorous. In fact, it preys on creatures few would dare mess with, such as the scorpion. But the werewolf mouse is uniquely equipped for that particular battle. It not only has a resistance to scorpion venom but can even convert the toxins into a painkiller!

There's something inspiring about the way this resilient little mouse seems custom-made to survive and even thrive in its harsh environment. As Paul explains in Ephesians 2:10, that kind of marvellous craftsmanship characterises God's designs for His people as well. Each of us is "God's handiwork" in Jesus, uniquely equipped to contribute to His kingdom. No matter how God has gifted you, you have much to offer. As you embrace with confidence who He's made you to be, you'll be a living witness to the hope and joy of life in Him.

So as you face whatever feels most menacing in your own life, take courage. You may feel small, but through the gifting and empowerment of the Spirit, God can use you to do mighty things.

MONICA LA ROSE

Is it easy or difficult for you to see yourself as God's marvellous handiwork? Why? In what areas of your life might remembering this truth give you renewed confidence and courage?

God, thank You for the incredible way You've designed me to live with joy and purpose. Help me to believe, and find courage in, the truth of who I am in You.

I urge you . . . to join me in my struggle by praying to God for me. [ROMANS 15:30]

THE PURPLE SHAWL

While serving as my mum's live-in carer at a cancer centre hundreds of miles away from my home, I asked people to pray for us. As the months passed, isolation and loneliness sapped my strength. How could I care for my mum if I gave in to my physical, mental and emotional exhaustion?

One day, a friend sent me an unexpected care package. Jodi had crocheted a purple prayer shawl, a warm reminder that we had people praying for us daily. Whenever I wrapped the soft yarn around my shoulders, I felt God hugging me with the prayers of His people. Years later, He still uses that purple shawl to comfort me and strengthen my resolve.

The apostle Paul affirmed the importance and spirit-refreshing power of praying for others. Through his passionate request for prayerful support and encouragement during his travels, Paul demonstrated how those who pray for others become partners in ministry (ROMANS 15:30). Offering specific requests, the apostle not only showed his dependence on the support of fellow believers but his trust that God powerfully answers prayer (VV. 31–33).

We'll all experience days when we feel alone. But Paul shows us how to ask for prayer as we pray for others. When we're wrapped in the intercessory prayers of God's people, we can experience God's strength and comfort no matter where life takes us.　　*XOCHITL DIXON*

Who has God used to encourage you through intercessory prayer? Who can you pray for today?

Loving God, thank You for the gift of intercessory prayers and for assuring me that You hear me and care for me wherever I go.

Whoever heeds life-giving correction will be at
home among the wise. [PROVERBS 15:31]

LOVING CORRECTION

For more than fifty years, my dad strove for excellence in his editing. His passion wasn't to just look for mistakes but also to make the copy better in terms of clarity, logic, flow and grammar. Dad used a green pen for his corrections, rather than a red one. A green pen he felt was 'friendlier', while slashes of red might be jarring to a novice or less confident writer. His objective was to gently point out a better way.

When Jesus corrected people, He did so in love. In some circumstances—such as when He was confronted with the hypocrisy of the Pharisees (MATTHEW 23)—He rebuked them harshly, yet still for their benefit. But in the case of his friend Martha, a gentle correction was all that was needed (LUKE 10:38–42). While the Pharisees responded poorly to His rebuke, Martha remained one of His dearest friends (JOHN 11:5).

Correction can be uncomfortable and few of us like it. Sometimes, because of our pride, it's hard to receive it graciously. The book of Proverbs talks much about wisdom and indicates that heeding correction is a sign of wisdom and understanding (15:31–32).

God's loving correction helps us to adjust our direction and to follow Him more closely. Those who refuse it are sternly warned (V. 10), but those who respond to it through the power of the Holy Spirit will gain wisdom and understanding (VV. 31–32).

CINDY HESS KASPER

> *How do you usually respond to loving correction from your heavenly Father? What correction have you received from someone that's made a significant difference in your life?*
>
> *Father, help me learn to graciously accept Your loving correction so I can grow in wisdom and understanding.*

Surely he was the Son of God!
[MATTHEW 27:54]

GOD AT WORK

"God is crying." Those were the words whispered by Bill Haley's ten-year-old daughter as she stood in the rain with a group of multi-ethnic believers in Jesus. They had come together to try and make sense of the legacy of racial discord in their country. As they stood on the grounds where former slaves were buried, they joined hands in prayer. Then suddenly the wind began to blow, and it started to rain. As the leader called out for racial healing, the rain began to fall even harder. Those gathered believed that God was at work to bring reconciliation and forgiveness.

And so was it at Calvary—God was at work. After the crucified Jesus breathed His last, "The earth shook, the rocks split and the tombs broke open" (MATTHEW 27:51–52). Though some had denied who Jesus was, a centurion assigned to guard Him had come to a different conclusion: "When the centurion and those with him . . . saw the earthquake and all that had happened, they were terrified, and exclaimed, 'Surely he was the Son of God!' " (V. 54).

In the death of Jesus, God was at work providing forgiveness of sin for all who believe in Him. "God was reconciling the world to himself in Christ, not counting people's sins against them" (2 CORINTHIANS 5:19). And what better way to demonstrate that we've been forgiven by God than to extend forgiveness to each other.   *ARTHUR JACKSON*

In what ways have you shared the forgiveness you've received from God with others, even those who are different from you? If you haven't received forgiveness from God through the death of Jesus, what's keeping you from doing so today?

Father, thank You for loving the world so much that You sent Jesus so I can be forgiven. Help me to demonstrate forgiveness towards others by the way I live.

How sweet are your words to my taste,
sweeter than honey to my mouth!
[PSALM 119:103]

SPIRITUAL FOOD

Awhile ago I attended a conference on the Middle Ages. In one seminar we actually prepared several foods that would have been common in medieval times. We used pestle and mortar to grind cinnamon and fruit to make jam. We cut orange rinds and broiled them with honey and ginger to produce a sweet snack. We crushed almonds with water and other ingredients to create almond milk. And, finally, we prepared a whole chicken to serve as a main dish with rice. As we sampled these dishes, we enjoyed a tasty culinary experience.

When it comes to spiritual food for our souls, God has given us a varied menu that we can chew on and savour. In doing so, we can be filled and satisfied. The historic books, poetry, wisdom literature, prophecy and other parts of the Bible strengthen us when we are weak, give us wisdom and encouragement and nourish us for the day's journey (PSALM 19:7-14; 119:97-104; HEBREWS 5:12). As the psalmist tells us: "How sweet are your words to my taste, sweeter than honey to my mouth!" (PSALM 119:103).

So what are we waiting for? God has set before us a banquet of delectable spiritual food and calls us to come and dine. We are all invited!   *DENNIS FISHER*

***How has your life changed when you've read the
Bible regularly? How could you ensure you don't lose
this practice in the busyness of your daily life?***

*Gracious God, You've given me the gift of Scripture.
Help me to read it, savour it and digest it, that I might
serve You faithfully.*

What do people get for all the toil and anxious
striving with which they labour under the sun?
[ECCLESIASTES 2:22]

THE REASON TO REST

I f you want to live longer, take a holiday! Forty years after a study
of middle-aged, male executives who each had a risk of heart
disease, researchers in Helsinki, Finland, followed up with their
study participants. The scientists discovered something they hadn't
been looking for in their original findings: the death rate was lower
among those who had taken time off for holidays.

Work is a necessary part of life—a part God appointed to us even
before our relationship with Him was fractured in Genesis 3. Solomon
wrote of the seeming meaninglessness of work experienced by those
not working for God's honour—recognising its "anxious striving"
and "grief and pain" (ECCLESIASTES 2:22–23). Even when they're not
actively working, he says their "minds do not rest" because they're
thinking about what still needs to be done (V. 23).

We too might at times feel like we're "chasing after the wind"
(V. 17) and grow frustrated by our inability to "finish" our work.
But when we remember that God is part of our labour—our purpose—we can both work hard *and* take time to rest. We can trust
Him to be our Provider, for He's the giver of all things. Solomon
acknowledges that "without him, who can eat or find enjoyment?"
(V. 25). Perhaps by reminding ourselves of that truth, we can work
diligently for Him (COLOSSIANS 3:23) and also allow ourselves times
of rest.　　　　　　　　　　　　　　　　　　*KIRSTEN HOLMBERG*

How can you invite God into your labours?
How might you allow Him to be your satisfaction
even when your work isn't "finished"?

God, You bring meaning and purpose to all my labours.

We are co-workers in God's service.
[1 CORINTHIANS 3:9]

SOMETHING MUCH BIGGER

More than two hundred volunteers assisted October Books, a bookstore in Southampton, England, move its inventory to an address down the street. Helpers lined the pavement and passed books down a 'human conveyor belt'. Having witnessed the volunteers in action, a shop assistant said, "It was . . . a really moving experience to see people [helping]. . . . They wanted to be part of something bigger."

We can also be part of something much bigger than ourselves. God uses us to reach the world with the message of His love. Because someone shared the message with us, we can turn to another person and pass it on. Paul compared this—the building of God's kingdom—to growing a garden. Some of us plant seeds while some of us water the seeds. We are, as Paul said, "co-workers in God's service" (1 CORINTHIANS 3:9).

Each job is important, yet all are done in the power of God's Spirit. By His Spirit, God enables people to thrive spiritually when they hear that He loves them and sent His Son to die in their place so that they can be free from their sin (JOHN 3:16).

God does much of His work on earth through 'volunteers' like you and me. Although we are a part of a community that's much bigger than any contribution we may make, we can help it grow by working together to share His love with the world.   *JENNIFER BENSON SCHULDT*

Do you see yourself as a part of God's plan or as someone who works alone in your service for God? How does this affect the way in which you serve Him and others?

Dear God, thank You for including me in Your plan to tell everyone about Your love. Help me to represent You well with my words and actions.

I am the good shepherd; I know my sheep and
my sheep know me. [JOHN 10:14]

KNOW HIS VOICE

One year for a holiday Bible club, Ken's church decided to bring in live animals to illustrate the Bible story. When he arrived to help, Ken was asked to bring a sheep inside. He had to practically drag the woolly animal by a rope into the church hall. But as the week went on, it became less reluctant to follow him. By the end of the week, Ken didn't have to hold the rope anymore; he just called the sheep and it followed, knowing it could trust him.

In the New Testament, Jesus compares Himself to a shepherd, stating that His people, the sheep, will follow Him because they know His voice (JOHN 10:4). But those same sheep will run from a stranger or thief (V. 5). Like sheep, we (God's children) get to know the voice of our Shepherd through our relationship with Him. And as we do, we see His character and learn to trust Him.

As we grow to know and love God, we'll be discerning of His voice and better able to run from the "the thief [who] comes only to steal and kill and destroy" (V. 10)—from those who try to deceive and draw us away from Him. Unlike those false teachers, we can trust the voice of our Shepherd to lead us to safety.　*JULIE SCHWAB*

***What's one thing you've learned about God's character
through reading Scripture? How did that impact you?
What will help you to discern God's voice?***

*Heavenly Father, thank You for being my loving Shepherd.
Help me to recognise and follow Your voice only.*

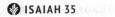

They will enter Zion with singing; everlasting
joy will crown their heads. [ISAIAH 35:10]

SLUM SONGS

Cateura is a small slum in Paraguay, South America. Its villagers survive by recycling items from its rubbish dump. But from these unpromising conditions something beautiful has emerged—an orchestra.

With a violin costing more than a house in Cateura, the orchestra had to get creative, crafting its own instruments from their rubbish supply. Violins are made from oil barrels with bent forks as tailpieces. Saxophones have come from drainpipes with bottle tops for keys. Cellos are made from tin drums with gnocchi rollers for tuning pegs. Hearing Mozart played on these contraptions is a beautiful thing. The orchestra has gone on tour in many countries, lifting the sights of its young members.

Violins from landfills. Music from slums. That's symbolic of what God does. For when the prophet Isaiah envisions God's new creation, a similar picture of beauty-from-poverty emerges, with barren lands bursting into blooming flowers (ISAIAH 35:1–2), deserts flowing with streams (VV. 6–7), castaway war tools crafted into garden instruments (2:4), and impoverished people becoming whole to the sounds of joyful songs (35:5–6, 10).

"The world sends us rubbish," Cateura's orchestra director says. "We send back music." And as they do, they give the world a glimpse of the future, when God will wipe away the tears of every eye and poverty will be no more.   *SHERIDAN VOYSEY*

*How have you seen God turn the 'rubbish' of your
life into something beautiful? How might He wish to
bring 'music' out of your pain?*

*Holy Spirit, turn the poverty in my life into
something beautiful.*

So in Christ Jesus you are all children of God
through faith. [GALATIANS 3:26]

HOSTING ROYALTY

Afterfter meeting the Queen at a ball in Scotland, Sylvia and her
husband received a message that the royal family would like
to visit them for tea. Sylvia started cleaning and prepping,
nervous about hosting the royal guests. Before they were due to
arrive, she went outside to pick some flowers for the table, her heart
racing. Then she sensed God reminding her that He's the King of
kings and that He's with her every day. Immediately she felt peaceful
and thought, "After all, it's only the Queen!"

Sylvia is right. As the apostle Paul noted, God is the "King of kings
and Lord of lords" (1 TIMOTHY 6:15) and those who follow Him are
"children of God" (GALATIANS 3:26). When we belong to Christ, we're
heirs of Abraham (V. 29). We no longer are bound by division—such
as that of race, social class, or gender—for we're "all one in Christ
Jesus" (V. 28). We're children of the King.

Although Sylvia and her husband had a marvellous meal with the
Queen, I don't anticipate receiving an invitation from her anytime
soon. But I love the reminder that the highest King of all is with me
every moment. And that those who believe in Jesus wholeheartedly
(V. 27) can live in unity, knowing they're God's children.

How could holding onto this truth shape the way we live today?

AMY BOUCHER PYE

What does it mean to you to be an heir of Abraham?
How could you invite others to become part of the family?

King of kings and Lord of lords, You are mighty and
glorious. Thank You for stooping down to love me and for
welcoming me as Your child.

From the lips of children and infants
you, Lord, have called forth your praise.
[MATTHEW 21:16]

WATCH ME!

"**W**atch my fairy princess dance, Grandma!" my three-year-old granddaughter gleefully called as she raced around the garden, a big grin on her face. Her 'dancing' brought a smile; and her big brother's glum, "She's not dancing, just running," didn't squelch her joy at being on holiday with family.

The first Palm Sunday was a day of highs and lows. When Jesus rode into Jerusalem on a donkey, the crowds enthusiastically shouted, "Hosanna! . . . Blessed is he who comes in the name of the Lord!" (MATTHEW 21:9). Yet many in the crowd were expecting a Messiah to free them from Rome, not a Saviour who would die for their sins that same week.

Later that day, despite the anger of the chief priests who questioned Jesus' authority, children in the temple expressed their joy by shouting, "Hosanna to the Son of David" (V. 15), perhaps leaping and waving palm branches as they ran around the courtyard. They couldn't help but worship Him, Jesus told the indignant leaders, for "from the lips of children and infants [God has] called forth [His] praise" (V. 16). They were in the presence of the Saviour!

Jesus invites us to also see Him for who He is. When we do, like a child overflowing with joy, we can't help but revel in His presence.

ALYSON KIEDA

> ***How do the daily distractions and discontent of others
> draw your focus away from the Lord? What will help you
> to keep your eyes on Jesus?***
>
> *Loving God, thank You for all You've done for me! I'm
> amazed at the great lengths You went to so that I could
> find joy in You. Help me to keep my focus firmly on You.*

In the LORD I take refuge.
[PSALM 11:1]

FACING THE BATTLES WITH GOD

The heroic deeds of US Army soldier Desmond Doss are featured in the 2016 movie *Hacksaw Ridge*. While Doss' convictions wouldn't allow him to take human life, as an army medic he committed himself to preserving life even at the risk of his own. The citation read at Doss' medal ceremony on 12 October, 1945, included these words: "Private First Class Doss refused to seek cover and remained in the fire-swept area with the many stricken, carrying them one by one to the edge of the escarpment. . . . He unhesitatingly braved enemy shelling and small arms fire to assist an artillery officer."

In Psalm 11, David's conviction that his refuge was in God compelled him to resist suggestions to flee rather than face his foes (VV. 2–3). Six simple words comprised his statement of faith: "In the LORD I take refuge" (V. 1). That well-rooted conviction would guide his conduct.

David's words in verses 4–7 amplified God's greatness. Yes, life can sometimes be like a battlefield, and hostile fire can send us scattering for cover when we're bombarded with health challenges or financial, relational and spiritual stresses. So, what should we do? Acknowledge that God is the king of the universe (V. 4); take delight in His amazing capacity to judge with precision (VV. 5–6); and rest in His delight in what's right, fair and equitable (V. 7). We can run swiftly to God for shelter!   *ARTHUR JACKSON*

> ***When have you experienced life's hostile fire and been tempted to find shelter in something other than God? Can you recall times when God came to your rescue and your hope in Him was renewed?***
>
> *Father, help me to see You more clearly than any force that opposes me and run to You for true safety and security.*

BIBLE IN A YEAR | JUDGES 7–8; LUKE 5:1-16

I will bring judgement on all the gods of Egypt.
[EXODUS 12:12]

GOT YOUR NOSE

" **W**hy are the statues' noses broken?" That's the number one question visitors ask at a museum displaying a range of ancient Egyptian art.

Bleiberg can't blame it on normal wear and tear; even two-dimensional painted figures are missing noses. He surmises that such destruction must have been intentional. Enemies meant to kill Egypt's gods. It's as if they were playing a game of 'got your nose' with them. Invading armies broke off the noses of these idols so they couldn't breathe.

Really? That's all it took? With gods like this, Pharaoh should have known he was in trouble. Yes, he had an army and the allegiance of a whole nation. The Hebrews were weary slaves led by a timid fugitive named Moses. But Israel had the living God, and Pharaoh's gods were pretenders. Ten plagues later, their imaginary lives were snuffed out.

Israel celebrated their victory with the Festival of Unleavened Bread, when they ate bread without yeast for a week (EXODUS 12:17; 13:7–9). Yeast symbolises sin, and God wanted His people to remember their rescued lives belong entirely to Him.

Our Father says to idols, "Got your nose," and to His children, "Got your life." Serve the God who gives you breath, and rest in His loving arms.   *MIKE WITTMER*

***What false god is suffocating your life? How might
you show God you're trusting only in Him?***

*Father of life, I give You my life. Help me recognise
that any perceived 'enemies' in my life are nothing
compared to Your power.*

Search me, God, and know my heart.
[PSALM 139:23]

WISELY WEEDING

My grandchildren are running around my back garden. Playing games? No, pulling weeds. "Pulling them up by the roots!" the youngest says, showing me a hefty prize. Her delight as we tackled weeds that day was how much we enjoyed plucking the weedy roots—clearing away each pesky menace. Before the joy, however, came the choice to go after them.

Intentional weeding is also the first step in removing personal sin. Thus, David prayed: "Search me, God, and know my heart. . . . See if there is any offensive way in me (PSALM 139:23–24).

What a wise approach, to go after our sin by asking God to show it to us. He above all knows everything about us. "You have searched me, LORD, and you know me," wrote the psalmist. "You know when I sit and when I rise; you perceive my thoughts from afar" (VV. 1–2).

"Such knowledge," David added, "is too wonderful for me, too lofty for me to attain" (V. 6). Even before a sin takes root, therefore, God can alert us to the danger. He knows our 'landscape'. So when a sneaky sinful attitude tries to take root, He's first to know and point it out.

"Where can I go from your Spirit," wrote David. "Where can I flee from your presence?" (V. 7). May we closely follow our Saviour to higher ground!   *PATRICIA RAYBON*

> ***When you ask God to search your heart, what personal wrongs do you discover? How does intentional 'weeding' help rid you of a relentless sin?***
>
> *Loving God, when You show me my personal sin, point me to Your plan to pull those weeds.*

FROM BITTER ROOT TO FLOWER OF FORGIVENESS

I didn't mean to grow up bitter. But my skin colour made me a target. In school, one teacher even called me "Nobody." The result? Bitterness. I knew Jesus, but I also knew hurt. Its sting fertilised my bitterness which, like a weed "springs up and causes trouble" (HEBREWS 12:15 ESV).

So, while I loved God and believed He loved me, my bitterness stood between us. I'd forgotten the Bible's call to "strive for peace with everyone, and for the holiness without which no one will see the Lord" (V. 14 ESV).

Instead, I was obsessed with racial hatred, ignoring Paul's call to "get rid of all bitterness, rage and anger, brawling and slander, along with every form of malice" (EPHESIANS 4:31). But how? God reveals three ways:

Take your bitterness to Him. Ask Him to banish it. In reply, I heard God say, "Forgive." But how?

Ask God to teach you. In fact, forgiveness isn't an act, it's a process. As scholar Lewis Smedes explained, forgiveness doesn't excuse offenders; it means "we are ready to be healed." How?

Rely on the Holy Spirit's great power. Then His work in us becomes His witness. Indeed, "But you will receive power when the Holy Spirit comes on you; and you will be my witnesses . . . to the ends of the earth (ACTS 1:8).

Then a bitter root can bloom, in Christ, into a beautiful flower. True, my "soil" always needs weeding. But God's love turns my bitter sin into grace.

Patricia Raybon, Our Daily Bread *author*

★ The topic of **FORGIVENESS** is discussed in the devotions for **April 1, 9, 16** and **23**. We hope these articles encourage you in your relationships with others.

Have mercy on me, my God, have mercy on me, for in you I take refuge. [PSALM 57:1]

REFUGE FOR THE REJECTED

George Whitefield (1714–1770) was one of the most gifted and effective preachers in history, leading thousands to faith in Jesus. But his life wasn't without controversy. His practice of preaching outdoors (to accommodate large crowds) was sometimes criticised by those who questioned his motives and felt he should speak only within the four walls of a church building. Whitefield's epitaph sheds light on his response to others' harsh words: "I am content to wait till the Day of Judgement for the clearing up of my character; and after I am dead, I desire no other epitaph than this, 'Here lies George Whitefield—what sort of a man he was, the great day will discover.' "

In the Old Testament, when David faced harsh criticism from others, he too entrusted himself to God. When Saul falsely accused David of leading a rebellion and he was forced to hide from Saul's approaching army in a cave, David described being "in the midst of lions," among "men whose teeth are spears and arrows, whose tongues are sharp swords" (PSALM 57:4). But even in that difficult place, he turned to God and found comfort in Him: "For great is your love, reaching to the heavens; your faithfulness reaches to the skies" (V. 10).

When others misunderstand or reject us, God is our "refuge" (V. 1). May He be forever praised for His unfailing and merciful love!

JAMES BANKS

> **How does dwelling on God's mercy help you when you're discouraged? How can you demonstrate His love to another?**
>
> *Abba Father, I praise You that I can be accepted by You forever because of Your Son. I take refuge in Your perfect love today.*

BIBLE IN A YEAR | JUDGES 13–15; LUKE 6:27–49

When he had received the drink, Jesus said, "It is finished." With that, he bowed his head and gave up his spirit. [JOHN 19:30]

THE COST

Michelangelo's works explored many facets of the life of Jesus, yet one of the most poignant was also one of the simplest. In the 1540s he sketched a pieta (a picture of Jesus' mother holding the body of the dead Christ) for his friend Vittoria Colonna. Done in chalk, the drawing depicts Mary looking to the heavens as she cradles her Son's still form. Rising behind Mary, the upright beam of the cross carries these words from Dante's *Paradise*, "There they don't think of how much blood it costs." Michelangelo's point was profound: when we contemplate the death of Jesus, we must consider the price He paid.

The price paid by Christ is captured in His dying declaration, "It is finished" (JOHN 19:30). The term for "it is finished" *(tetelestai)* was used in several ways—to show a bill had been paid, a task finished, a sacrifice offered, a masterpiece completed. Each of them applies to what Jesus did on our behalf on the cross! Perhaps that's why the apostle Paul wrote, "May I never boast except in the cross of our Lord Jesus Christ, through which the world has been crucified to me, and I to the world" (GALATIANS 6:14).

Jesus' willingness to take our place is the eternal evidence of how much God loves us. As we contemplate the price He paid, may we also celebrate His love—and give thanks for the cross. *BILL CROWDER*

> *How could each meaning of* tetelestai *be applied to the cross of Jesus and what He accomplished there? Why does each one have meaning to you?*
>
> *Father, when I consider the sacrifice Jesus made on my behalf, I am humbled and deeply grateful. Thank You for Jesus, and thank You for the cross.*

Who is like you, LORD God Almighty?
You, LORD, are mighty and your faithfulness
surrounds you. [PSALM 89:8]

RIDING THE WAVES

As my husband strolled down the rocky beach taking photos of the Hawaiian horizon, I sat on a large rock fretting over another medical setback. Though my problems would be waiting for me when I returned home, I needed peace in that moment. I stared at the incoming waves crashing against the black, jagged rocks. A dark shadow in the curve of the wave caught my eye. Using the zoom option on my camera, I identified the shape as a sea turtle riding the waves peacefully. Its flippers spread wide and still. Turning my face into the salty breeze, I smiled.

The "heavens praise [God's] wonders" (PSALM 89:5). Our incomparable God rules "over the surging sea; when its waves mount up, [God] stills them" (V. 9). He "founded the world and all that is in it" (V. 11). He made it all, owns it all, manages it all and purposes it all for His glory and our enjoyment.

Standing on the foundation of our faith—the love of our unchanging Father—we can "walk in the light of [His] presence" (V. 15). God remains mighty in power and merciful in His dealings with us. We can rejoice in His name all day long (V. 16). No matter what obstacles we face or how many setbacks we have to endure, God holds us as the waves rise and fall.

XOCHITL DIXON

***When facing rough waves in life, how can reflecting on God's
wonders fill you with peace, courage and confidence in His
ongoing presence and sufficient care? What situations do you
need to release to God as you ride the waves of life?***

*Father, thank You for empowering me to ride the waves of life
with courageous faith, anchored in Your proven faithfulness.*

Share with the Lord's people who are in need.
Practise hospitality. [ROMANS 12:13]

"SO HELPFUL"

The caller to the Christian radio station said that his wife was coming home from the hospital following surgery. Then he shared something that spoke deeply to my heart: "Everyone in our church family has been so helpful in taking care of us during this time."

When I heard this simple statement, it reminded me of the value and necessity of Christian hospitality and care. I began to think that the love and support of fellow believers for one another is one of the greatest ways to demonstrate the life-changing power of the gospel.

In 1 Peter, the apostle was writing a letter to be circulated among the first-century churches in what's now the country of Turkey. In that letter, he compelled his readers to do something that his friend Paul wrote about in Romans 12:13: "Practise hospitality." Peter said, "Love each other deeply . . . offer hospitality," and he told them to use the gifts God gave them to "serve others" (1 PETER 4:8–10). These are clear directions to all believers in Jesus for how we're to treat fellow believers.

All of us know people like that caller's wife—those who need someone to come alongside and show concern and Christ-like love. In God's strength, may we be among the ones who are noted for being "so helpful."   *DAVE BRANON*

What has God equipped you to do for those in need?
How has God revealed His own hospitable nature?

Loving God, help me to look around for people who
need an encouraging word or action from me.
Then help me offer hospitality to them.

I will drive him like a peg into a firm place.
[ISAIAH 22:23]

ANCHORED IN TRUTH

My family lives in a nearly century-old house with a lot of character, including wonderfully textured plaster walls. A builder cautioned me that with these walls, to hang a picture up I'd have to either drill the nail into a wood support or use a plaster anchor for support. Otherwise, I'd risk the picture crashing to the ground, leaving an ugly hole behind.

The prophet Isaiah used the imagery of a nail driven firmly into a wall to describe a minor biblical character named Eliakim. Unlike the corrupt official Shebna (ISAIAH 22:15–19), as well as the people of Israel—who looked to themselves for strength (VV. 8–11)—Eliakim trusted in God. Prophesying Eliakim's promotion to palace administrator for King Hezekiah, Isaiah wrote that Eliakim would be driven like a "peg into a firm place" (V. 23). Being securely anchored in God's truth and grace would also allow Eliakim to be a support for his family and his people (VV. 22–24).

Yet Isaiah concluded this prophecy with a sobering reminder that no person can be the ultimate security for friends or family—we all fail (V. 25). The only completely trustworthy anchor for our lives is Jesus (PSALM 62:5–6; MATTHEW 7:24). As we care for others and share their burdens, may we also point them to Him, the anchor who will never fail.   *LISA M. SAMRA*

> *How can you stay firmly anchored in God's truth and grace?*
> *In what ways can you support those feeling weighed down*
> *by life's burdens?*

Dear Jesus, thank You for being my anchor. As Your child,
I know that I'm firmly planted in You.

I thank my God every time I remember you.
[PHILIPPIANS 1:3]

COMPANIONS IN CHRIST

The Harvard Study of Adult Development is a decades-long project that's resulted in a greater understanding of the importance of healthy relationships. The research began with a group of 268 university students in the 1930s and has since expanded across different cities. Researchers have conducted interviews with the participants and pored over their medical records every few years. They discovered that close relationships are the biggest factor in predicting happiness and health. It turns out that if we surround ourselves with the right people, we'll likely experience a deeper sense of joy.

This appears to reflect what the apostle Paul is describing in Philippians 1. Writing from prison, Paul can't help but tell his friends that he thanks God for them every time he remembers them, praying "with joy" (V. 4). But these aren't just any friends; these are brothers and sisters in Jesus who "share in God's grace," partners in the gospel with Paul (V. 7). Their relationship was one of sharing and mutuality—a true fellowship shaped by God's love and the gospel itself.

Yes, friends are important, but fellow companions in Christ are catalysts of a true and deep joy. The grace of God can bind us together like nothing else. And even through the darkest seasons of life, the joy that comes from that bond will last.　　*GLENN PACKIAM*

Who are the friends that surround you? What's the substance of your relationships? How has the grace of God shaped your choice of companions?

Dear God, thank You for the gift of friendship. Help me to express my gratitude to those who have been faithful companions to me. Give me the grace to strengthen and encourage them.

The cloud of the LORD was over the tabernacle by day, and fire was in the cloud by night, in the sight of all the Israelites during all their travels.
[EXODUS 40:38]

THROUGH THICK AND THIN

O n 28 January 1986, the Space Shuttle *Challenger* broke apart seventy-three seconds after take-off. In a speech offering comfort, American President Reagan quoted from the poem "High Flight" in which John Gillespie Magee, a World War II pilot, had written of "the high untrespassed sanctity of space" and the sense of putting out his hand to touch "the face of God."

Although we can't literally touch God's face, we sometimes experience a stunning sunset or a place of meditation in nature that gives us an overwhelming sense that He's near. Some people call these moments "thin places." The barrier separating heaven and earth seems to grow a little thinner. *God feels a little closer.*

The Israelites may have experienced a "thin place" as they sensed the nearness of God in the desert wilderness. God provided a pillar of cloud by day and pillar of fire by night to lead them through the desert (EXODUS 40:34–38). When they were staying in the camp, "the glory of the LORD filled the tabernacle" (V. 35). Throughout all their travels, they knew God was with them.

As we enjoy the incredible beauty of God's creation, we grow conscious that He's present everywhere. As we talk with Him in prayer, listen to Him and read the Scriptures, we can enjoy fellowship with Him anytime and anywhere.　　　　*CINDY HESS KASPER*

> **What places in nature make you feel especially close to God? How can you seek Him anytime and anywhere?**
>
> *Father, help me to seek and find You even when I'm lost in a desert wilderness.*

It is better not to . . . do anything . . . that will cause
your brother or sister to fall. [ROMANS 14:21]

LOVE REINS US IN

Most young Samoan boys receive a tattoo signalling their responsibility to their people and their chief. Naturally, then, the marks cover the arms of the Samoan men's rugby team members. Travelling to Japan where tattoos can carry negative connotations, the teammates realised their symbols presented a problem for their hosts. In a generous act of friendship, the Samoans wore skin-coloured sleeves covering the designs. "We're respectful and mindful to . . . the Japanese way," the team captain explained. "We'll be making sure that what we're showing will be okay."

In an age emphasising individual expression, it's remarkable to encounter self-limitation—a concept Paul wrote about in the book of Romans. He told us that love sometimes requires us to lay down our rights for others. Rather than pushing our freedom to the boundaries, sometimes love reins us in. The apostle explained how some people in the church believed they were free "to eat anything," but others ate "only vegetables" (ROMANS 14:2). While this might seem like a minor issue, in the first century, adherence to Old Testament dietary laws was controversial. Paul instructed everyone to "stop passing judgement on one another" (V. 13), before concluding with particular words for those who ate freely. "It is better not to eat meat or drink wine or to do anything else that will cause your brother or sister to fall" (V. 21).

At times, loving another means limiting our own freedoms. We don't have to always do everything we're free to do. Sometimes love reins us in. *WINN COLLIER*

> *When have you seen people limit their freedom for the sake of other believers in Jesus? What was that like? What's difficult about those situations where love reins us in?*
>
> *God, I want to love well. Help me see where I need to encourage others to experience freedom—and where I need to limit how I use my own freedoms.*

Mary Magdalene went to the disciples
with the news: "I have seen the Lord!"
[JOHN 20:18]

IN THE GARDEN

My dad loved to sing the old hymns. One of his favourites was "In the Garden." A few years back, we sang it at his funeral. The chorus is simple: "And He walks with me, and He talks with me, and He tells me I am His own, and the joy we share as we tarry there none other has ever known." That song brought joy to my dad—as it does to me.

Hymn writer C. Austin Miles says he wrote this song in spring 1912 after reading chapter 20 of the gospel of John. "As I read it that day, I seemed to be part of the scene. I became a silent witness to that dramatic moment in Mary's life when she knelt before her Lord and cried, 'Rabboni [Teacher].' "

In John 20, we find Mary Magdalene weeping near Jesus' empty tomb. There she met a man who asked why she was crying. Thinking the man was the gardener, she spoke with the risen Saviour—*Jesus!* Her sorrow turned to joy, and she ran to tell the disciples, "I have seen the Lord!" (V. 18).

We too have the assurance that Jesus is risen! He's now in heaven with the Father, but He hasn't left us on our own. Believers in Christ have His Spirit inside us, and through Him we have the assurance and joy of knowing He's with us, and we are "His own."　　*ALYSON KIEDA*

> ***How is it comforting to know that you don't have to
> do this life on your own? When have you intimately
> felt Jesus' presence?***
>
> *Jesus, I'm so thankful You're alive and that as Your child
> You live in me!*

Yet I will rejoice in the LORD. [HABAKKUK 3:18]

FINDING JOY IN PRAISE

When the famous writer C. S. Lewis first gave his life to Jesus, he initially resisted praising God. In fact, he called it "a stumbling block." His struggle was "in the suggestion that God Himself demanded it." Yet Lewis finally realised "it is in the process of being worshipped that God communicates His presence" to His people. Then we, "in perfect love with God," find joy in Him no more separable "than the brightness a mirror receives" from the "brightness it sheds."

The prophet Habakkuk arrived at this conclusion centuries earlier. After complaining to God about evils aimed at the people of Judah, Habakkuk came to see that praising Him leads to joy—not in what God does, but in who He is. Thus, even in a national or world crisis, God is still great. As the prophet declared:

"Though the fig tree does not bud and there are no grapes on the vines, though the olive crop fails and the fields produce no food, though there are no sheep in the pen and no cattle in the stalls, yet I will rejoice in the LORD" (HABAKKUK 3:17–18). "I will be joyful in God my Saviour," he added.

As C. S. Lewis realised, "The whole world rings with praise." Habakkuk, likewise, surrendered to praising God always, finding rich joy in the One who "marches on forever" (V. 6).   *PATRICIA RAYBON*

When you praise God, what's the impact on your spirit? Reflecting on God's goodness, name three things you can praise Him for today.

Loving God, even during hard times, stir in my heart—and on my lips—the rich spirit of joyful praise to You.

Many are the plans in a person's heart,
but it is the LORD's purpose that prevails.
[PROVERBS 19:21]

IMPERFECT PLANS

was exploring a library on the bottom floor of a new community centre when an overhead crash suddenly shook the room. A few minutes later it happened again, and then again. An agitated librarian finally explained that a weight-lifting area was positioned directly above the library, and the noise occurred every time someone dropped a weight. Architects and designers had carefully planned many aspects of this state-of-the-art facility, yet someone had forgotten to locate the library away from all the action.

In life as well, our plans are often flawed. We overlook important considerations. Our plans don't always account for accidents or surprises. Although planning helps us avoid financial shortfalls, time crunches and health issues, even the most thorough strategies can't eliminate all problems from our lives. We live in a post-Eden world.

With God's help, we can find the balance between prudently considering the future (PROVERBS 6:6–8) and responding to difficulties. God often has a purpose for the trouble He allows into our lives. He may use it to develop patience in us, to increase our faith, or simply to bring us closer to Him. The Bible reminds us, "Many are the plans in a person's heart, but it is the LORD's purpose that prevails" (PROVERBS 19:21). As we submit our goals and hopes for the future to Jesus, He'll show us what He wants to accomplish in us and through us.

JENNIFER BENSON SCHULDT

How do you respond when your plans don't work out or when your expectations are unmet? What might God want you to learn through those experiences?

God, I believe You're in control of everything. Help me to live wisely in this world, committing all my plans to You.

The King will reply, "Truly I tell you, whatever you did for one of the least of these brothers and sisters of mine, you did for me."
[MATTHEW 25:40]

SERVING THE LEAST

His name is Spencer. But everybody calls him "Spence." He was a state track champion in high school; then he went on to attend a prestigious university. He lives now in a large city and is highly respected in the field of chemical engineering. But if you were to ask Spence his greatest achievements to date, he wouldn't mention any of those things. He would excitedly tell you about the trips he makes to Nicaragua every few months to check in on the kids and teachers in the tutoring programme he helped establish in one of the poorest areas of the country. And he'd tell you how enriched his life has been by serving them.

"The least of these." It's a phrase people use in a variety of ways, yet Jesus used it to describe those who, according to the world's standards, have little or nothing to offer us in return for our service. They are the men and women and children the world often overlooks—if not forgets completely. Yet it's exactly those people Jesus elevates to such a beautiful status by saying, "Whatever you did [for them], you did for me" (MATTHEW 25:40). You don't have to have a degree from a prestigious university to understand Christ's meaning: serving "the least" is the same as serving Him. All it really takes is a willing heart.   *JOHN BLASE*

Who comes to mind when you hear the phrase "the least of these"? What's something you could do for them?

King Jesus, I'm afraid I make serving You harder than it is. Your words are clear—You call me to the least and the littlest, perhaps in Nicaragua or maybe in my neighbourhood. Give me courage to serve.

I am reminded of your sincere faith, which first
lived in your grandmother Lois and in your
mother Eunice and, I am persuaded, now lives
in you also. [2 TIMOTHY 1:5]

THE ICING OF FAITH

Hand in hand, my grandson and I skipped across the carpark
to find a special back-to-school outfit. A pre-schooler now, he
was excited about *everything*, and I was determined to ignite
his happiness into joy. I'd just seen a coffee mug with the inscription,
"Grandmas are mums with lots of icing." Icing equals fun, glitter, joy!
That's my job description as his grandma, right? That . . . and more.

In his second letter to his spiritual son Timothy, Paul calls out his
sincere faith—and then credits its lineage both to Timothy's grandmother, Lois, and his mother, Eunice (2 TIMOTHY 1:5). These women
lived out their faith in such a way that Timothy also came to believe
in Jesus. Surely, Lois and Eunice loved Timothy and provided for his
needs. But clearly, they did more. Paul points to the faith living in
them as the source of the faith later living in Timothy.

My job as a grandmother includes the 'icing' moment of a back-
to-school outfit. But even more, I'm called to the icing moments
when I share my faith: bowing our heads over chicken nuggets.
Noticing angelic cloud formations in the sky as God's works of art.
Chirping along with a song about Jesus on the radio. Let's be wooed
by the example of mums and grandmas like Eunice and Lois to let
our faith become the icing in life so others will want what we have.

ELISA MORGAN

> **How have you been influenced by the faith of others?**
> **How are you living out your faith so that others**
> **might be influenced?**
>
> *Dear God, help me to invest my time in living out my*
> *faith before others.*

The fruit of the light consists in all goodness,
righteousness and truth. [EPHESIANS 5:9]

LIVE LIKE IT'S MORNING

When I have to travel across time zones by air, I try various
remedies to avoid jet lag. I think I've tried them all! On
one occasion, I decided to adjust my in-flight eating to
the time zone where I was heading. Instead of eating dinner with
the rest of the passengers, I kept watching a movie and tried to fall
asleep. The hours of elective fasting were difficult, and the breakfast
that came right before we landed left much to be desired. But living
"out of sorts" with those around me *worked.* It jolted my body clock
into a new time zone.

Paul knew that if believers in Jesus were to truly reflect Him
in their lives, they would need to live out of step with the world
around them. They "were once darkness" but now they were to live
as "children of light" (EPHESIANS 5:8). And what might that look like?
Paul goes on to fill out the picture: "The fruit of the light consists
in all goodness, righteousness and truth" (V. 9).

Sleeping through dinner may have seemed foolish to the people
on my flight, but even as it's midnight in the world, as believers,
we're called to live like it's morning. This may provoke scorn and
opposition, but in Jesus we can "walk in the way of love," following
the example of the One who "love[s] us and gave himself up for us
as a fragrant offering and sacrifice to God" (V. 2).   *GLENN PACKIAM*

**Where have your actions and choices lined up too closely
with the world around you? What would the fruit of
goodness, righteousness and truth look like in your life?**

*Jesus, wake me up to the new day that has come in You.
Fill me with Your power to live in a 'different time zone'.
Open my eyes to choose goodness, righteousness and beauty.*

Love them as yourself, for you were foreigners
in Egypt. [LEVITICUS 19:34]

THE BAGGAGE ACTIVITY

Karen, a secondary school teacher, created an activity to teach
her students how to better understand one another. In "The
Baggage Activity" the children wrote down some of the emotional
weights they were carrying. The notes were shared anonymously,
giving the students insight into each other's hardships, often with
a tearful response from their peers. The classroom has since been
filled with a deeper sense of mutual respect among the young
teens, who now have a greater sense of empathy for one another.

Throughout the Bible, God has nudged His people to treat one
another with dignity and show empathy in their interaction with
others (ROMANS 12:15). As early in the history of Israel as the book of
Leviticus, God pointed the Israelites towards empathy—especially
in their dealings with foreigners. He said to "love them as [them-
selves]" because they too had been foreigners in Egypt and knew
that hardship intimately (LEVITICUS 19:34).

Sometimes the burdens we carry make us feel like foreigners—
alone and misunderstood—even among our peers. We don't always
have a similar experience to draw on as the Israelites did with the
foreigners among them. Yet we can always treat those God puts in our
paths with the respect and understanding that we, ourselves, desire.
Whether a modern-day middle schooler, an Israelite or anything in
between, we honour God when we do.   *KIRSTEN HOLMBERG*

Who around you might need your empathy for the burdens
they carry? How can you "love them as yourself"?

God, You know the weight in my heart and You graciously
unburden me as I put my trust in You. Help me to offer care
and compassion toward those in my life.

If your brother or sister sins against you,
rebuke them; and if they repent, forgive them.
[LUKE 17:3]

EXTENDING MERCY

Reflecting on how she forgave Manasseh, the man who killed her husband and some of her children in the Rwandan genocide, Beata said, "My forgiving is based on what Jesus did. He took the punishment for every evil act throughout all time. His cross is the place we find victory—the only place!" Manasseh had written to Beata from prison more than once, begging her—and God—for forgiveness as he detailed the regular nightmares that plagued him. At first she could extend no mercy, saying she hated him for killing her family. But then "Jesus intruded into her thoughts," and with God's help, around two years later, she forgave him.

In this, Beata followed Jesus' instruction to His disciples to forgive those who repent. He said that even if they "sin against you seven times in a day and seven times come back to you saying 'I repent,' you must forgive them" (LUKE 17:4). But to forgive can be extremely difficult, as we see by the disciples' reaction: "Increase our faith!" (V. 5).

Beata's faith increased as she wrestled in prayer over her inability to forgive. If, like her, we're struggling to forgive, we can ask God through His Holy Spirit to help us to do so. As our faith increases, He helps us to forgive.   *AMY BOUCHER PYE*

If someone who wronged you later repented, how
did you react? How could God help you to forgive in
these situations?

Jesus, thank You for releasing me from the consequences of
my sin through Your death on the cross. I give You the glory!

You will go out in joy and be led forth in
peace. [ISAIAH 55:12]

WINDOWS

Near the foothills of the Himalayas, a visitor noticed a row
of houses without windows. His guide explained that some
of the villagers feared that demons might sneak into their
homes while they slept, so they built impermeable walls. You could
tell when a homeowner began to follow Jesus because he put in
windows to let in the light.

A similar dynamic may take place in us, though we might not
see it quite that way. We live in scary, polarising times. Satan and
his demons instigate angry divisions that split families and friends.
I often feel like hiding behind my walls. But Jesus wants me to cut
out a window.

Israel sought refuge in higher walls, but God said their security
lay with Him. He reigns from heaven, and His word governs all
(ISAIAH 55:10–11). If Israel would return to Him, God would "have mercy
on them" (V. 7) and restore them as His people to bless the world
(GENESIS 12:1–3). He would lift them up, ultimately leading them in a
triumphal parade. Their celebration "will be for the LORD's renown,
for an everlasting sign, that will endure forever" (ISAIAH 55:13).

Sometimes walls are necessary. Walls with windows are best. They
show the world that we trust God for the future. Our fears are real.
Our God is greater. Windows open us to Jesus—"the light of the
world" (JOHN 8:12)—and to others who need Him.   *MIKE WITTMER*

> ***Would you say your life is more wall or window?***
> ***Why? Is there a person or situation you need to be***
> ***more open to?***

> *Almighty Father, flood my heart with the confidence*
> *of Your love.*

Praise be to the LORD.
[RUTH 4:14]

HARD GROUND AND TENDER MERCY

When James was just six years old, his older brother David died tragically in an ice-skating accident. It was the day before David's fourteenth birthday. In the years that followed, James tried his best to console his mother, Margaret, who in her deep grief sometimes reminded herself that her elder son would never have to face the challenges of growing up. In James Barrie's fertile imagination, decades later that same idea would burgeon into inspiration for a much-loved children's story character who never aged: Peter Pan. Like a flower pushing its way through pavement, good emerged even from the hard ground of unthinkable heartache.

How comforting is the thought that God, in an infinitely more creative way, is able to bring good out of our most difficult circumstances. A beautiful illustration of this occurs in the Old Testament story of Ruth. Naomi lost her two sons, leaving her without means or support. Her widowed daughter-in-law Ruth chose to remain with Naomi to help provide for her and to serve her God (RUTH 1:16). In the end, God's provision brought them unexpected joy. Ruth remarried and had a child, "and they named him Obed. He was the father of Jesse, the father of David" (4:17). He would also be listed among the ancestors of Jesus (MATTHEW 1:5).

God's tender mercy reaches beyond our ability to fathom and meets us in surprising places. Keep looking! Perhaps you'll see it today. *JAMES BANKS*

When have you seen God bring unexpected good out of difficult circumstances in your life? How can you share what He's done with others?

Loving God, I thank You that one day You'll wipe every tear from my eyes because You're greater than every heartache or difficulty I'll ever face.

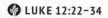
Seek his kingdom.
[LUKE 12:31]

QUARANTINED BY FEAR

In 2020, an outbreak of the coronavirus left the world in fear. People were quarantined, countries were put under lockdown, flights and events were cancelled. Those living in areas with no known cases still feared they might get the virus. Graham Davey, an expert in anxiety, believes that negative news broadcasts are "likely to make you sadder and more anxious." A meme that circulated on social media showed a man watching the news on TV, and he asked how to stop worrying. In response, another person in the room reached over and flipped off the TV, suggesting that the answer might be a shift in focus!

Luke 12 gives us some advice to help us stop worrying: "Seek his kingdom" (V. 31). We seek God's kingdom when we focus on the promise that His followers have an inheritance in heaven. When we face difficulty, we can shift our focus and remember that God sees us and knows our needs (VV. 24–30).

Jesus encourages His disciples: "Do not be afraid, little flock, for your Father has been pleased to give you the kingdom" (V. 32). God enjoys blessing us! Let's worship Him, knowing He cares for us more than the birds of the air and the flowers of the field (VV. 22–29). Even in difficult times, we can read the Scriptures, pray for God's peace, and trust in our good and faithful God.　　　*JULIE SCHWAB*

What's causing you to fear today? What's one thing you can do to seek God's kingdom when you begin to worry?

Loving God, instead of living in fear or worry, help me to focus on Your care for me.

He will give you another advocate to help you
and be with you forever. [JOHN 14:16]

JESUS' PROMISE TO YOU

Jason wailed as his parents handed him over to Amy. It was the
two-year-old's first time in the nursery—and he was *not* happy.
Amy assured them he'd be fine. She tried to soothe him with toys
and books, by rocking in a chair, walking around, standing still and
talking about what fun he could have. But everything was met with
bigger tears and louder cries. Then she whispered five simple words
in his ear: "I will stay with you." Peace and comfort quickly came.

Jesus offered His friends similar words of comfort during the week
of His crucifixion: "The Father . . . will give you another advocate to
help you and be with you forever—the Spirit of truth" (JOHN 14:16–17).
After His resurrection He gave them this promise: "Surely I am with
you always, to the very end of the age" (MATTHEW 28:20). Jesus was
soon to ascend to heaven, but He would send the Spirit to "stay"
and live within His people.

We experience the Spirit's comfort and peace when our tears flow.
We receive His guidance when we're wondering what to do (JOHN 14:26).
He opens our eyes to understand more of God (EPHESIANS 1:17–20),
and He helps us in our weakness and prays for us (ROMANS 8:26–27).

He stays with us forever.   *ANNE CETAS*

What do you need from the Holy Spirit today?
How can knowing He's always near help you?

How thankful I am that You remain always by my
side, Jesus! I need You.

A gentle answer turns away wrath, but a harsh
word stirs up anger. [PROVERBS 15:1]

DIFFICULT PEOPLE

Lucy Worsley is a British historian and TV presenter. Like most people in the public eye, she sometimes receives nasty mail—in her case, over a mild speech impediment that makes her *r*'s sound like *w*'s. One person wrote this: "Lucy, I'll be blunt: please try harder to correct your lazy speech or remove *r*'s from your scripts—I couldn't sit through your TV series because it made me so annoyed. Regards, Darren."

For some people, an insensitive comment like this might trigger an equally rude reply. But here's how Lucy responded: "Oh Darren, I think you've used the anonymity of the internet to say something you probably wouldn't say to my face. Please reconsider your unkind words! Lucy."

Lucy's measured response worked. Darren apologised and vowed not to send anyone such an email again.

"A gentle answer turns away wrath," Proverbs says, "but a harsh word stirs up anger" (15:1). While the hot-tempered person stirs things up, the patient person calms them down (V. 18). When we get a critical comment from a colleague, a snide remark from a family member or a nasty reply from a stranger, we have a choice: to speak angry words that fuel the flames or gentle words that douse them.

May God help us to speak words that turn away wrath—and perhaps even help difficult people to change.   *SHERIDAN VOYSEY*

> **Think of a time you got defensive with someone.**
> **Why do you think you reacted that way? How could**
> **you respond differently in God's power?**
>
> *Loving God, give me the ability to respond to*
> *quarrelsome people with patient, gentle words.*

[God] comforts us in all our troubles, so
that we can comfort those in any trouble.
[2 CORINTHIANS 1:4]

THE GOD OF ALL COMFORT

Radamenes was just a kitten when his owner dropped him off at an animal shelter, thinking he was too ill to recover. The kitten was nursed back to health and adopted by the vet. He then became a full-time resident at the shelter and now spends his days 'comforting' cats and dogs—just out of surgery or recovering from an illness—through his warm presence and gentle purr.

That story is a small picture of what our loving God does for us—and what we can do for others in return. He cares for us in our sickness and struggles, and He soothes us with His presence. The apostle Paul in 2 Corinthians calls our God, "the Father of compassion and the God of all comfort" (1:3). When we are discouraged, depressed or mistreated, He's there for us. When we turn to Him in prayer, He "comforts us in all our troubles" (v. 4).

But verse 4 doesn't end there. Paul, who had experienced intense suffering, continues, "so that we can comfort those in any trouble with the comfort we ourselves receive from God." Our Father comforts us, and when we've experienced His comfort, we're enabled to comfort others.

Our compassionate Saviour, who suffered for us, is more than able to comfort us in our suffering and distress (v. 5). He helps us through our pain and equips us to do the same for others.   *ALYSON KIEDA*

> **When have you experienced God's comfort during a difficult time? When have you offered God's comfort to others?**
>
> *Dear God, thank You for Your comforting presence in my pain and sorrow. Help me in turn to be a comfort to others.*

[Don't look] to your own interests but
each of you to the interests of . . . others.
[PHILIPPIANS 2:4]

SEEING WITH NEW EYES

A video game, one that's become a cultural phenomenon, places a hundred players on a virtual island to compete until one player remains. Whenever a player eliminates you from the contest, you can continue to watch through that player's vantage point. As one journalist notes, "When you step into another player's shoes and inhabit their point of view, the emotional register . . . shifts from self-preservation to . . . communal solidarity. . . . You begin to feel invested in the stranger who, not too long ago, did you in."

Transformation happens whenever we open ourselves to see another's experience, looking beyond our own vision and encountering another's pain, fear, or hopes. When we follow Jesus' example and "do nothing out of selfish ambition or vain conceit" and instead "in humility value others above [our]selves," then we notice things we would have missed otherwise (PHILIPPIANS 2:3). Our concerns broaden. We ask different questions. Rather than being preoccupied with only our own needs or angst, we become invested in others' wellbeing. Rather than looking to "[our] own interests," we become committed "to the interests of . . . others" (V. 4). Rather than protecting what we assume we need to thrive, we joyfully pursue whatever helps others flourish.

With this transformed vision, we gain compassion for others. We discover new ways to love our family. We may even make a friend out of an enemy!   *WINN COLLIER*

How can the Holy Spirit help you avoid becoming small, narrow or selfish? How do you think God's inviting you to see others with new eyes?

Jesus, too often what I see is only my fear, my pain, or my lack. Help me to see my sisters and brothers. I want to truly see them and love them.

BIBLE IN A YEAR | 2 SAMUEL 16–18; LUKE 17:20-37   119

Wisdom and power are his.
[DANIEL 2:20]

BETTER WITH GOD

On her university volleyball team, my granddaughter learned a winning principle. When the ball came her way, no matter what, she could "better the ball." She could make a play that left her teammates in a better situation—without throwing tantrums, blaming or making excuses. Always make the situation better.

That was Daniel's response when he and three Hebrew friends were taken into captivity by Babylon's king Nebuchadnezzar. Although they were given pagan names and ordered to take three years of training in the enemy's palace, Daniel didn't rage. Instead, he asked permission not to defile himself in God's sight by eating the king's rich food and wine. As this intriguing Bible story shows, after consuming nothing but vegetables and water for ten days (DANIEL 1:12), Daniel and his friends "looked healthier and better nourished than any of the young men who ate the royal food" (V. 15).

Another time, Nebuchadnezzar threatened to kill Daniel and all palace wise men if they couldn't repeat the king's disturbing dream and interpret it. Again, Daniel didn't panic, but sought mercy "from the God of heaven," and the mystery was revealed to him in a vision (2:19). As Daniel declared of God, "wisdom and power are his" (V. 20). Throughout his captivity, Daniel sought God's best despite the conflicts he faced. In our own troubles, may we follow that example, making the situation better by taking it to God.   *PATRICIA RAYBON*

> **What battles are you facing now? As you turn
> from those troubles and seek God, how does He
> make your journey better?**

> *Loving God, life's challenges feel overwhelming
> today. As I turn to You, inspire me to shed my
> despair to journey better with You.*

Have you eaten from the tree that
I commanded you not to eat from?
[GENESIS 3:11]

A TREE TO HEAL

For just over £200,000, you can buy a new McLaren 720S sports car. The vehicle comes with a V8 engine pumping 710 horsepower—considerably more than you'll need for your morning commute.

Of course, you might be tempted to use all that power. One driver learned his McLaren was so "fast" it could go from an upscale showroom to the scrap heap in just twenty-four hours! One day after buying the car, he slammed it into a tree. (Thankfully, he survived.)

Just three chapters into the story of the Bible, we learn how a different bad choice and a tree marred God's good creation. Adam and Eve ate from the one tree they were to leave alone (GENESIS 3:11). The story had barely begun, and paradise was cursed (VV. 14–19).

Another tree would play a role in undoing this curse—the cross Jesus endured on our behalf. His death purchased our future with Him (DEUTERONOMY 21:23; GALATIANS 3:13).

The story comes full circle in the Bible's last chapter. There we read of "the tree of life" growing beside the "river of the water of life" (REVELATION 22:1–2). As John describes it, this tree will be "for the healing of the nations" (V. 2). And he assures us, "No longer will there be any curse" (V. 3). God's story comes with the happily-ever-after we all long for.   *TIM GUSTAFSON*

> **How do we already experience the reality of Jesus'
> victory over sin and death today? What do you think is an
> appropriate response to His sacrifice for us?**
>
> *Father, don't let me forget the price it cost Your Son to undo
> the curse we set in motion way back in the garden of Eden.
> All I can say is thank You. All I can give You is my life.*

Be completely humble and gentle; be
patient, bearing with one another in love.
[EPHESIANS 4:2]

AT OUR WORST

"**S**he is tolerable, but not handsome enough to tempt *me*." This sentence, pronounced by Mr. Darcy in Jane Austen's *Pride and Prejudice*, is the reason I will never forget that novel and its impact on me. Because after reading that one sentence, I firmly decided I would never like Mr. Darcy.

But I was wrong. Like Austen's character Elizabeth Bennet, I had the humbling experience of slowly—and quite reluctantly—changing my mind. Like her, I'd been unwilling to get to know Darcy's character as a whole; I preferred to hang onto my reaction to one of his worst moments. After finishing the novel, I wondered who I'd made that same mistake with in the real world. What friendships had I missed because I wouldn't let go of a snap judgement?

At the heart of faith in Jesus is the experience of being seen, loved and embraced by our Saviour—at our worst (ROMANS 5:8; 1 JOHN 4:19). It's the wonder of realising we can surrender our old, false selves for who we truly are in Christ (EPHESIANS 4:23–24). And it's the joy of understanding that we are no longer alone but part of a family, a "body" of those learning to walk the "way of love"—real, unconditional love (5:2).

When we remember what Christ has done for us (V. 2), how can we not long to see others the way He sees us?　　*MONICA LA ROSE*

Why do you think you sometimes cling to negative judgements about others? What experiences have you had of being wrong about someone?

God, it's really hard, sometimes, to let go of that impulse to judge and compare, to resist that need to see myself as better than others. Help me to grasp, deep in my heart, the truth that I don't need to compete and that I am loved.

The heart of the wise inclines to the right,
but the heart of the fool to the left. Even as
fools walk along the road, they lack sense.
[ECCLESIASTES 10:2–3]

LEARNING FROM FOOLISHNESS

A man walked into a convenience store in Wollongong, Australia, put a $20 cash note on the counter and asked for change. When the shop assistant opened the till, the man pulled a gun and asked for all the cash in the register, which the assistant promptly provided. The man took the cash and fled, leaving his original $20 note on the counter. The total amount of cash he got from the till? *Fifteen dollars.*

We all act foolishly at times—even if, unlike this thief, we're trying to do the right thing. The key is how we learn from our foolish behaviour. Without correction, our poor choices can become habits, which will negatively shape our character. We'll become "fools . . . [who] lack sense" (ECCLESIASTES 10:3).

Sometimes it's hard to admit our foolishness because of the extra work it requires. Perhaps we need to reflect on a particular character flaw, and that's painful. Or maybe we need to admit that a decision was made hastily and next time we should take more care. Whatever the reason, it never pays to ignore our foolish ways.

Thankfully, God can use our foolishness to discipline and shape us. Discipline isn't "pleasant at the time," but its training yields good fruit in the long run (HEBREWS 12:11). Let's accept our Father's discipline for our foolish behaviour and ask Him to make us more like the sons and daughters He intends us to be.   *CON CAMPBELL*

What's a recent foolish choice you've made?
What do you think God wants you to learn from it?

*Thank You, Father, for using my foolishness to train
me. May I accept Your discipline graciously as You
continue to work in me.*

BIBLE IN A YEAR | 1 KINGS 1–2; LUKE 19:28–48

Return to your rest, my soul, for the LORD has been good to you. [PSALM 116:7]

CUDDLING IN

"**D**addy, will you read to me?" my daughter asked. It's not an unusual question for a child to make of a parent. But my daughter is eleven now. These days, such requests are fewer than they were when she was younger. "Yes," I said happily, and she curled up next to me on the couch.

As I read to her (from *The Fellowship of the Ring*), she practically melted into me. It was one of those glorious moments as a parent, when we feel perhaps just an inkling of the perfect love our Father has for us and His deep desire for us to 'cuddle in' to His presence and love for us.

I realised in that moment that I'm a lot like my eleven-year-old. Much of the time, I'm focused on being independent. It's so easy to lose touch with God's love for us, a tender and protective love that Psalm 116 describes as "gracious and righteous . . . full of compassion" (V. 5). It's a love where, like my daughter, I can curl up in God's lap, at home in His delight for me.

Psalm 116:7 suggests that we might need to regularly remind ourselves of God's good love, and then crawl up into His waiting arms: "Return to your rest, my soul, for the LORD has been good to you." And indeed, He has.   *ADAM R. HOLZ*

> ***When was the last time you rested quietly in God's love?***
> ***What barriers, if any, might keep you from experiencing***
> ***the Father's delight for you?***

> *Father, thank You for Your perfect love for me. Help me*
> *to remember that love and to rest in Your goodness and*
> *delight in me.*

If you do this and God so commands, you
will be able to stand the strain, and all these
people will go home satisfied. [EXODUS 18:23]

WORKING TOGETHER

J oe worked more than twelve hours a day, often without taking
breaks. Starting a charitable business demanded so much time
and energy that he had little left to offer his wife and children
when he got home. After the toll of chronic stress landed Joe in the
hospital, a friend offered to organise a team to help him. Though he
dreaded giving up control, Joe knew he couldn't keep up his current
pace. He agreed to trust his friend—and God—as he delegated
responsibilities to the group of people they chose together. A year
later, Joe admitted that the charity and his family could never have
prospered if he'd refused the help God had sent him.

God didn't design people to thrive without the support of a loving community. In Exodus 18, Moses led the Israelites through the
wilderness. He tried serving God's people as a teacher, a counsellor
and a judge all on his own. When his father-in-law visited, he offered
Moses advice: "You and these people who come to you will only
wear yourselves out," said Jethro. "The work is too heavy for you;
you cannot handle it alone" (EXODUS 18:18). He encouraged Moses
to share the workload with faithful people. Moses accepted help
and the whole community benefited.

When we trust that God works in and through *all* His people as
we work together, we can find true rest.   *XOCHITL DIXON*

> **How can you trust God by asking for help or offering
> help to someone in leadership this week? How has He
> provided you the support of trustworthy people?**
>
> *Father God, thank You for never asking me to handle
> life without Your help or the support of others.*

Solid food is for the mature.
[HEBREWS 5:14]

MILK COMES FIRST

Back in the seventh century the United Kingdom was many kingdoms often at war. When one king, Oswald of Northumbria, became a believer in Jesus, he called for a missionary to bring the gospel to his region. A man named Corman was sent, but things didn't go well. Finding the English "stubborn", "barbarous" and uninterested in his preaching, he returned home frustrated.

"I am of the opinion," a monk named Aidan told Corman, "that you were more severe to your unlearned hearers than you ought to have been." Instead of giving the Northumbrians "the milk of more easy doctrine," Corman had given them teaching they couldn't yet grasp. Aidan went to Northumbria, adapted his preaching to the people's understanding, and thousands became believers in Jesus.

Aidan got this sensitive approach to mission from Scripture. "I gave you milk, not solid food," Paul told the Corinthians, "for you were not yet ready for it" (1 CORINTHIANS 3:2). Before right living can be expected from people, Hebrews says, basic teaching about Jesus, repentance, and baptism must be grasped (HEBREWS 5:13–6:2). While maturity should follow (5:14), let's not miss the order. Milk comes before meat. People can't obey teaching they don't understand.

The faith of the Northumbrians ultimately spread to the rest of the country and beyond. Like Aidan, when sharing the gospel with others, we meet people where they are. *SHERIDAN VOYSEY*

In simple terms, how would you explain the gospel?
How can you avoid expecting people who aren't
believers in Jesus to think or behave as you do?

Jesus, thank You for reaching me in ways I could understand.

NO NEED TO ARGUE

I spent a year trying to persuade Li Jun that God existed. I told her that our beautiful world must have had a Designer and that the moral law requires a Lawgiver. She was unmoved. Later, as I was reading Romans chapter one, I noted that it says everyone knows God's "eternal power and divine nature," and that those who say they don't "are without excuse" (V. 20). *That's interesting!* I thought. The next time Li Jun raised the subject, I was ready.

"Professor Wittmer," she asked. "Why do you believe in God?"

I returned the question. "Tell me, Li Jun, why do you?"

"Oh!" she said. And suddenly, she realised that deep down, she really did believe in God. Several months later, Li Jun chose to follow Jesus!

Of course, not everyone will respond this way. We need the Holy Spirit to stop our suppression of the truth and open our hearts to Jesus (V. 18). But everyone intuitively knows that God exists, and that He's powerful and righteous (VV. 20, 32).

This knowledge frees us to avoid arguments. We don't have to prove something that people already know. The pressure's off! We're free to ask questions about their beliefs, buying another round of coffee to keep the conversation going. Perhaps our discussion will put a pebble in their shoe, and down the road they'll shake it out and give their life to Christ. When we remember what people already know, we realise we don't need to debate them. We're free to be their friend.

Mike Wittmer, Our Daily Bread *author*

★ The topic of **DEFENDING OUR FAITH** is explored in the above feature article and the devotions for **May 1, 9, 16** and **23**. We hope these articles will inspire you as you witness for Christ.

Faith is confidence in what we hope for
and assurance about what we do not see.
[HEBREWS 11:1]

WHAT CAN'T BE SEEN

Historians say the Atomic Age began on 16 July, 1945, when the first nuclear weapon was detonated in a remote desert of New Mexico. But Greek philosopher Democritus (c. 460–370 BC) was exploring the existence and power of the atom long before the invention of anything that could even see these tiny building blocks of the universe. Democritus comprehended more than he could see and atomic theory was the result.

The Scriptures tell us that the essence of faith is embracing what can't be seen. Hebrews 11:1 affirms, "Now faith is confidence in what we hope for and assurance about what we do not see." This assurance isn't the result of wishful or positive thinking. It's confidence in the God we can't see but whose existence is the truest reality in the universe. His reality is displayed in His creative works (PSALM 19:1) and made visible by revealing His invisible character and ways in His Son, Jesus, who came to show the Father's love to us (JOHN 1:18).

This is the God in whom "we live and move and have our being," as the apostle Paul put it (ACTS 17:28). As such, "we live by faith, not by sight" (2 CORINTHIANS 5:7). Yet we don't walk alone. The unseen God walks with us every step of the way.   *BILL CROWDER*

> *In a world where seeing is believing, in what ways do you struggle to live by faith in God? What has strengthened your faith, and in what areas do you need to rest in Him more fully?*

> *Father, sometimes it's a struggle to believe what I can't see. Nevertheless, You've promised Your faithful love and that You'll never leave me or forsake me. Help me to rest in that promise.*

I pray that . . . he may strengthen you with
power through his Spirit in your inner being,
so that Christ may dwell in your hearts
through faith. [EPHESIANS 3:16–17]

DWELLING IN OUR HEARTS

Sometimes the words of children can jolt us into a deeper understanding of God's truth. One evening when my daughter was young, I told her about one of the great mysteries of the Christian faith—that God through His Son and Spirit dwells in His children. As I tucked her into bed, I said that Jesus was with her and in her. "He's in my tummy?" she asked. "Well, you haven't swallowed Him," I replied. "But He's right there with you."

My daughter's literal translation of Jesus being 'in her tummy' made me stop and consider how when I asked Jesus to be my Saviour, He came and took residence within me.

The apostle Paul referred to this mystery when he prayed that the Holy Spirit would strengthen the believers in Ephesus so that Christ would "dwell in [their] hearts through faith" (EPHESIANS 3:17). With Jesus living within, they could grasp how deeply He loved them. Fuelled by this love, they would mature in their faith and love others with humility and gentleness while speaking the truth in love (4:2, 25).

Jesus dwelling inside His followers means that His love never leaves those who've welcomed Him into their lives. His love that surpasses knowledge (3:19) roots us to Him, helping us to understand how deeply He loves us.

Words written for children can say it best: "Yes, Jesus loves me!"

AMY BOUCHER PYE

How does Jesus dwelling inside you give you great
comfort? How can you grow closer to God knowing
that His power gives you strength?

God, You're not far off, but are close to me.
May I delight in Your love and share it with others.

BIBLE IN A YEAR | 1 KINGS 12–13; LUKE 22:1–20

Give to the one who asks you.
[MATTHEW 5:42]

JESUS' UNPOPULAR IDEAS

For fifteen years, Mike Burden held hate-filled meetings in the memorabilia shop he ran in his small town. But in 2012 when his wife began to question his involvement, his heart softened. He realised how wrong his racist views were and didn't want to be that person any longer. The militant group retaliated by kicking his family out of the flat they'd been renting from one of the members.

Where did he turn for help? Surprisingly, he went to a local black pastor with whom he'd clashed. The pastor and his church provided housing and groceries for Mike's family for some time. When asked why he agreed to help, Pastor Kennedy explained, "Jesus Christ did some very unpopular things. When it's time to help, you do what God wants you to do." Later Mike spoke at Kennedy's church and apologised to the black community for his part in spreading hatred.

Jesus taught some unpopular ideas in the Sermon on the Mount: "Give to the one who asks you . . . . Love your enemies and pray for those who persecute you" (MATTHEW 5:42, 44). That's the upside-down way of thinking God calls us to follow. Though it looks like weakness, it's actually acting out of God's strength.

The One who teaches us is the One who gives the power to live out this upside-down life in whatever way He asks of us. *ANNE CETAS*

*How are you living out Jesus' words of giving
to those who ask and loving your enemies?
What would you like to change?*

*God, help me to love others as You love me.
Show me how to do that today.*

If we are thrown into the blazing furnace,
the God we serve is able to deliver us . . . .
But even if he does not . . . we will not serve
your gods. [DANIEL 3:17–18]

FUELLED BY FIRE

When two firefighters, weary and sooty, stopped at a restaurant for breakfast, the waitress recognised the men from the news and realised they'd spent the night battling a warehouse fire. To show her appreciation, she wrote a note on their receipt, "Your breakfast is on me today. Thank you . . . for serving others and for running into the places everyone else runs away from. . . . Fuelled by fire and driven by courage, what an example you are."

In the Old Testament, we see an example of courage in the actions of three young men: Shadrach, Meshach and Abednego (DANIEL 3). Instead of obeying the mandate to bow down to a statue of the Babylonian king, these young men courageously showed their love for God through their refusal. Their penalty was to be thrown into a blazing furnace. Yet the men didn't back down: "If we are thrown into the blazing furnace, the God we serve is able to deliver us from it, and he will deliver us from Your Majesty's hand. But even if he does not . . . we will not serve your gods or worship the image of gold" (VV. 17–18).

God did rescue them and even walked with them in the fire (VV. 25–27). In our fiery trials and troubles today, we too have the assurance that God is with us. He is able.   *ALYSON KIEDA*

> ***When have you felt God's presence during a
> difficult trial? What gives you confidence to
> press on when challenges come?***
>
> *Almighty God, thank You for being with me in the
> fire and for comforting me with Your presence.*

I consider everything a loss because of the surpassing worth of knowing Christ Jesus my Lord. [PHILIPPIANS 3:8]

IT'S WHO YOU KNOW

In early 2019, Charlie VanderMeer died at the age of eighty-four. For many decades, he was known to thousands and thousands of people as Uncle Charlie, the host of a radio show called *Children's Bible Hour*. The day before Uncle Charlie slipped into eternity, he told a good friend, "It's not *what* you know, it's *who* you know. Of course, I'm talking about Jesus Christ."

Even as he faced the end of his life, Uncle Charlie couldn't help but talk about Jesus and the necessity for people to receive Him as their Saviour.

The apostle Paul considered knowing Jesus his most important task: "I consider everything a loss because of the surpassing worth of knowing Christ Jesus my Lord, for whose sake I have lost all things. I consider them garbage, that I may gain Christ and be found in him" (PHILIPPIANS 3:8–9). And how do we know Jesus? "If you declare with your mouth, 'Jesus is Lord,' and believe in your heart that God raised him from the dead, you will be saved" (ROMANS 10:9).

We may know facts about Jesus, we may know all about the church, and we may even be familiar with the Bible. But the only way to know Jesus as Saviour is to accept His free gift of salvation. He's the Who we need to know.   *DAVE BRANON*

In your relationship with Jesus, how have you experienced that it's Who you know, not what? What has Christ's forgiveness meant to you?

Father God, I pray for all who've yet to come to know Jesus by believing in Him and accepting His sacrifice on their behalf. And if I'm one who hasn't received Jesus as my Saviour, may I confess with my mouth "Jesus is Lord" today.

LORD, you are the God who saves me.
[PSALM 88:1]

HEAVY BUT HOPEFUL

In a *Peanuts* comic strip, the very enterprising character Lucy advertised "psychiatric help" for five pounds. Linus found his way to her office and acknowledged his "deep feelings of depression." When he asked her what he could do about his condition, Lucy's quick reply was, "Snap out of it! Five pounds, please."

While such light-hearted entertainment brings a momentary smile, the sadness and gloom that can grip us when real life happens is not that easily dismissed. Feelings of hopelessness and despair are real, and sometimes professional attention is needed.

Lucy's advice wasn't helpful in addressing real anguish. However, the writer of Psalm 88 does offer something instructive and hopeful. A mountain of trouble had arrived at his doorstep. And so, with raw honesty, he poured out his heart to God. "I am overwhelmed with troubles and my life draws near to death" (V. 3). "You have put me in the lowest pit, in the darkest depths" (V. 6). "Darkness is my closest friend" (V. 18). We hear, feel and perhaps identify with the psalmist's pain. Yet, that's not all. His lament is laced with hope. "LORD, you are the God who saves me; day and night I cry out to you. May my prayer come before you; turn your ear to my cry" (VV. 1–2; SEE VV. 9, 13). Heavy things do come and practical steps such as counsel and medical care may be needed. But never abandon hope in God.   *ARTHUR JACKSON*

When have you turned to God in the midst of your despair?
What's keeping you from crying out to Him now?

Father, help me to see Your open, welcome arms
regardless of my situation.

Pray for me, too. Ask God to give me the right words so I can boldly explain God's mysterious plan. [EPHESIANS 6:19 NLT]

THE RIGHT WORDS

In the past year or so, a number of authors have urged believers to take a fresh look at the 'vocabulary' of our faith. One writer, for example, emphasised that even theologically rich words of faith can lose their impact when, through overfamiliarity and over-use, we lose touch with the depths of the gospel and our need for God. When that happens, he suggested, we may need to relearn the language of faith "from scratch", letting go of our assumptions until we can see the good news for the first time.

The invitation to learn to 'speak the language of the Bible from scratch' reminds me of Paul, who devoted his life to "[becoming] all things to all people . . . for the sake of the gospel" (1 CORINTHIANS 9:22–23). He never assumed he knew best how to communicate what Jesus had done. Instead, he relied on constant prayer and pleaded for fellow believers to pray for him as well—to help him find "the right words" (EPHESIANS 6:19 NLT) to share the good news.

The apostle also knew the need for each believer in Christ to remain humble and receptive each day to their need for deeper roots in His love (3:16–17). It's only as we deepen our roots in God's love, each day becoming more aware of our dependence on His grace, that we can begin to find the right words to share the incredible news of what He's done for us.　　　　　　　*MONICA LA ROSE*

When have you had an experience of seeing the gospel in a new way for the first time? How can prayer keep your heart receptive to your constant need for God's grace?

Loving God, forgive me for, far too often, taking Your grace and goodness for granted. Help me to daily grasp in new ways the depths of Your grace and love. And help me find the right words to share what You've done.

　　BIBLE IN A YEAR | 2 KINGS 1–3; LUKE 24:1–35

The Spirit you received brought about your
adoption to sonship. [ROMANS 8:15]

LEGALLY HIS

Liz cried for joy when she and her husband received the birth
certificate and passport for their child, making the adoption
legally binding. Now Milena would always be their daughter,
forever part of their family. As Liz pondered the legal process, she
also thought of the true exchange that happens when we become
part of Jesus' family: no longer are we held down by our birth right
of sin and brokenness. *Rather*, she reflected, *we enter into the fullness of God's kingdom legally when we are adopted as His children*.

In the apostle Paul's day, if a Roman family adopted a son, his
legal status would change completely. Any debts from his old life
would be cancelled and he would gain all of the rights and privileges
of his new family. Paul wanted the Roman believers in Jesus to understand that this new status applied to them too. No longer were
they bound to sin and condemnation but now they lived "according
to the Spirit" (ROMANS 8:4). And those the Spirit leads are adopted
as God's children (VV. 14–15). Their legal status changed when they
became citizens of heaven.

If we have received the gift of salvation, we too are God's children,
heirs of His kingdom and united with Christ. Our debts have been
cancelled by the gift of Jesus' sacrifice. We no longer need to live
in fear or condemnation.   *AMY BOUCHER PYE*

> **How does your status as a child of God affect
> how you live? What could you do to embrace this
> central part of your identity?**
>
> *Father God, You created me in my mother's womb,
> and You know and love me. May I never doubt how
> much You care for me.*

BIBLE IN A YEAR | 2 KINGS 4-6; LUKE 24:36-53

Look at the birds of the air; they do not sow
or reap or store away in barns, and yet your
heavenly Father feeds them. [MATTHEW 6:26]

NOTICING NATURE

Afriend and I recently visited a favourite walking spot of mine.
Climbing a windswept hill, we crossed a field of wildflowers
into a forest of towering pines, then descended into a valley
where we paused a moment. Clouds floated softly above us. A stream
trickled nearby. The only sounds were birdsongs. Jason and I stood
there silently for fifteen minutes, taking it all in.

As it turns out, our actions that day were deeply therapeutic.
According to research from one university, people who stop to contemplate nature experience higher levels of happiness, lower levels
of anxiety and a greater desire to care for the earth. Walking through
the forest isn't enough, though. You have to *watch* the clouds, *listen*
to the birds. The key isn't *being in* nature, but *noticing* it.

Could there be a spiritual reason for nature's benefits? Paul said
that creation reveals God's power and nature (ROMANS 1:20). God told
Job to look at the sea, sky and stars for evidence of His presence
(JOB 38–39). Jesus said that contemplating the "birds of the air" and
"flowers of the field" could reveal God's care and reduce anxiety
(MATTHEW 6:25–30). In Scripture, noticing nature is a spiritual practice.

Scientists wonder why nature affects us so positively. Maybe one
reason is that by noticing nature we catch a glimpse of the God who
created it and who created us.   *SHERIDAN VOYSEY*

> ***Since nature isn't God, and vice-versa, how do
> you think He can be seen through it? How can
> you take a few minutes today to notice His care
> through His creation?***
>
> *God of heaven, earth, streams and
> birdsongs, I worship You today.*

[He] will rejoice over you with singing.
[ZEPHANIAH 3:17]

SINGING OVER US

A young father held his baby boy in his arms, singing to him and rocking him in soothing rhythm. The baby was hearing-impaired, unable to hear the melody or the words. Yet the father sang anyway, in a beautiful, tender act of love towards his son. And his efforts were rewarded with a delightful smile from his little boy.

The imagery of the father-son exchange bears a striking resemblance to the words of Zephaniah. The Old Testament prophet says that God will joyfully sing over His daughter, the people of Jerusalem (ZEPHANIAH 3:17). God enjoys doing good things for His beloved people, such as taking away their punishment and turning back their enemies (V. 15). Zephaniah says they no longer have any reason for fear and instead have cause for rejoicing.

We, as God's children redeemed by the sacrifice of Jesus Christ, sometimes are hard of hearing—unable, or perhaps unwilling, to tune our ears to the exuberant love God sings over us. His adoration of us is like that of the young father, who lovingly sang to his son despite his inability to hear. He has taken away our punishment too, giving us further reason to rejoice. Perhaps we might try to listen more closely to hear the joy ringing loudly in His voice. *Father, help us to hear Your loving melody and savour being held safely in Your arms.*

KIRSTEN HOLMBERG

What keeps you from hearing God? How can you tune your ears to hear His delight in you?

Thank You, God, for taking great delight in me. May I always listen to your voice as You joyfully sing over me.

He calls his own sheep by name and
leads them out. [JOHN 10:3]

MORE THAN GOOD ADVICE

A few years ago, I was invited to speak on the subject of guidance. In my preparation, I opened my concordance to look up the word guidance, expecting to find a long list of verses promising guidance from God. To my surprise, guidance wasn't there. Instead, I found the word guide and a number of verses promising that God Himself would be the guide of His people.

This discovery added fresh insight to my Christian walk. I was reminded that people who are blind need guide dogs, not guidance dogs! Even if dogs were capable of talking, how unsatisfactory it would be if they were mere bystanders, shouting warnings to the blind from a distance: "Careful now! You're approaching a hole. Watch out for the curb!" No, these mute but faithful creatures escort their sightless companions every step of the way, being their eyes and steering them safely along precarious pathways.

Some people want God to be like a glorified advice bureau. But when our sight is dim and our way is dark, as it often is, we need more than good advice—we need the Good Shepherd to lead us (JOHN 10:3, 11).

As we follow Christ each day, we'll have all the guidance we'll ever need.   *JOANIE YODER*

How does reading the Bible help you learn to hear Jesus' voice? How does it encourage you that God is right here to guide you through every situation?

God of wisdom, teach me Your ways and help me to listen to Jesus' voice. Thank You that my Good Shepherd leads me.

My heart rejoices in the LORD; in the LORD my
horn is lifted high. [1 SAMUEL 2:1]

RENEWED VISION

After a painful minor surgery on my left eye, my doctor recommended a vision test. With confidence, I covered my right eye
and read each line on the chart with ease. Covering my left
eye, I gasped. How could I not realise I'd been so blind?

While adjusting to new glasses and renewed vision, I thought of
how daily trials often caused me to be spiritually near sighted. Focusing only on what I could see up-close—my pain and ever-changing
circumstances—I became blind to the faithfulness of my eternal and
unchanging God. With such a limited perspective, hope became an
unattainable blur.

We're told the story in 1 Samuel 1 of another woman who failed
to recognise God's trustworthiness while focusing on her current
anguish, uncertainty and loss. For years, Hannah had endured child-
lessness and endless torment from Peninnah, the other wife of her
husband Elkanah. Hannah's husband adored her, but contentment
evaded her. One day, she prayed with bitter honesty. When Eli the
priest questioned her, she explained her situation. As she left, he
prayed that God would grant her request (1 SAMUEL 1:17). Though
Hannah's situation didn't change immediately, she walked away
with confident hope (V. 18).

Her prayer in 1 Samuel 2:1–2 reveals a shift in Hannah's focus.
Even before her circumstances improved, Hannah's renewed vision
changed her perspective and her attitude. She rejoiced in the ongoing
presence of God—her Rock and everlasting hope.　*XOCHITL DIXON*

> ***Why can you experience hope when focusing on your
> unchanging God instead of your ever-changing circumstances,
> desires and feelings? In what situation are you currently
> struggling with spiritual near sightedness?***

> *God, please renew my vision so I can focus on Your constant
> presence and live with an eternal perspective in all circumstances.*

BIBLE IN A YEAR | 2 KINGS 15–16; JOHN 3:1–18

Strike the rock, and water will come out of it
for the people to drink. [EXODUS 17:6]

ABUNDANT WATERS

I n Australia, a report outlined "a grim story" of extreme drought,
heat and fire. The account described a horrific year with only
minuscule rainfall, turning parched brush into tinder. Raging fires
torched the countryside. Fish died. Crops failed. All because they
didn't have a simple resource we often take for granted—water,
which we all need in order to live.

Israel found itself in its own terrifying dilemma. As the people
camped in the dusty, barren desert, we read this alarming line:
"There was no water for the people to drink" (EXODUS 17:1). The
people were afraid. Their throats were dry. The sand sizzled. Their
children suffered thirst. Terrified, the people "quarrelled with Moses," demanding water (V. 2). But what could Moses do? He could
only go to God.

And God gave Moses odd instructions: "Take . . . the staff [and]
. . . strike the rock, and water will come out of it for the people to
drink" (VV. 5–6). So Moses hit the rock, and out gushed a river, plenty
for the people and their cattle. That day, Israel knew that their God
loved them. Their God provided abundant water.

If you're experiencing a drought or wilderness in life, know that
God is aware of it and He's with you. Whatever your need, whatever your lack, may you find hope and refreshment in His abundant
waters.   *WINN COLLIER*

> **Where are the parched and barren places in your world?**
> **How can you look for and trust in God's abundant waters?**
>
> *I need Your water, God, Your provision. If You don't help me,*
> *I don't think I'll make it. Will You bring me the water I need?*

People who . . . lack understanding are like the
beasts that perish. [PSALM 49:20]

TAKEN IN

My old dog sits by my side and stares off into space. A penny
for her thoughts. One thing I know she *isn't* thinking about
is dying because dogs don't 'understand'. They don't think
about future things. But we do. No matter our age or health or
wealth, we at some point think about dying. That's because we,
unlike beasts, have "understanding", according to Psalm 49:20.
We know that we will die, and there's nothing we can do about it.
"No one can redeem the life of another or give to God a ransom
for them" (V. 7). No one has enough money to buy himself or herself
out of the grave.

But there is a way out of the finality of death: "God will redeem
me from the realm of the dead," insists the psalmist. "He will surely
take me to himself"; literally, "He will take me in" (V. 15). Robert Frost
said, "Home is the place where, when you have to go there, they
have to take you in." God has redeemed us from death through His
Son, "who gave himself as a ransom for all people" (1 TIMOTHY 2:6).
Thus Jesus promised that when our time comes, He will greet us
and take us in (JOHN 14:3).

When my time comes, Jesus, who gave to God the price of my
life, will welcome me into His Father's house with open arms.

DAVID H. ROPER

How do you deal with the thought of dying?
On what do you base your confidence of heaven?

I'm grateful, God, that You have provided a place for
Your children. I look forward to being at home with You.

You will shine among them like stars in the sky as you hold firmly to the word of life.
[PHILIPPIANS 2:15–16]

SHINING STARS

I can close my eyes and go back in time to the house where I grew up. I remember stargazing with my father. We took turns squinting through his telescope, trying to focus on glowing dots that shimmered and winked. These pinpricks of light, born of heat and fire, stood out in sharp contrast to the smooth, ink-black sky.

Do you consider yourself to be a shining star? I'm not talking about reaching the heights of human achievement, but standing out against a dark background of brokenness and evil. The apostle Paul told the Philippian believers that God would shine in and through them as they held "firmly to the word of life" and avoided grumbling and arguing (PHILIPPIANS 2:14–16).

Our unity with other believers and our faithfulness to God can set us apart from the world. The problem is that these things don't come naturally. We constantly strive to overcome temptation so we can maintain a close relationship with God. We wrestle against selfishness to have harmony with our spiritual brothers and sisters.

But still, there's hope. Alive in each believer, God's Spirit empowers us to be self-controlled, kind and faithful (GALATIANS 5:22–23). Just as we are called to live beyond our natural capacity, God's supernatural help makes this possible (PHILIPPIANS 2:13). If every believer became a "shining star" through the power of the Spirit, just imagine how the light of God would repel the darkness around us!

JENNIFER BENSON SCHULDT

What causes your light for Jesus to dim?
What do you need to do to brighten it?

Loving God, I ask Your Spirit to empower me to shine in the darkness. Make me into someone who is known for my love of others and my faithfulness to You.

They show that the requirements of the law
are written on their hearts. [ROMANS 2:15]

GUILT AND FORGIVENESS

I n his book *Human Universals,* anthropologist Donald Brown lists
more than four hundred behaviours that he considers common
across humanity. He includes such things as toys, jokes, dances
and proverbs, wariness of snakes, and tying things with string!
Likewise, he believes all cultures have concepts of right and wrong,
where generosity is praised, promises are valued and things like
meanness and murder understood to be wrong. We all have a sense
of conscience, wherever we're from.

The apostle Paul made a similar point many centuries ago. While
God gave the Jewish people the Ten Commandments to clarify right
from wrong, Paul noted that since gentiles could do right by obeying
their conscience, God's laws were evidently written on their hearts
(ROMANS 2:14–15). But that didn't mean people always *did* what was
right. The gentiles rebelled against their conscience (1:32), the Jews
broke the Law (2:17–24), leaving both guilty. But through faith in
Jesus, God removes the death penalty from all our rule-breaking
(3:23–26; 6:23).

Since God created all humans with a sense of right and wrong,
each of us will likely feel some guilt over a bad thing we've done or a
good thing we failed to do. When we confess those sins, God wipes
away the guilt like a whiteboard wiped clean. All we have to do is
ask Him—whoever we are, wherever we're from.   *SHERIDAN VOYSEY*

***Where do you think humanity's sense of right and wrong
comes from? What guilt feelings are you wanting Jesus'
forgiveness for today?***

*Jesus, I've failed to do right and succeeded in doing wrong.
Forgive me. Thank You for dying my death so I don't have to.*

I will say, "Salvation comes from the LORD."
[JONAH 2:9]

PURSUED BY LOVE

" I fled Him, down the nights and down the days," opens the famous poem "The Hound of Heaven" by English poet Francis Thompson. Thompson describes Jesus' unceasing pursuit—despite his efforts to hide, or even run away, from God. The poet concludes, "I am he whom Thou seekest!"

The pursuing love of God is a central theme of the book of Jonah. The prophet received an assignment to tell the people of Nineveh (notorious enemies of Israel) about their need to turn to God, but instead "Jonah ran away from the LORD" (JONAH 1:3). He secured passage on a ship sailing in the opposite direction of Nineveh, but the vessel was soon overcome by a violent storm. To save the ship's crew, Jonah was thrown overboard before being swallowed by a large fish (1:15–17).

In his own beautiful poem, Jonah recounted that despite his best efforts to run away from God, God pursued him. When Jonah was overcome by his situation and needed to be saved, he cried out to God in prayer and turned toward His love (2:2, 8). God answered and provided rescue not only for Jonah, but for his Assyrian enemies as well (3:10).

As described in both poems, there may be seasons of our lives when we try to run from God. Even then Jesus loves us and is at work guiding us back into restored relationship with Him (1 JOHN 1:9).

LISA M. SAMRA

When have you tried to run from God?
How did He provide rescue?

Jesus, thank You for lovingly pursuing me
to offer rescue.

The people walking in darkness have seen a
great light. [ISAIAH 9:2]

FACING THE DARKNESS

I n the mid-1960s, two people participated in research on the effects
of darkness on the human psyche. They entered separate caves,
while researchers tracked their eating and sleeping habits. One
remained in total darkness for 88 days, the other 126 days. Each
guessed how long they could remain in darkness and were off by
months. One took what he thought was a short nap only to discover
he'd slept for *30 hours.* Darkness is disorienting.

The people of God found themselves in the darkness of impending
exile. They waited, unsure of what would take place. The prophet
Isaiah used darkness as a metaphor for their disorientation and as
a way of speaking about God's judgment (ISAIAH 8:22). Previously, the
Egyptians had been visited with darkness as a plague (EXODUS 10:21–29).
Now Israel found herself in darkness.

But a light would come. "The people walking in darkness have seen
a great light; on those living in the land of deep darkness a light has
dawned" (ISAIAH 9:2). Oppression would be broken, disorientation
would end. A Child would come to change everything and bring
about a new day—a day of forgiveness and freedom (V. 6).

Jesus did come! And although the darkness of the world can be
disorienting, may we experience the comfort of the forgiveness,
freedom and light found in Christ.

GLENN PACKIAM

**What would it look like to embrace a new day of
freedom and forgiveness? How can you welcome
the light of Christ today?**

*Dear Jesus, shine Your light into my life. Bring
forgiveness and freedom. Help me to live in the
light of Your arrival.*

She did what she could. She poured perfume
on my body beforehand to prepare for my
burial. [MARK 14:8]

SHE DID WHAT SHE COULD

She loaded the plastic container of cupcakes onto the conveyor belt, sending it towards the shop assistant. Next came the birthday card and various bags of crisps. Hair escaped from her ponytail, crowning her fatigued forehead. Her toddler clamoured for attention. The assistant announced the total and the mum's face fell. "Oh, I guess I'll have to put something back. But these are for her party," she sighed, glancing regretfully at her child.

Standing behind her in line, another customer recognised this mother's pain. This scene is familiar in Jesus' words to Mary of Bethany: "She did what she could" (MARK 14:8). After anointing Him with a bottle of expensive nard before His death and burial, Mary was ridiculed by the disciples. Jesus corrected His followers by celebrating what she had done. He didn't say, "She did *all* she could," but rather, "She did *what* she could." The lavish cost of the perfume wasn't His point. It was Mary's investment of her love in action that mattered. A relationship with Jesus results in a response.

In that moment, before the mum could object, the second customer leaned forward and inserted her credit card into the reader, paying for the purchase. It wasn't a large expense, and she had extra funds that month. But to that mum, it was everything. A gesture of pure love poured out in her moment of need.   *ELISA MORGAN*

> *In what unexpected ways has Jesus helped you?*
> *What might you do—not* all, *but* what—*to love*
> *Jesus back in a need you see today?*
>
> *Father, open my eyes to see You inviting me to do*
> *what I can do today.*

Walk humbly with your God.
[MICAH 6:8]

WALK, DON'T RUN

'd see her welcoming the dawn each day. She was our local power walker. As I drove my kids to school, she'd be there on the road's shoulder. Equipped with an oversized pair of headphones and knee-high, colourful socks, she walked with an alternating movement of arms and feet, always with one foot in contact with the ground. The sport is different from running or jogging. Power walking involves an intentional restraint, a reining in of the body's natural inclination to run. Although it doesn't look like it, there's just as much energy, focus and power involved as in running or jogging. But it's under control.

Power under control—that's the key. Biblical humility, like power walking, is often viewed as weakness. The truth is, it's not. Humility isn't diminishing our strengths or abilities, but rather allowing them to be reined in much like the arms and legs and feet guided by the mind of an early morning power walker.

Micah's words "walk humbly" are a call for us to rein in our inclination to go ahead of God. He says "to act justly and to love mercy" (6:8), and that can bring with it a desire to do something and do it fast. That's fair since the daily injustices in our world are so overwhelming. But we are to be controlled and directed by God. Our goal is to see *His* will and purposes accomplished in the dawning of *His* kingdom here on earth.

JOHN BLASE

> **In what circumstance have you 'run ahead'**
> **of God? Do you usually view humility as a**
> **strength or a weakness? Why?**

> *To walk humbly with You, O God, is not always*
> *easy. Train me, so that my steps are in tune with*
> *You and Your will.*

Peace, be still!
[MARK 4:39 NKJV]

SAFELY ASHORE

In Papua New Guinea, the Kandas tribe awaited with excitement the arrival of New Testament Bibles printed in their language. To reach the village, however, the people bringing the books had to travel on the ocean in small boats.

What gave them courage to travel across great waters? Their seafaring skills, yes. But they also knew who created the seas. He's the One who guides each of us across our life's churning waves and deepest waters.

As David wrote, "Where can I go from your Spirit?" (PSALM 139:7). "If I go up to the heavens, you are there; . . . if I settle on the far side of the sea, even there your hand will guide me, your right hand will hold me fast" (VV. 8–10).

These words would resonate deeply with the Kandas, who live on an island nation whose tropical coasts, dense rainforests, and rugged mountains have been called "The Last Unknown." Yet as believers there and everywhere know, no place or problem is too remote for God. "Even the darkness will not be dark to you," says Psalm 139:12, and "the night will shine like the day, for darkness is as light to you."

On stormy waters, therefore, our God speaks, "Peace, be still!" and the waves and wind obey (MARK 4:39 NKJV). So, don't fear life's deep or turbulent waters today. Our God safely leads us ashore.

PATRICIA RAYBON

**What tempts you not to trust God? What do you
need to trust Him with today?**

*Dear heavenly Father, You rule life's winds and waves,
and I thank You for guiding me safely to shore.*

Whoever drinks the water I give them will
never thirst. [JOHN 4:14]

WATER WHERE WE NEED IT

Lake Baikal, the world's deepest lake, is vast and magnificent.
Measuring one-mile-deep and nearly 400 miles (636 km) by
49 miles (79 km) across, it contains one-fifth of all the surface
fresh water in the world. But this water is largely inaccessible. Lake
Baikal is located in Siberia—one of the most remote areas of Russia.
With water so desperately needed for much of our planet, it's ironic
that such a vast supply of water is tucked away in a place where not
many people can access it.

Although Lake Baikal may be remote, there is an endless source
of life-giving water that is available and accessible to those who
need it most. When at a well in Samaria, Jesus engaged a woman
in conversation, probing at the edges of her deep spiritual thirst.
The solution to her heart-need? Jesus Himself.

In contrast to the water she had come to draw from the well, Jesus
offered something better: "Everyone who drinks this water will be
thirsty again, but whoever drinks the water I give them will never
thirst. Indeed, the water I give them will become in them a spring
of water welling up to eternal life" (JOHN 4:13–14).

Many things promise satisfaction but never fully quench our
thirsty hearts. Jesus alone can truly satisfy our spiritual thirst, and
His provision is available to everyone, everywhere.　　*BILL CROWDER*

***Where are you seeking fulfilment or satisfaction in
life? Why is the search for true satisfaction impossible
apart from Christ?***

*Loving God, thank You for the life You provide and the
purpose and meaning You give to me. Teach me to find
my truest satisfaction in You and Your love.*

If they do not listen to Moses and the
Prophets, they will not be convinced even if
someone rises from the dead. [LUKE 16:31]

SIGHT UNSEEN

After Yuri Gagarin became the first man in space, he parachuted
into the Russian countryside. A woman spotted the orange-clad
cosmonaut, still wearing his helmet and dragging two para-
chutes. "Can it be that you have come from outer space?" she asked
in surprise. "As a matter of fact, I have," he said.

Soviet leaders sadly turned the historic flight into anti-religious
propaganda. "Gagarin went into space, but he didn't see any god
there," their premier declared. (Gagarin himself never said such a
thing.) As C. S. Lewis observed, "Those who do not find [God] on
earth are unlikely to find Him in space."

Jesus warned us about ignoring God in this life. He told a story
of two men who died—a rich man who had no time for God, and
Lazarus, a destitute man rich in faith (LUKE 16:19–31). In torment, the
rich man pleaded with Abraham for his brothers still on earth. "Send
Lazarus," he begged Abraham. "If someone from the dead goes to
them, they will repent" (VV. 27, 30). Abraham got to the heart of the
problem: "If they do not listen to Moses and the Prophets, they
will not be convinced even if someone rises from the dead" (V. 31).

"Seeing is never believing," wrote Oswald Chambers. "We interpret
what we see in the light of what we believe."   *TIM GUSTAFSON*

**What do you believe about the existence of God and the
reality of Christ's resurrection? How do your beliefs affect
your day-to-day choices?**

*Father, I pray today for those who don't yet believe in You.
Draw them by the gentle power and love of Your Holy Spirit.*

In their hearts humans plan their course,
but the LORD establishes their steps.
[PROVERBS 16:9]

GOT PLANS?

Caden, a young man of almost eighteen, was anticipating attending his first-choice university. He was involved in a Christian union in school and looked forward to participating in a similar ministry in the new environment. He'd saved money from his part-time job and also had an excellent lead on a new job. He'd established some great goals, and everything was coming together exactly on schedule.

And then in the spring of 2020 a global health crisis changed everything.

The school let Caden know that his first term would probably be online. The campus ministry was on hiatus. The job prospect dried up when the business closed. As he despaired, his friend glibly quoted words from a well-known professional boxer: "Yeah, everyone has a plan until they get punched in the mouth."

Proverbs 16 tells us that when we commit all we do to God, He'll establish our plans and work things out according to His will (VV. 3–4). True commitment, however, can be difficult. It involves an open heart to God's direction, along with a willingness to resist charting our course independently (V. 9; 19:21).

Dreams that don't come to fruition can bring disappointment, but our limited vision for the future can never compete with God's all-knowing ways. As we yield ourselves to Him, we can be certain that He's still lovingly directing our steps even when we don't see the path ahead (16:9).   *CINDY HESS KASPER*

What disappointment changed your plans for the future?
What can you do to seek God's guidance today?

Loving and wise Father, help me to trust You even in my
disappointments knowing that You're a good and faithful
God and You'll establish my steps.

And after the fire came a gentle whisper.
[1 KINGS 19:12]

SHIFT INTO NEUTRAL

The man ahead of me at the carwash was on a mission. He purposefully strode around his car to check nothing would snag the high-powered rolling brushes. He paid the attendant then pulled onto the automated track—where he left his automatic car in drive. The attendant shouted after him, "Neutral! Neutral!" but the man's windows were up and he couldn't hear. He zipped through the car wash in four seconds flat. His car barely got wet.

Elijah was on a mission too. He was busy serving God in big ways. He had just defeated the prophets of Baal in a supernatural showdown, which left him drained (SEE 1 KINGS 18:16–39). He needed time in neutral. God brought Elijah to Mount Horeb, where He had appeared to Moses long before. Once again God shook the mountain. But He wasn't in the rock-shattering wind, earthquake or raging fire. Instead, God came to Elijah in a gentle whisper. "When Elijah heard it, he pulled his cloak over his face and went out" to meet God (1 KINGS 19:13).

You and I are on a mission. We put our lives in drive to accomplish big things for our Saviour. But if we never shift down to neutral, we can zip through life and miss the outpouring of His Spirit. God whispers, "Be still, and know that I am God" (PSALM 46:10). Neutral! Neutral!   *MIKE WITTMER*

How do you slow down to spend time with your Father?
Why is time in neutral necessary for driven people?

Father, I am still, because You are God.

Do everything in love. [1 CORINTHIANS 16:14]

BRAVE LOVE

The four chaplains weren't known as heroes. But on a frigid February night in 1943, when their transport ship, the SS *Dorchester,* was torpedoed off the coast of Greenland during World War II, the four gave their all to calm hundreds of panicked soldiers. With the ship sinking and injured men jumping for over-crowded lifeboats, the four chaplains calmed the pandemonium by "preaching courage", a survivor said.

When life jackets ran out, each took his off, giving it to a frightened young man. They had determined to go down with the ship so that others might live. One survivor said, "It was the finest thing I have seen or hope to see this side of heaven."

Linking arms as the ship began to sink, the chaplains prayed aloud together, offering encouragement to those perishing with them.

Bravery marks their saga. Love, however, defines the gift the four offered. Paul urged such love of all believers, including those in the storm-tossed church at Corinth. Roiled by conflict, corruption and sin, Paul urged them to "be on your guard; stand firm in the faith; be courageous; be strong" (1 CORINTHIANS 16:13). Then he added, "Do everything in love" (V. 14).

It's a sterling command for every believer in Jesus, especially dur-ing a crisis. In life, when upheaval threatens, our bravest response reflects Christ—giving to others His love.　　　　*PATRICIA RAYBON*

> **Why does selfless love reflect Jesus? How can His love influence how you respond in a turbulent situation?**
>
> *Jesus, when I don't feel brave, which is often, stir up my courage to boldly offer love.*

The more they were oppressed, the more
they multiplied and spread. [EXODUS 1:12]

FLOURISH AGAIN

Given enough sunlight and water, certain vibrant wildflowers
carpet areas of California. But what happens when drought
strikes? Scientists have discovered that certain wildflowers
store large quantities of their seeds underground instead of allowing
them to push through the soil and bloom. After the drought, the
plants use the seeds they have saved to begin to flourish again.

The ancient Israelites thrived in the land of Egypt, despite harsh
conditions. Slave masters forced them to work in fields and make
bricks. Ruthless overseers required them to build entire cities for
Pharaoh. The king of Egypt even tried to use infanticide to reduce
their numbers. However, because God sustained them, "the more
they were oppressed, the more they multiplied and spread"
(EXODUS 1:12). Many Bible scholars estimate that the population of
Israelite men, women and children grew to two million (or more)
during their time in Egypt.

God, who preserved His people *then*, is upholding us *today* as
well. He can help us in any environment. We may worry about enduring through another season. But the Bible assures us that God,
who "cares so wonderfully for wildflowers that are here today and
[are gone] tomorrow," can provide for our needs (MATTHEW 6:30 NLT).

JENNIFER BENSON SCHULDT

**Why is it so hard to trust God during life's 'dry' seasons?
How has God provided for you in the past, and how might
the story of His faithfulness encourage someone you know?**

*Father, sometimes it's so hard to keep going. Please meet
my needs today, and help me to persevere through the
power of Your Holy Spirit.*

My rainbow . . . will be the sign of the covenant
between me and the earth. [GENESIS 9:13]

RAINBOW HALO

On a hike in the mountains, Adrian found himself above some
low-lying clouds. With the sun behind him, Adrian looked
down and saw not only his shadow but also a brilliant display
known as a Brocken spectre. This phenomenon resembles a rainbow halo, encircling the shadow of the person. It occurs when the
sunlight reflects back off the clouds below. Adrian described it as a
"magical" moment, one that delighted him immensely.

We can imagine how similarly stunning seeing the first rainbow
must have been for Noah. More than just a delight to his eyes, the
refracted light and resulting colours came with a promise from God.
After a devastating flood, God assured Noah, and all the "living
creatures" who've lived since, that "never again [would] the waters
become a flood to destroy all life" (GENESIS 9:15).

Our earth still experiences floods and other frightening weather
that results in tragic loss, but the rainbow is a promise that God will
never judge the earth again with a worldwide flood. This promise
of His faithfulness can remind us that though we individually will
experience personal losses and physical death on this earth—whether
by disease, natural disaster, wrongdoing or advancing age—God
bolsters us with His love and presence throughout the difficulties
we face. Sunlight reflecting colours through water is a reminder of
His faithfulness to fill the earth with those who bear His image and
reflect His glory to others.   *KIRSTEN HOLMBERG*

> ***How does God's promise reassure you in the midst of***
> ***weather-related catastrophes? Who in your life needs***
> ***your reflection of God's glory?***
>
> *Thank You, God, for Your faithfulness to protect and provide*
> *for me by sustaining the natural laws of Your creation.*
> *Help me to reflect Your glory to those around me.*

But David remained in Jerusalem.
[2 SAMUEL 11:1]

DEATH ZONE

I n 2019, a climber saw his last sunrise from the peak of Mount Everest. He survived the dangerous ascent, but the high altitude squeezed his heart, and he passed away on the trek down. One medical expert warns climbers not to think of the summit as their journey's end. They must get up and down quickly, remembering "they're in the Death Zone."

David survived his dangerous climb to the top. He killed lions and bears, slew Goliath, dodged Saul's spear and pursuing army, and conquered Philistines and Ammonites to become king of the mountain.

But David forgot he was in the death zone. At the peak of his success, as "the LORD gave David victory wherever he went" (2 SAMUEL 8:6), he committed adultery and murder. His initial mistake? He lingered on the mountaintop. When his army set out for new challenges, he "remained in Jerusalem" (11:1). David once had volunteered to fight Goliath; now he relaxed in the accolades of his triumphs.

It's hard to stay grounded when everyone, including God, says you're special (7:11–16). But we must. If we've achieved some success, we may appropriately celebrate the accomplishment and accept congratulations, but we must keep moving. We're in the death zone. Come down the mountain. Humbly serve others in the valley—asking God to guard your heart and your steps.   *MIKE WITTMER*

Are you climbing your mountain or near the top?
How might you avoid the pitfalls that come with success?

Father, grant me success, and protect me from its excess.

Worthy is the Lamb, who was slain.
[REVELATION 5:12]

WORTH IT, OR WORTHY?

Helen Roseveare, an English missionary in the African Congo, was taken prisoner by rebels during the Simba Rebellion in 1964. Beaten and abused by her captors, she suffered terribly. In the days that followed, she found herself asking, "Is it worth it?"

As she began to ponder the cost of following Jesus, she sensed God speaking to her about it. Years later she explained to an interviewer, "When the awful moments came during the rebellion and the price seemed too high to pay, the Lord seemed to say to me, 'Change the question. It's not, 'Is it worth it?' It's 'Am I worthy?'" She concluded that in spite of the pain she had endured, "Always the answer is 'Yes, He is worthy.'"

Through God's grace at work within her during her harrowing ordeal, Helen Roseveare decided that the Saviour who had suffered even death for her was worthy to be followed no matter what she faced. Her words, "He is worthy" echo the cries of those surrounding Jesus' throne in the book of Revelation: "In a loud voice they were saying: 'Worthy is the Lamb, who was slain, to receive power and wealth and wisdom and strength and honour and glory and praise!'" (5:12).

Our Saviour suffered and bled and died for us, giving Himself entirely, so that we may freely receive eternal life and hope. His all deserves our all. He is worthy!   *JAMES BANKS*

> **How does Jesus' death and resurrection prove He's greater than any circumstance you face? In what ways will you tell Him He's worthy today?**
>
> *You are always worthy to be worshipped, Jesus! Please help me to live today in Your presence with a grateful heart.*

Be careful not to practise your righteousness
in front of others to be seen by them.
[MATTHEW 6:1]

SECRET GIVER

F or Christopher, a physically disabled military veteran, everyday
activities had become more challenging, took longer to finish
and increased his pain. Still, he did his best to serve his wife
and child. Passers-by would see him pushing along a mower to cut
his lawn every week.

One day, Christopher received a letter—and an expensive riding
lawnmower—from an anonymous donor. The secret giver's satisfaction came through the privilege of helping someone in need.

Jesus doesn't say that all of our giving should be in secret, but He
does remind us to check our motives when we give (MATTHEW 6:1).
He also said: "When you give to the needy, do not announce it
with trumpets, as the hypocrites do in the synagogues and on the
streets, to be honoured by others" (V. 2). While God expects us to be
openhanded givers, He encourages us to avoid doing good deeds
in front of people for the purpose of receiving accolades or special
recognition (V. 3).

When we realise everything we have comes from God, we can
be secret givers who don't need to pat our own backs or gain the
admiration of others. Our all-knowing Giver of all good things delights
in the genuine generosity of His people. Nothing beats the reward
of His approval.　　　　　　　　　　　　　　　　*XOCHITL DIXON*

> **How has God helped you through someone else's secret
> giving? Who can you help with an anonymous gift today?**
>
> *Loving God, please bless me with opportunities to give as
> selflessly and sacrificially as You have given to me*

GROWING IN CHRIST

How do we grow in our relationship with Jesus?

■ **LISTEN TO HIM**. As we read the Bible, God speaks to us through His own words.

All Scripture is God-breathed and is useful for teaching, rebuking, correcting and training in righteousness, so that the servant of God may be thoroughly equipped for every good work. (2 TIMOTHY 3:16–17)

■ **RESPOND TO HIM.** As we receive understanding from Him, we respond to Him with the affections and needs of our hearts.

If you remain in me and my words remain in you, ask whatever you wish, and it will be done for you. (JOHN 15:7)

■ **FELLOWSHIP WITH OTHERS.** As we connect with others who share our faith in Christ, we experience mutual encouragement to love others as we ourselves have been loved.

And let us consider how we may spur one another on towards love and good deeds, not giving up meeting together, as some are in the habit of doing, but encouraging one another—and all the more as you see the Day approaching. (HEBREWS 10:24–25)

■ **SHARE OUR FAITH.** Christ desires for us to be His representatives to those who haven't yet believed. One of the best ways to do this is to show honest concern for them. If they see our changed life and that we're genuinely interested in them, they're more likely to be curious about the difference they see in us.

A genuine believer will have a desire to listen to God, to respond to Him, to fellowship with other believers, and to share their faith to those who don't yet know Christ. Ask God to guide your path to a growing relationship with Him.

Dennis Fisher, Discovery Series author

★ The topic of **GROWING IN CHRIST** is the focus of the above feature article and the devotions for **June 1, 9, 16** and **23**. We hope these articles will encourage you as you grow in your relationship with Jesus.

Be careful to live properly among your
unbelieving neighbours. [1 PETER 2:12 NLT]

A REMARKABLE LIFE

I came to learn about Catherine Hamlin, a remarkable Australian
surgeon, through reading her obituary. In Ethiopia, Catherine and
her husband established the world's only hospital dedicated to
curing women from the devastating physical and emotional trauma
of obstetric fistulas, a common injury in the developing world that
can occur during childbirth. Catherine is credited with overseeing
the treatment of more than 60,000 women.

Still operating at the hospital when she was ninety-two years
old, and still beginning each day with a cup of tea and Bible study,
Hamlin told curious questioners that she was an ordinary believer
in Jesus who was simply doing the job God had given her to do.

I was grateful to learn about her remarkable life because she
powerfully exemplified for me Scripture's encouragement to believers to live our lives in such a way that even people who actively
reject God "may see your good deeds and glorify God" (1 PETER 2:12).

The power of God's Spirit that called us out of spiritual darkness
into a relationship with Him (V. 9) can also transform our work or
areas of service into testimonies of our faith. In whatever passion
or skill God has gifted us, we can embrace added meaning and
purpose in doing all of it in a manner that has the power to point
people to Him.   *LISA M. SAMRA*

What has God called you to do?
How might you do it today in Jesus' name?

*Jesus, may Your love and grace be evident in
my words and deeds today.*

I trust in your unfailing love.
[PSALM 13:5]

GOD OF JUSTICE

She was perhaps the greatest 'scapecow' in history. We don't know if her name was Daisy, Madeline or Gwendolyn (each name has been suggested), but Mrs. O'Leary's cow was blamed for a fire in 1871 that left every third resident of Chicago city homeless. Carried by strong winds through wooden structures, the fire burned for three days and took the lives of nearly three-hundred people.

For years, many believed the fire began when the cow knocked over a lantern left burning in a shed. After further investigation—126 years later—the city's Committee on Police and Fire passed a resolution exonerating the cow and her owners and suggesting the activities of a neighbour warranted scrutiny.

Justice often takes time, and Scripture acknowledges how difficult that can be. The refrain, "How long?" is repeated four times in Psalm 13: "How long, LORD? Will you forget me forever? How long will you hide your face from me? How long must I wrestle with my thoughts and day after day have sorrow in my heart? How long will my enemy triumph over me?" (VV. 1–2). But in the middle of his lament, David finds reason for faith and hope: "But I trust in your unfailing love; my heart rejoices in your salvation" (V. 5).

Even when justice is delayed, God's love will never fail us. We can trust and rest in Him not just for the moment but for eternity.

JAMES BANKS

**In what ways has God shown you His unfailing love?
How will you demonstrate trust in Him today?**

*Loving God, help me to trust You even when I can't see what
You're doing. I'm thankful I can rest in Your goodness and
faithfulness today.*

The LORD is good to those whose hope
is in him. [LAMENTATIONS 3:25]

IT'S OKAY TO LAMENT

I dropped to my knees and let my tears fall to the floor. "God, why aren't you taking care of me?" I cried. It was during the COVID-19 pandemic in 2020. I'd been laid-off for almost a month, and something had gone wrong with my unemployment application. I hadn't received any money yet. Deep down, I trusted that God would work out everything. I believed He truly loved me and would take care of me, but in that moment, I felt abandoned.

The book of Lamentations reminds us it's okay to lament. The book was probably written during or soon after the Babylonians destroyed Jerusalem in 587 BC. It describes the affliction (3:1, 19), oppression (1:18) and starvation (2:20; 4:10) the people faced. Yet, in the middle of the book the author remembers why he could hope: "Because of the LORD's great love we are not consumed, for his compassions never fail. They are new every morning; great is your faithfulness" (3:22–23). Despite the devastation, the author remembered that God remains faithful.

Sometimes it feels impossible to believe that "the LORD is good to those whose hope is in him, to the one who seeks him" (V. 25), especially when we don't see an end to our suffering. But we can cry out to Him, trusting that He hears us and that He'll be faithful to see us through.   *JULIE SCHWAB*

***What's making it difficult for you to trust God today?
What will help you feel comfortable enough to cry out to Him?***

*Father, I need You right now. Please help me to trust You to
come through for me in my difficult situation.*

All [God's] ways are just.
[DEUTERONOMY 32:4]

PERFECT JUSTICE

n 1983, three teens were arrested for the murder of a fourteen-year-old. According to news reports, the younger teen was "shot . . . because of his [athletic] jacket." Sentenced to life in prison, the three spent thirty-six years behind bars before evidence surfaced that revealed their innocence. Another man had committed the crime. Before the judge released them as free men, he issued an apology.

No matter how hard we try (and no matter how much good is done by our officials), human justice is often flawed. We never have all the information. Sometimes dishonest people manipulate the facts. Sometimes we're just wrong. And often, evils may take years to be righted, if they ever are in our lifetime. Thankfully, unlike fickle humans, God wields perfect justice. "His works are perfect," says Moses, "and all his ways are just" (DEUTERONOMY 32:4). God sees things as they truly are. In time, after we've done our worst, God will bring about final, ultimate justice. Though uncertain of the timing, we have confidence because we serve a "faithful God who does no wrong, upright and just is he" (V. 4).

We may be dogged by uncertainty regarding what's right or wrong. We may fear that the injustices done to us or those we love will never be made right. But we can trust the God of justice to one day—either in this life or the next—enact justice for us.

WINN COLLIER

Where have you seen justice abused or misrepresented?
Where does your heart cry out for God to bring justice?

God, I see injustice all around me: in the news, in my
relationships, on social media. Thank You for the hope
I can have in You and Your just ways.

Be joyful in hope, patient in affliction,
faithful in prayer. [ROMANS 12:12]

WAITING IN HOPE

Rogelio served as our waiter during our weeklong holiday. In one conversation, he credited Jesus for blessing him with Kaly, a compassionate wife with strong faith. After they had their first baby, God gave them the opportunity to help care for their niece who had Down syndrome. Soon after, Rogelio's mother-in-law needed live-in care.

Rogelio works with joy, often taking on double shifts to ensure his wife can stay home to care for the people God entrusted to them. When I shared how the couple inspired me to love better because of the way they opened their hearts and home to serve their family members, he said, "It is my pleasure to serve them . . . and you."

Rogelio's life affirms the power of living with generosity and trusting God to provide as we serve one another selflessly. The apostle Paul urged God's people to be "devoted to one another in love . . . joyful in hope, patient in affliction, [and] faithful in prayer" as we "share with the Lord's people who are in need [and] practise hospitality" (ROMANS 12:10–13).

Our life can change in an instant, leaving us or those we love in circumstances that feel impossible to bear. But when we're willing to share all God has given us while we wait on Him, we can cling to His enduring love . . . together.   *XOCHITL DIXON*

> *How can you prayerfully and physically support someone in need today? How has God used someone to offer you tangible support while you waited for Him?*
>
> *God, please help me love others while I wait for You to work in and through my circumstances.*

We know that when Christ appears,
we shall be like him. [1 JOHN 3:2]

OUR TRUE SELVES

Inside my parents' old photo album is a picture of a young boy. He has a round face, freckles and straight, light-blond hair. He loves cartoons, hates avocados and owns just one record, by Abba. Also inside that album are pictures of a teenager. His face is long, not round; his hair is wavy, not straight. He has no freckles, likes avocados, watches movies rather than cartoons, and would never admit to owning an Abba record! The boy and the teenager are little alike. According to science they have different skin, teeth, blood and bones. And yet they are both me. This paradox has baffled philosophers. Since we change throughout our lives, who is the real us?

The Scriptures provide the answer. From the moment God began knitting us together in the womb (PSALM 139:13–14), we've been growing into our unique design. While we can't yet imagine what we'll finally become, we know that if we're children of God we'll ultimately be like Jesus (1 JOHN 3:2)—our body with His nature, our personality but His character, all our gifts glistening, all our sins gone.

Until the day Jesus returns, we're being drawn towards this future self. By His work, step by step, we can reflect His image ever more clearly (2 CORINTHIANS 3:18). We aren't yet who we're meant to be, but as we become like Him, we become our true selves.

SHERIDAN VOYSEY

When songs and films encourage us to find our true selves, what do you think they miss? In what area can you step towards Christ-likeness today?

Jesus, make me more like You today and every day.

The wise woman builds her house, but with her own hands the foolish one tears hers down. [PROVERBS 14:1]

A WISE BUILDER

Sojourner Truth, whose birth name was Isabella Baumfree, was born a slave in 1797 in New York. Though nearly all her children were sold as slaves, she escaped to freedom in 1826 with one daughter and lived with a family who paid the money for her freedom. Instead of allowing an unjust system to keep her family apart, she took legal action to regain her small son Peter—an amazing feat for an African American woman in that day. Knowing she couldn't raise her children without God's help, she became a believer in Christ and later changed her name to Sojourner Truth to show that her life was built on the foundation of God's truth.

King Solomon, the writer of Proverbs 14, declares, "The wise woman builds her house" (V. 1). In contrast, one without wisdom "tears hers down." This building metaphor shows the wisdom God provides to those willing to listen. How does one build a house with wisdom? By saying "only what is helpful for building others up" (Ephesians 4:29; see also 1 Thessalonians 5:11). How does one tear down? Proverbs 14 gives the answer: "A fool's mouth lashes out with pride" (V. 3).

Sojourner had a "secure fortress" (V. 26) in a turbulent time, thanks to the wisdom of God. You may never have to rescue your children from an injustice. But you can build your house on the same foundation Sojourner did—the wisdom of God.   *LINDA WASHINGTON*

> **What foundation is your house established upon?**
> **How will you build your house this week?**
>
> *Father, I need Your wisdom to build a lasting*
> *legacy for Your glory.*

I have come down to rescue them.
[EXODUS 3:8]

DIVINE RESCUE

After being informed of an emergency call from a concerned citizen, a police officer drove alongside the train tracks, shining his floodlight into the dark until he spotted the vehicle straddling the iron rails. The officer's dashboard camera captured the harrowing scene as a train barrelled towards the car. "That train was coming fast," the officer said, "Fifty to eighty miles per hour." Acting without hesitation, he pulled an unconscious man from the car mere seconds before the train slammed into it.

Scripture reveals God as the One who rescues—often precisely when all seems lost. Trapped in Egypt and withering under suffocating oppression, the Israelites imagined no possibility for escape. In Exodus, however, we find God offering them words resounding with hope: "I have indeed seen the misery of my people in Egypt," He said. "I have heard them crying out . . . and I am concerned about their suffering" (3:7). And God not only *saw*—God acted. "I have come down to rescue them" (V. 8). God led Israel out of bondage. This was a divine rescue.

God's rescue of Israel reveals God's heart—and His *power*—to help all of us who are in need. He assists those of us who are destined for ruin unless God arrives to save us. Though our situation may be dire or impossible, we can lift our eyes and heart and watch for the One who loves to rescue.

WINN COLLIER

Where does all seem lost and where do you need God's rescue?
How can you turn your hope to Him in this dire place?

God, I'm in real trouble, and if You don't help me, I don't see a
good ending. Will You help me? Will You rescue me?

Become mature, attaining to the whole measure
of the fullness of Christ. [EPHESIANS 4:13]

MOVING TOWARDS MATURITY

A recent survey asked respondents to identify the age at which they believed they became adults. Those who considered themselves adults pointed to specific behaviours as evidence of their status. Having a budget and buying a house topped the list as being marks of 'adulting'. Other adult activities ranged from cooking dinner every weeknight and scheduling one's own medical appointments, to the more humorous ability to choose to eat snacks for dinner or being excited to stay at home on a Saturday evening instead of going out.

The Bible says we should press on towards spiritual maturity as well. Paul wrote to the church at Ephesus, urging the people to "become mature, attaining to the whole measure of the fullness of Christ" (EPHESIANS 4:13). While we're 'young' in our faith, we're vulnerable to "every wind of teaching" (V. 14), which often results in division among us. Instead, as we mature in our understanding of the truth, we function as a unified body under "him who is the head, that is, Christ" (V. 15).

God gave us His Spirit to help us grow into a full understanding of who He is (JOHN 14:26), and He equips pastors and teachers to instruct and lead us towards maturity in our faith (EPHESIANS 4:11–12). Just as certain characteristics are evidence of physical maturity, our unity as His body is evidence of our spiritual growth.   *KIRSTEN HOLMBERG*

In what ways are you still vulnerable to "every wind of teaching"? How can you continue to grow spiritually?

Loving God, You're the author of my growth and maturity. Please help me to see where my understanding of You is still immature and teach me more of Your wisdom.

You are like a lion among the nations; you are like a monster in the seas. [EZEKIEL 32:2]

WHO ARE YOU?

The leader of our video conference said, "Good morning!" I said "Hello" back, but I wasn't looking at him. I was distracted by my own image on the screen. *Do I look like this?* I looked at the smiling faces of the others on the call. That looks like them. So yes, this must be me. *I should lose some weight. And get a haircut.*

In his mind, Pharaoh was pretty great. He was "a lion among the nations . . . a monster in the seas" (EZEKIEL 32:2). But then he caught a glimpse of himself from God's perspective. God said he was in trouble and that He would expose his carcass to wild animals, causing "many peoples to be appalled at you, and their kings [to] shudder with horror because of you" (V. 10). Pharaoh was much less impressive than he thought.

We may think we're 'spiritually handsome'—until we see our sin as God sees it. Compared to His holy standard, even "our righteous acts are like filthy rags" (ISAIAH 64:6). But God also sees something else, something even more true: He sees Jesus, and He sees us *in* Jesus.

Feeling discouraged about *how you are*? Remember this is not *who you are*. If you have put your trust in Jesus, then you're in Jesus, and His holiness drapes over you. You're more beautiful than you imagine.   MIKE WITTMER

What image do you have of yourself? How does that compare to the image God has of you?

Jesus, I cling to You. Your love and goodness transform me.

Though you have not seen him, you love him;
and even though you do not see him now, you
believe in him. [1 PETER 1:8]

UNSEEN WONDER

In the twilight of her years, Mrs. Goodrich's thoughts came in and out of focus along with memories of a challenging and grace-filled life. Sitting by a window overlooking the waters of a lake, she reached for her notepad. In words she soon wouldn't recognise as her own she wrote: "Here I am in my favourite chair, with my feet on the sill and my heart in the air. The sun-struck waves on the water below, in constant motion—to where I don't know. But thank You—dear Father above—for Your innumerable gifts and Your undying love! It always amazes me—How can it be? That I'm so in love with One I can't see."

The apostle Peter acknowledged such wonder. He had seen Jesus with his own eyes, but those who would read his letter had not. "Though you have not seen him . . . you believe in him and are filled with an inexpressible and glorious joy" (1 PETER 1:8). We love Jesus not because we're commanded to, but because with the help of the Spirit (V. 11) we begin to see how much He loves us.

It's more than hearing that He cares for people like us. It's experiencing for ourselves the promise of Christ to make the wonder of His unseen presence and Spirit real to us at every stage of life.

MART DEHAAN

**Read 1 Peter 1:3–9 again. In what ways do these words show
you how our God makes the inexpressible real to us? How open
are you to the Spirit of Jesus, who lives in and among us?**

*Our Father in heaven, please help me to see the miracle of Your
love and presence in Your Son and to believe in Your Spirit.*

I have summoned you by name; you are mine.
[ISAIAH 43:1]

HE KNOWS YOUR NAME

After breaking with our church, my husband and I reunited with the fellowship after three long years. *But how would people treat us? Would they welcome us back? Love us? Forgive us for leaving?* We got our answer on a sunny Sunday morning. As we walked through the big church doors, we kept hearing our names. "Pat! Dan! It's so great to see you!" As children's author Kate DiCamillo wrote in one of her popular books, "Reader, nothing is sweeter in this sad world than the sound of someone you love calling your name."

The same assurance was true for the people of Israel. We had chosen a different church for a time, but they had turned their backs on God. Yet He welcomed them back. He sent the prophet Isaiah to assure them, "Do not fear, for I have redeemed you; I have summoned you by name; you are mine" (ISAIAH 43:1).

In this world—where we can feel unseen, unappreciated and even unknown—be assured that God knows each of us by name. "You are precious and honoured in my sight," He promises (V. 4). "When you pass through the waters, I will be with you; and when you pass through the rivers, they will not sweep over you" (V. 2). This promise isn't just for Israel. Jesus ransomed His life for us. He knows our names. Why? In love, we are His.   *PATRICIA RAYBON*

> **Why does God welcome His people back to Him?**
> **How has He shown that He knows you by name?**

> *Jesus, when I stray from Your arms and Your fellowship,*
> *summon me home by name. I'm so grateful to be Yours.*

The kingdom of God belongs to such as these.
[MARK 10:14]

THE KINGDOM OF GOD

My mother has been committed to many things over the course of her life, but one that has remained constant is her desire to see little children introduced to Jesus. Of the few times I've witnessed my mother display disagreement publicly, all were when someone attempted to cut a children's ministry budget in favour of what they felt were more 'serious' expenditures. "I took one summer off when I was pregnant with your brother, but that's it," she told me. I did a little family maths and I realised my mum had been working with children in the church for fifty-five years.

Mark 10 records one of the endearing stories in the Gospels commonly titled "The Little Children and Jesus." People were bringing children to Jesus that He might touch and bless them. But the disciples tried to prevent this from happening. Mark records Jesus as "indignant"—and rebuking His very own disciples: "Let the little children come to me, and do not hinder them, for the kingdom of God belongs to such as these" (V. 14).

Charles Dickens wrote, "I love these little people; and it's not a slight thing when they, who are so fresh from God, love us." And it's not a slight thing when we, who are older, do all we can to make sure the little children are never hindered from the ever-fresh love of Jesus.

JOHN BLASE

If you were introduced to Jesus as a child, who were the supporting adults in that memory? What kind of impression does Jesus being indignant in this story make on you?

Jesus, help me to reveal Your love and presence to all people, including children. Make me mindful of ways to ensure that they can always come to You.

My help comes from the LORD, the Maker of
heaven and earth. [PSALM 121:2]

THE POWER OF GOD

Rebecca and Russell's doctors told them they couldn't have
children. But God had other ideas—and ten years later
Rebecca conceived. The pregnancy was a healthy one; and
when the contractions started, the couple excitedly rushed to the
hospital. Yet the hours of labour grew long and more intense, and
Rebecca's body still wasn't progressing enough for delivery. Finally,
the doctor decided she needed to perform an emergency C-section.
Fearful, Rebecca sobbed for her baby and herself. The doctor calmly
assured her, saying, "I will do my best, but we're going to pray to
God because He can do more." She prayed with Rebecca, and fifteen
minutes later, Bruce, a healthy baby boy, was born.

That doctor understood her dependence on God and His power.
She recognised that although she had the training and skill to do
the surgery, she still needed God's wisdom, strength and help to
guide her hands (PSALM 121:1–2).

It's encouraging to hear about highly skilled people, or of anyone,
who recognise they need Him—because, honestly, we all do. He's
God; we're not. He alone "is able to do immeasurably more than
all we ask or imagine" (EPHESIANS 3:20). Let's have a humble heart
to learn from Him and to trust Him in prayer "because He can do
more" than we ever could.   *ANNE CETAS*

> **How have you gained an understanding of your own
> need for God and His power? How is this dependence
> seen in your daily life?**
>
> *I need You and Your wisdom and power, God,
> for decisions, skill, work, relationships—all of my life.*

Are not two sparrows sold for a penny? Yet
not one of them will fall to the ground outside
your Father's care. [MATTHEW 10:29]

OUR FATHER'S CARE

Thwack! I looked up and strained my ears towards the sound.
Spotting a smudge on the windowpane, I peered out onto the
deck and discovered the still-beating body of a bird. My heart
hurt. I longed to help the fragile feathered being.

In Matthew 10, Jesus described His Father's care for sparrows in
order to comfort the disciples as He warned of upcoming dangers.
He offered instructions to the twelve as He "gave them authority to
drive out impure spirits and to heal every disease and sickness" (V. 1).
While the power to do such deeds might have seemed grand to the
disciples, many would oppose them, including governing authorities,
their own families and the ensnaring grip of the evil one (VV. 16–28).

Then in 10:29–31, Jesus told them not to fear whatever they faced
because they would never be out of their Father's care. "Are not
two sparrows sold for a penny?" He asked. "Yet not one of them
will fall to the ground outside your Father's care. . . . So don't be
afraid; you are worth more than many sparrows."

I checked on the bird throughout the day, each time finding it alive
but unmoved. Then, late into the evening, it was gone. I prayed it had
survived. Surely, if I cared this much about the bird, God cared even
more. Imagine how much He cares for you and me! *ELISA MORGAN*

> *How have you seen God care for you in the past? How
> can you gain courage for all you face by understanding
> that you're never outside your Father's care?*
>
> *Dear Father, thank You for always watching over and
> caring for me.*

If you hold to my teaching, you are really
my disciples. [JOHN 8:31]

THE JESUS CHAIR

When my friend Marge met Tami at a Bible study meeting,
she noticed that they seemed to have little in common.
But Marge befriended her, and she learned a valuable
lesson from her new friend.

Tami had never been to a Bible study, and she was having a hard
time understanding something the other women in the study talked
about: that God communicated with them—something she'd never
experienced.

She so desired to hear from God that she took action. Later,
she told Marge. "I set aside an old wooden chair, and every time I
study my Bible, I ask Jesus to come sit in it." Then Tami explained
that whenever a verse stood out to her, she would write out the
verse in chalk on the chair. It's become her special 'Jesus chair', and
she's filled it up with God's messages to her directly from the Bible.

Marge says, "[The Jesus Chair] has changed [Tami's] life. She's
growing spiritually because Scripture is becoming personal."

While speaking to Jewish believers, Jesus said, "If you hold to
my teaching, you are really my disciples. Then you will know the
truth, and the truth will set you free" (JOHN 8:31–32). Let's hold to His
teaching, whether it means writing His words on a chair, memorising
them or seeking to put them into action. The truth and wisdom of
Christ's messages help us grow in Him and set us free. *DAVE BRANON*

> **What can you do in a practical way to more regularly take
> in the wisdom found in the Bible? How does the Holy Spirit
> help you understand Scripture?**
>
> *Help me, God, to connect with You more and more through
> the wisdom You've given me in the Bible. And then help me
> apply what I learn to help me grow more and more like Jesus.*

BIBLE IN A YEAR | NEHEMIAH 4–6; ACTS 2:22–47   175

The LORD said to Gideon, "You have too many men. I cannot deliver Midian into their hands, or Israel would boast against me." [JUDGES 7:2]

THE WAY OF FAITH

I n a 2018 football World Cup qualifying match that pitted the US against Trinidad and Tobago, the Soca Warriors shocked the world when they beat the US men's national team, a team ranked *fifty-six* places higher. The 2-1 upset eliminated the US team from the 2018 World Cup.

Trinidad and Tobago's victory was so unexpected in part because the United States' population and resources dwarfed those of the small Caribbean nation. But those seemingly insurmountable advantages weren't enough to defeat the passionate Soca Warriors.

The story of Gideon and the Midianites features a similar upset, one between a small group of fighters and a large army. The Israelite army actually had more than thirty-thousand fighters, but the Lord whittled the army down to just three hundred warriors so the nation would learn that their success was dependent on God—not the size of their army, the amount of money in their treasury or the skill of their leaders (JUDGES 7:1–8).

It can be tempting to put our trust and confidence in things we can see or measure, but that's not the way of faith. Though it's often difficult, when we are willing to depend on God, to "be strong in the Lord and in his mighty power" (EPHESIANS 6:10), we can go into situations with courage and confidence, even when we feel overwhelmed and unqualified. His presence and power can do amazing things in and through us.   LISA M. SAMRA

When have you faced seemingly insurmountable odds? Whether you tasted victory or defeat, how did you experience God's provision for you?

God, when life gets challenging, help me learn to rely more and more on Your mighty power and grace.

The peace of God, which transcends all
understanding, will guard your hearts and
your minds in Christ Jesus. [PHILIPPIANS 4:7]

THE LIFE OF PEACE

In Perth, Australia, there's a place called Shalom House where men
struggling with addictions go to find help. At Shalom House, they'll
meet caring staff members who introduce them to God's *shalom*
(Hebrew for *peace*). Lives crushed under the weight of addictions
to drugs, alcohol, gambling and other destructive behaviours are
being transformed by the love of God.

Central to this transformation is the message of the cross. The
broken people of Shalom House discover that through the resurrection of Jesus, they can find their own lives resurrected. In Christ,
we gain true peace and healing.

Peace isn't merely the absence of conflict; it's the presence of God's
wholeness. All of us need this *shalom*, and it's only found in Christ and
His Spirit. This is why Paul pointed the Galatians to the Spirit's transfor-
mational work. As the Holy Spirit operates in our lives, He generates
His fruit that includes love, joy, patience and more (GALATIANS 5:22–23).
He gives us that vital element of true, enduring peace.

As the Spirit enables us to live in God's *shalom,* we learn to bring
our needs and concerns to our heavenly Father. This in turn brings
us "the peace of God, which transcends all understanding"—the
peace that "will guard [our] hearts and [our] minds in Christ Jesus"
(PHILIPPIANS 4:7).

In Christ's Spirit, our hearts experience true *shalom*. BILL CROWDER

What things tend to rob you of God's peace? How will you
allow the Spirit to produce His peace in your heart?

God of shalom, thank You that Your desire is for peace to reign in
my life. Thank You for the work of Jesus to make peace available
and the work of the Spirit whose fruit in my life brings peace.

Look at Behemoth, which I made along
with you. [JOB 40:15]

BIGGER THAN OUR PROBLEMS

What do you imagine dinosaurs looked like when they were
alive? Big teeth? Scaly skin? Long tails? Artist Karen Carr
recreates these extinct creatures in large murals. One of
her panoramas is over twenty feet tall and sixty feet long. Because
of its size, it required a crew of experts to install it in sections where
it resides in a museum.

It would be hard to stand in front of this mural without feeling
dwarfed by the dinosaurs. I get a similar sensation when I read God's
description of the powerful animal called "Behemoth" (JOB 40:15).
This big guy munched grass like an ox and had a tail the size of a tree
trunk. His bones were like iron pipes. He lumbered through the hills
grazing, stopping occasionally to relax at the local swamp. When
floodwaters surged, Behemoth never raised an eyebrow.

No one could tame this incredible creature—except its Maker (V. 19).
God reminded Job of this truth during a time when Job's problems
had cast ominous shadows over his life. Grief, bewilderment and
frustration filled his field of vision until he began to question God.
But God's response helped Job see the real size of things. God was
bigger than all his issues and powerful enough to handle problems
that Job couldn't resolve on his own. In the end, Job conceded, "I
know that you can do all things" (42:2).   *JENNIFER BENSON SCHULDT*

*Which is bigger, your worst problem or the God who
made everything? How does your view of God affect the
way in which you handle problems?*

*Dear God, I believe You can help me with the things I'm
facing today. Help me to be open to Your power and
goodness when I feel overwhelmed by trouble.*

Jesus often withdrew to lonely places
and prayed. [LUKE 5:16]

SPENDING TIME WITH GOD

A *River Runs Through It* is Norman Maclean's masterful story of two boys growing up with their father, a Presbyterian minister. On Sunday mornings, Norman and his brother, Paul, went to church where they heard their father preach. Once Sunday evening rolled around, there was another service and their father would preach again. But between those two services, they were free to walk the hills and streams with him "while he unwound between services." It was an intentional withdrawing on their father's part to "restore his soul and be filled again to overflowing for the evening sermon."

Throughout the Gospels, Jesus is seen teaching multitudes on hillsides and cities, and healing the sick and diseased who were brought to Him. All this interaction was in line with the Son of Man's mission "to seek and to save the lost" (LUKE 19:10). But it's also noted that He "often withdrew to lonely places" (5:16). His time there was spent communing with the Father, being renewed and restored to step back once more into His mission.

In our faithful efforts to serve, it's good for us to remember that Jesus often withdrew. If this practice was important for Jesus, how much more so for us? May we regularly spend time with our Father, who can fill us again to overflowing.   *JOHN BLASE*

What comes to mind when you think of a "lonely" place?
When and where can you withdraw to simply spend
time with the Father?

Thank You for the reminder, Father, of my need for time
spent with You. I need Your grace and strength to renew
my often-weary soul.

The horse is made ready for the day of
battle, but victory rests with the LORD.
[PROVERBS 21:31]

HE WILL FIGHT FOR YOU

The wounded horse was named Drummer Boy, one of 112
mounts carrying British soldiers into battle during the famed
Charge of the Light Brigade. The animal showed such bravery
and stamina that his assigned commander, Lieutenant Colonel de
Salis, decided his horse deserved a medal as much as his valiant
men. This was done even though their military action against enemy
forces failed. Yet the cavalry's valour, matched by the courage of
their horses, established the clash as one of Britain's most historic
military moments.

The confrontation, however, shows the wisdom of an ancient
Bible proverb: "The horse is made ready for the day of battle,
but victory rests with the LORD" (PROVERBS 21:31). Scripture affirms
this principle clearly. "For the LORD your God is the one who goes
with you to fight for you against your enemies to give you victory"
(DEUTERONOMY 20:4). Indeed, even against the sting of death, wrote
the apostle Paul, "Thanks be to God! He gives us the victory through
our Lord Jesus Christ" (1 CORINTHIANS 15:56-57).

Knowing this, our task still is to be prepared for life's tough tests.
To build a ministry, we study, work and pray. To create beautiful art,
we master a skill. To conquer a mountain, we secure our tools and
build our strength. Then prepared, we're more than conquerors
through Christ's strong love. *PATRICIA RAYBON*

**What battles or challenges are you preparing for now?
If your victory rests in God, why should you prepare for
this life test?**

*Heavenly Father, as I approach life's great tests, inspire
me to prepare my heart so that You get the victory.*

If God will be with me and watch over
me . . . then the LORD will be my God.
[GENESIS 28:20–21]

GOD IS THERE

Aubrey bought a fleece-lined coat for her ageing father, but
he died before he could wear it. So she tucked a letter of
encouragement with a £20 note into the pocket and donated
the jacket to charity.

Ninety miles away, unable to endure his family's dysfunction any
longer, nineteen-year-old Kelly left his house without grabbing a
coat. He knew of only one place to turn—the home of his grandmother who prayed for him. Hours later he stepped off a bus and
into his grandma's arms. Shielding him from the winter wind, she
said, "We've got to get you a coat!" At the charity shop, Kelly tried
on a coat he liked. Slipping his hands into the pockets he found an
envelope—with a £20 note and Aubrey's letter.

Jacob fled his dysfunctional family in fear for his life (GENESIS 27:41–45).
When he stopped for the night, God revealed Himself to Jacob in a
dream. "I am with you and will watch over you wherever you go,"
God told him (28:15). Jacob vowed, "If God will . . . give me food to eat
and clothes to wear . . . , then the LORD will be my God" (VV. 20–21).

Jacob made a rudimentary altar and named the spot "God's house"
(V. 22). Kelly takes Aubrey's letter and that £20 note wherever he
goes. Each serves as a reminder that no matter where we run, God
is there. *TIM GUSTAFSON*

**When you've had to 'run', whether literally or
metaphorically, where did you go and who did you turn to?
How can you remind yourself of God's presence in your life?**

*Father, You're the One I can always run to.
Help me turn to You first.*

I will create new heavens and a new earth.
[ISAIAH 65:17]

IMAGE THIS!

During the course of a popular home renovation television programme, viewers often hear the host say, "Imagine this!" Then she unveils what could be when old things are restored and drab walls and floors are painted or stained. In one episode, after the renovation the homeowner was so overjoyed that, along with other expressions of elation, the words "That's beautiful!" gushed from her lips three times.

One of the stunning "Imagine this!" passages in the Bible is Isaiah 65:17–25. What a dazzling re-creation scene! The future renovation of heaven and earth is in view (V. 17), and it's not merely cosmetic. It's deep and real, life-altering and life-preserving. "They will build houses and dwell in them; they will plant vineyards and eat their fruit" (V. 21). Violence will be a thing of the past: "They will neither harm nor destroy on all my holy mountain" (V. 25).

While the reversals envisioned in Isaiah 65 will be realised in the future, the God who will orchestrate universal restoration is in the business of life-change now. The apostle Paul assures us, "If anyone is in Christ, the new creation has come: The old has gone, the new is here!" (2 CORINTHIANS 5:17). In need of restoration? Has your life been broken by doubt, disobedience and pain? Life-change through Jesus is real and beautiful and available to those who ask and believe.
ARTHUR JACKSON

> *What changes can you imagine the God of restoration making in your life? What's keeping you from believing in Jesus for life-change today?*

> *God of restoration and renovation, You know what changes are needed in my life for me to look more like You. Please work in my heart and life today.*

　BIBLE IN A YEAR | ESTHER 9–10; ACTS 7:1–21

My grace is sufficient for you, for my power is made perfect in weakness.
[2 CORINTHIANS 12:9]

SHARING YOUR FAITH

When author and evangelist Becky Pippert lived in Ireland, she longed to share the good news of Jesus with Heather, who'd done her nails for two years. But Heather hadn't seemed remotely interested. Feeling unable to start a conversation, Becky prayed before her appointment.

While Heather worked on her nails, Becky flipped through an old magazine and paused at a picture of one of the models. When Heather asked why she was so riveted, Becky told her the photograph was of a close friend who'd years before been a *Vogue* cover model. Becky shared some of her friend's story of coming to faith in God, which Heather listened to with rapt attention.

Becky left for a trip, and later when she returned to Ireland, she learned that Heather had moved to a new location. Becky reflected, "I had asked God to provide an opportunity to share the gospel, and He did!"

Becky looked to God for help in her weakness, inspired by the apostle Paul. When Paul was weak and pleaded with God to remove the thorn in his flesh, the Lord said, "My grace is sufficient for you, for my power is made perfect in weakness" (2 CORINTHIANS 12:9). Paul had learned to rely on God in all things—the big and the small.

When we depend on God to help us love those around us, we too will find opportunities to share our faith authentically.

AMY BOUCHER PYE

When has God helped you to share your faith with someone? How could you pray for someone today who you wish would come to know God?

Loving Jesus, You work through my weaknesses to bring glory to Your Father. Move in my life today, that I might share Your good news of grace.

BIBLE IN A YEAR | JOB 1–2; ACTS 7:22–43

Follow God's example, therefore, as dearly
loved children and walk in the way of love.
[EPHESIANS 5:1–2]

CHILDREN OF GOD

I once spoke at a secular conference for childless couples. Heartbroken over their infertility, many attendees despaired at their
future. Having walked the childless path too, I tried to encourage them. "You can have a meaningful identity without becoming
parents," I said. "I believe you are fearfully and wonderfully made,
and there's new purpose for you to find."

A woman later approached me in tears. "Thank you," she said. "I've
felt worthless being childless and needed to hear that I'm fearfully
and wonderfully made." I asked the woman if she was a believer in
Jesus. "I walked away from God years ago," she said. "But I need a
relationship with Him again."

Times like this remind me how profound the gospel is. Some iden-
tities, like 'mother' and 'father', are hard for some to attain. Others,
like those based on a career, can be lost through unemployment.
But through Jesus we become God's "dearly loved children"—an
identity that can never be stolen (EPHESIANS 5:1). And then we can
"walk in the way of love"—a life purpose that transcends any role
or employment status (V. 2).

All human beings are "fearfully and wonderfully made" (PSALM 139:14),
and those who follow Jesus become children of God (JOHN 1:12–13).
Once in despair, that woman left in hope—about to find an identity
and purpose bigger than this world can give.　　　　*SHERIDAN VOYSEY*

*Is there someone in despair whom you can affirm
as "wonderfully made" today? With whom can you
share the offer of becoming a child of God?*

*Father, life in all its fullness is Yours alone to give.
I open my hands to accept it.*

Then you will call on me and come and pray to me, and I will listen to you. [JEREMIAH 29:12]

HE HEARS US

American President Franklin D. Roosevelt often endured long receiving lines at the White House. As the story is told, he complained that no one paid attention to what was said. So, he decided to experiment at a reception. To everyone who passed down the line and shook his hand, he said, "I murdered my grandmother this morning." The guests responded with phrases like, "Marvellous! Keep up the good work. God bless you, Sir." It wasn't until the end of the line, greeting the ambassador from Bolivia, that his words were actually heard. Nonplussed, the ambassador whispered, "I'm sure she had it coming."

Do you ever wonder if people are really listening? Or worse, do you fear that God isn't listening? We can tell if people are listening based on their responses or eye contact. But how do we know if God is listening? Should we rely on feelings? Or see if God answers our prayers?

After seventy years of exile in Babylon, God promised to bring His people back to Jerusalem and secure their future (JEREMIAH 29:10–11). When they called upon Him, He heard them (V. 12). They knew that God heard their prayers because He promised to listen. And the same is true for us (1 JOHN 5:14). We don't need to rely on feelings or wait for a sign to know that God listens to us. He's promised to listen, and He always keeps His promises (2 CORINTHIANS 1:20).

CON CAMPBELL

> **When have you felt that God wasn't listening?**
> **Why did you feel that way?**
>
> *Dear God, thank You for hearing my prayers, though*
> *I may sometimes doubt it. Help me to trust Your*
> *promise that You listen to me.*

All the widows stood around him, crying and
showing him the robes and other clothing
that Dorcas had made while she was still
with them. [ACTS 9:39]

LEGACY OF KINDNESS

Martha served as a teaching assistant at a primary school for over thirty years. Every year, she saved money to buy new coats, scarves and gloves for students in need. After she lost her fight with leukaemia, we celebrated her life with a thanksgiving service. In lieu of flowers, people donated hundreds of brand-new winter coats to the students she loved and served for decades. Many people shared stories about the countless ways Martha encouraged others with kind words and thoughtful deeds. Her fellow teachers honoured her memory with an annual coat drive for three years after her life ended on this side of eternity. Her legacy of kindness still inspires others to generously serve those in need.

In Acts 9, the apostle Luke shares a story about Dorcas, a woman who was "always doing good and helping the poor" (V. 36). After she got sick and died, the grieving community urged Peter to visit. All the widows showed Peter how Dorcas had lived to serve (V. 39). In a miraculous act of compassion, Peter brought Dorcas back to life. The news of Dorcas' resurrection spread, and "many people believed in the Lord" (V. 42). But it was Dorcas' commitment to serving others in practical ways that touched the hearts in her community and revealed the power of loving generosity.　　　　　　*XOCHITL DIXON*

*How can you love someone with your kind words and deeds
today? How has God used someone else's kindness to draw
you closer to Him?*

*Loving God, please help me to love others in practical ways
each day so I can leave a legacy of kindness that points
others straight to You.*

I sing in the shadow of your wings. I cling
to you; your right hand upholds me.
[PSALM 63:7–8]

GOD'S PROTECTION

Needles, milk, mushrooms, lifts, births, bees and bees in blenders—these are just a fraction of the many phobias attributed to Mr. Adrian Monk, detective and title character of the TV show *Monk*. But when he and his rival Harold Krenshaw find themselves locked in a car boot, Monk has a breakthrough that allows him to cross off at least one fear from his list—claustrophobia.

It's while Monk and Harold are both panicking that the epiphany comes, abruptly interrupting Monk's angst. "I think we've been looking at this the wrong way," he tells Harold. "This [boot], these walls . . . they're not closing in on us . . . they're protecting us, really. They're keeping the bad stuff out . . . germs, and snakes and harmonicas." Eyes widening, Harold sees what he means and whispers in wonder, "This [boot] is our *friend*."

In Psalm 63, it's almost as if David has a similar epiphany. Despite being in a "dry and parched land," when David remembers God's power, glory and love (VV. 1–3), it's as if the desert transforms into a place of God's care and protection. Like a baby bird hiding in the shelter of a mother's wings, David finds that when he clings to God, even in that barren place, he can feast "as with the richest of foods" (V. 5), finding nourishment and strength in a love that "is better than life" (V. 3).

MONICA LA ROSE

> **When have you experienced God's care for you while you were in a difficult place? In what current struggles might you learn to "sing in the shadow of [God's] wings"?**
>
> *Loving Creator, Sustainer and Nourisher, thank You for the miraculous way Your love seeps into my heart in even the most difficult places, transforming them into the shelter of Your wings.*

BIBLE IN A YEAR | JOB 11–13; ACTS 9:1–21

The love of money is a root of all kinds
of evil. . . . Flee from all this, and pursue
righteousness. [1 TIMOTHY 6:10–11]

YOUR LIFE'S PASSION

One evening years ago, my wife and I were making our way
down a mountain trail, accompanied by two friends. The trail
was narrow and wound around a slope with a steep drop on
one side and an unclimbable bank on the other.

As we came around a bend, I saw a large bear moseying along,
swinging his head from side to side, and quietly huffing. We were
downwind, and he hadn't detected our presence, but he would soon.

Our friend began to rummage around in her jacket for a camera.
"Oh, I must take a picture!" she said. I, being less comfortable with
our odds, said, "No, we must get out of here." So we backed up
quietly until we were out of sight—and ran.

That's how we should feel about the dangerous passion to get
rich. There's nothing wrong with money; it's just a medium of exchange. But those who *desire* to get rich "fall into temptation and
a trap and into many foolish and harmful desires that plunge them
into ruin and destruction," Paul wrote (1 TIMOTHY 6:9). Wealth is only
a goad to get more.

Instead, we should "pursue righteousness, godliness, faith, love,
endurance and gentleness" (V. 11). These traits grow in us as we
pursue them and ask God to form them within us. This is how we
secure the deep satisfaction we seek in God.   *DAVID H. ROPER*

> **What's your passion in life? How might you pursue traits
> that will make you more like Jesus?**
>
> *God, I want to grow to become more Christlike.
> Help me cooperate with what You're trying to teach me.*

I have learned the secret of being content in any and every situation. [PHILIPPIANS 4:12]

THE SECRET OF CONTENTMENT

When Joni Eareckson Tada returned home after suffering a swimming accident that left her a quadriplegic, her life was vastly different. Now doorways were too narrow for her wheelchair and sinks were too high. Someone had to feed her, until she decided to relearn how to feed herself. Lifting the special spoon to her mouth from her arm splint the first time, she felt humiliated as she smeared applesauce on her clothes. But she pressed on. As she says, "My secret was learning to lean on Jesus and say, 'Oh God, help me with this!' " Today she manages a spoon very well.

Joni says her confinement made her look at another captive—the apostle Paul, who was imprisoned in a Roman jail—and his letter to the Philippians. Joni strives for what Paul achieved: "I have learned to be content whatever the circumstances" (PHILIPPIANS 4:11). Note that Paul had to *learn* to be at peace; he wasn't naturally peaceful. How did he find contentment? Through trusting in Christ: "I can do all this through him who gives me strength" (V. 13).

We all face different challenges throughout our days; and we all can look to Jesus moment by moment for help, strength and peace. He will help us to hold back from snapping at our loved ones; He will give us the courage to do the next hard thing. Look to Him and find contentment.

AMY BOUCHER PYE

> *How has leaning on Jesus helped you to find peace?*
> *In what areas of your life are you struggling right now?*
> *How could you commit them to God?*

Saving Christ, thank You for giving me courage and hope.
When I feel weak, help me to find strength in You.

LED BY THE SPIRIT

The teaching about the Holy Spirit, the third person of the Trinity, is at the core of the Christian faith. Included in this teaching is the Spirit's leading in our lives, for He guides us in our everyday living.

Romans 8 refers to the Spirit twenty-one times. Verse 14 says, "For those who are led by the Spirit of God are the children of God." This is in the section that speaks of the believer in Jesus' battle against our sinful human nature, "the flesh" (SEE VV. 12–13). The Spirit's leading is invisible, internal, and informed by Scripture (the "sword of the Spirit"; SEE EPHESIANS 6:17).

Believers in Jesus are not without God's help as they seek to honour Him in their earthly living. The dynamics and privileges of family membership continue in Romans 8:15: "The Spirit you received does not make you slaves . . . ; rather, the Spirit you received brought about your adoption to sonship. And by him we cry, 'Abba, Father.' "

Far from being the privilege of an elite group, the Spirit's leading is the heritage of every child of God. Practically speaking, what does His leading look like? It looks like a shepherd lovingly leading his sheep as expressed in Psalm 23:3: "He guides me along right paths for his name's sake." The Spirit of God leads us along "right paths." As we spend time in prayer and the Scriptures, we learn how to live by His leading and walk in step with Him. Then our light shines, and He gets the glory.

Arthur Jackson, Our Daily Bread *author*

★ The devotions for **July 1, 9, 16** and **23** speak about **THE SPIRIT'S LEADING** in our lives. We trust these articles will encourage you as you learn more about how the Spirit guides us along our path as we journey through life.

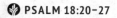
To the faithful you show yourself faithful.
[PSALM 18:25]

CHOOSING TO HONOUR GOD

In the novella *Family Happiness* by Leo Tolstoy, main characters Sergey and Masha meet when Masha is young and impressionable. Sergey is an older, well-travelled businessman who understands the world beyond the rural setting where Masha lives. Over time, the two fall in love and marry.

They settle in the countryside, but Masha becomes bored with her surroundings. Sergey, who adores her, arranges a trip to St. Petersburg. There, Masha's beauty and charm bring her instant popularity. Just as the couple is about to return home, a prince arrives in town, wanting to meet her. Sergey knows he can force Masha to leave with him, but he lets her make the decision. She chooses to stay, and her betrayal breaks his heart.

Like Sergey, God will never force us to be faithful to Him. Because He loves us, he lets us choose *for* or *against* Him. Our first choice *for* Him happens when we receive His Son, Jesus Christ, as the sacrifice for our sin (1 JOHN 4:9–10). After that, we have a lifetime of decisions to make.

Will we choose faithfulness to God as His Spirit guides us, or let the world entice us? David's life wasn't perfect, but he often wrote about keeping "the ways of the LORD" and the good outcomes that came from doing so (PSALM 18:21–24). When our choices honour God, we can experience the blessing David described: to the faithful, God shows Himself faithful.   *JENNIFER BENSON SCHULDT*

When was the last time you made a difficult decision that honoured God? How did it affect your relationship with Him?

*Dear God, help me to honour You with the choices I make.
Thank You for loving me faithfully throughout my life.*

Be still, and know that I am God.
[PSALM 46:10]

NOT RUSHING PRAYER

Alice Kaholusuna recounts a story of how the Hawaiian people would sit outside their temples for a lengthy amount of time preparing themselves before entering in. Even after entering, they would creep to the altar to offer their prayers. Afterwards, they would sit outside again for a long time to "breathe life" into their prayers. When missionaries came to the island, the Hawaiians sometimes considered their prayers odd. The missionaries would stand up, utter a few sentences, call them "prayer", say *amen*, and be done with it. The Hawaiians described these prayers as "without breath."

Alice's story speaks of how God's people may not always take the opportunity to "be still, and know" (PSALM 46:10). Make no mistake—God hears our prayers, whether they're quick or slow. But often the pace of our lives mimics the pace of our hearts, and we need to allow ample time for God to speak into not only our lives but the lives of those around us. How many life-giving moments have we missed by rushing, saying amen, and being done with it?

We're often impatient with everything from slow people to the slow lane in traffic. Yet, I believe God in His kindness says, "Be still. Breathe in and out. Go slow, and remember that I am God, your refuge and strength, an ever-present help in trouble." To do so is to know that God is God. To do so is to trust. To do so is to live.

JOHN BLASE

Recall a time when you slowed down and listened to God in your prayer time. How did that feel? What actions can you put into place to still yourself in God's presence and know Him?

Father, thank You for being my ever-present help in good times and bad. Give me the grace to be still and know that You're God.

Wash your hands, you sinners, and purify
your hearts. [JAMES 4:8]

CLEANING METHOD

At the sink, two little children cheerfully sing the "Happy Birthday" song—two times each—while washing their hands. "It takes that long to wash away the germs," their mother tells them. So even before the COVID-19 pandemic, they'd learned to take time to clean dirt from their hands.

Keeping things clean can be a tedious process, as we learned in the pandemic. Scrubbing away sin, however, means following focused steps back to God.

James urged believers in Jesus scattered throughout the Roman Empire to turn their focus back to God. Beset by quarrels and fights, their battles for one-upmanship, possessions, worldly pleasures, money and recognition made them an enemy of God. He warned them, "Submit yourselves, then to God. Resist the devil, and he will flee from you. . . . Wash your hands, you sinners, and purify your hearts, you double-minded" (JAMES 4:7–8). But how?

"Come near to God and he will come near to you" (V. 8). These are sanitising words describing the necessity of turning to God to scour away the soil of sin from our lives. James then further explained the cleaning method: "Grieve, mourn and wail. Change your laughter to mourning and your joy to gloom. Humble yourselves before the Lord, and he will lift you up" (VV. 9–10).

Dealing with our sin is humbling. But, hallelujah, God is faithful to turn our 'washing' into worship.

PATRICIA RAYBON

**Where in your life does sin persist? Have you turned
back to God to let Him clean you up?**

*Holy God, thank You that Your cleaning methods for
purifying sin draw me back to You. Wash my hands
and purify my heart as I return.*

In repentance and rest is your salvation,
in quietness and trust is your strength.
[ISAIAH 30:15]

IN GOD WE TRUST

I n the early days of the American Revolutionary War, an expedition
was launched against British forces in Quebec. When the expedition
passed through Massachusetts, on the way to Canada, they visited
the tomb of the renowned evangelist George Whitefield. Whitefield's
coffin was opened and his clerical collar and cuffs were removed.
The clothing was cut in pieces and distributed in the mistaken belief
that it could somehow give the soldiers success.

The expedition failed. But what the soldiers did demonstrates our
human tendency to trust in something less than a relationship with
God—money or human strength or even religious traditions—for
our ultimate wellbeing. God cautioned His people against this when
invasion from Assyria threatened, and they sought Pharaoh's help
instead of turning from their sins and turning personally to Him:
"This is what the Sovereign LORD, the Holy One of Israel, says: 'In
repentance and rest is your salvation, in quietness and trust is your
strength, but you would have none of it. You said, "No, we will flee
on horses." Therefore you will flee!'" (ISAIAH 30:15–16).

Their 'expedition' failed as well (just as God said it would) and
Assyria overwhelmed Judah. But God also told His people, "The LORD
longs to be gracious to you." Even when we have trusted in lesser
things, God still holds out His hand to help us return to Him. "Blessed
are all who wait for him!" (V. 18)   JAMES BANKS

*In what other than God are you sometimes tempted to
place your trust? How will you rely on Him today?*

*I trust You, God! Please help me to always rely on You
because You're always faithful!*

My message and my preaching were not
with wise and persuasive words, but with
a demonstration of the Spirit's power.
[1 CORINTHIANS 2:4]

THE 'WHAT' IN SHARING OUR FAITH

Alan came to me for advice on how to deal with his fear of
public speaking. Like so many others, his heart would begin to race, his mouth would feel sticky and dry, and his face
would flush bright red. *Glossophobia* is among the most common
social fears people have—many even joke that they're more fearful
of public speaking than of dying! To help Alan conquer his fear of
not 'performing' well, I suggested he focus on the substance of his
message instead of how well he'd deliver it.

Shifting the focus to *what* will be shared, instead of one's ability
to share it, is similar to Paul's approach to pointing others to God.
When he wrote to the church at Corinth, he remarked that his
message and preaching "were not with wise and persuasive words"
(1 CORINTHIANS 2:4). Instead, he'd determined to focus solely on the
truth of Jesus Christ and His crucifixion (V. 2), trusting the Holy Spirit
to empower his words, not his eloquence as a speaker.

When we've come to know God personally, we'll want to share
about Him with those around us. Yet we sometimes shy away from
it because we're afraid of not presenting it well—with the 'right'
or eloquent words. By focusing instead on the 'what'—the truth
of who God is and His amazing works—we can, like Paul, trust
God to empower our words and share without fear or reluctance.

KIRSTEN HOLMBERG

*What has prevented you at times from sharing the truth of God with
others? How can Paul's approach embolden you to share the gospel?*

*Father in heaven, thank You for revealing Yourself to me through
the Bible and those You put in my life to share with me. Please help
me to share with others, trusting You to empower my words.*

BIBLE IN A YEAR | JOB 30–31; ACTS 13:26–52

The Spirit himself testifies with our spirit that
we are God's children. [ROMANS 8:16]

NOT FATHERLESS

J ohn Sowers in his book *Fatherless Generation* writes that "No
generation has seen as much voluntary father absence as this
one with [millions of] kids growing up in single-parent homes."
In my own experience, if I'd bumped into my father on the street,
I wouldn't have known him. My parents were divorced when I
was very young, and all the photos of my dad were burned. So for
years I felt fatherless. Then at thirteen, I heard the Lord's Prayer
(MATTHEW 6:9–13) and said to myself, *You may not have an earthly
father, but now you have God as your heavenly Father.*

In Matthew 6:9 we're taught to pray, "Our Father in heaven,
hallowed be your name." Previously verse 7 says not to "keep on
babbling" when praying, and we may wonder how these verses are
connected. I realised that because God remembers, we don't need
to repeat. He truly understands, so we don't need to explain. He
has a compassionate heart, so we don't need to be uncertain of His
goodness. And because He knows the end from the beginning, we
know His timing is perfect.

Because God is our Father, we don't need to use "many words"
(V. 7) to move Him. Through prayer, we're talking with a Father who
loves and cares for us and made us His children through Jesus.

ALBERT LEE

**When have you tried to 'move God' in prayer by using
many words? How does having a relationship with Him
as your Father help you to trust Him?**

*Dear heavenly Father, thank You for making me Your
child and for being a Father that welcomes me into Your
presence through prayer.*

Fear of the LORD is the foundation of true knowledge. [PROVERBS 1:7 NLT]

THE WISDOM WE NEED

Ellen received a bulky envelope with her dear friend's return address on. Just a few days prior, she'd shared a relational struggle with that friend. Curious, she unwrapped the package and found a colourful beaded necklace on a simple jute string. Attached was a card with a company's slogan, "Say It in Morse Code," and words translating the necklace's hidden and wise message, "Seek God's Ways." Ellen smiled as she fastened it around her neck.

The book of Proverbs is a compilation of wise sayings—many written by Solomon, who was acclaimed as the wisest man of his era (1 KINGS 10:23). Its thirty-one chapters call the reader to listen to wisdom and avoid folly, starting with the core message of Proverbs 1:7: "The fear of the LORD is the beginning of knowledge." Wisdom—knowing what to do when—comes from honouring God by seeking His ways. In the introductory verses, we read, "Listen when your father corrects you. Don't neglect your mother's instruction. What you learn from them will crown you with grace and be a chain of honour around your neck" (VV. 8–9 NLT).

Ellen's friend had directed her to the Source of the wisdom she needed: seek God's ways. Her gift focused Ellen's attention on where to discover the help she needed.

When we honour God and seek His ways, we'll receive the wisdom we need for all the matters we face in life. Each and every one.

ELISA MORGAN

Where do you go when you need wisdom? How can you keep God's words in the forefront of your mind?

God, please remind me that You're the Source of all the wisdom I need.

When you stand praying, if you hold anything
against anyone, forgive them, so that your Father
in heaven may forgive you your sins. [MARK 11:25]

BLOCKED PRAYERS

For fourteen years, the Mars rover *Opportunity* faithfully communicated with the people at NASA's Jet Propulsion Laboratory. After it landed in 2004, it traversed twenty-eight miles of the Martian surface, took thousands of images and analysed many materials. But in 2018, communication between *Opportunity* and scientists ended when a major dust storm coated its solar panels, causing the rover to lose power.

Is it possible that we can allow 'dust' to block our communication with Someone outside of our world? When it comes to prayer—communicating with God—there are certain things that can get in the way.

Scripture says that sin can block our relationship with God. "If I had cherished sin in my heart, the Lord would not have listened" (PSALM 66:18). Jesus instructs, "When you stand praying, if you hold anything against anyone, forgive them, so that your Father in heaven may forgive you your sins" (MARK 11:25). Our communication with God can also be hindered by doubt and relationship problems (JAMES 1:5–7; 1 PETER 3:7).

Opportunity's blockage of communication seems to be permanent. But our prayers don't have to be blocked. By the work of the Holy Spirit, God lovingly draws us to restored communication with Him. As we confess our sins and turn to Him, by God's grace we experience the greatest communication the universe has ever known: one-to-one prayer between us and our holy God.   *DAVE BRANON*

**How can prayer, specifically confessing your sins to God,
improve your communication with Him? What can you do
to enrich your prayer life this week?**

*Heavenly Father, please guide me to discover whatever
might be limiting my communication with You. Thank
You for helping me connect with You!*

Make every effort to add to your faith
goodness; and to goodness, knowledge.
[2 PETER 1:5]

GROWING IN GOD'S GRACE

The English preacher Charles H. Spurgeon (1834–1892) lived
life 'full throttle'. He became a pastor at nineteen—and soon
was preaching to large crowds. He personally edited all of his
sermons, which eventually filled sixty-three volumes, and wrote many
commentaries, books on prayer and other works. And he typically
read six books a week! In one of his sermons, Spurgeon said, "The
sin of doing nothing is about the biggest of all sins, for it involves
most of the others. . . . Horrible idleness! God save us from it!"

Charles Spurgeon lived with diligence, which meant he "[made]
every effort" (2 PETER 1:5) to grow in God's grace and to live for Him.
If we're Christ's followers, God can instil in us that same desire and
capacity to grow more like Jesus, to "make every effort to add to
[our] faith goodness; and to goodness, knowledge . . . self-control,
perseverance . . . godliness" (VV. 5–7)

We each have different motivations, abilities and energy levels—not
all of us can, or should, live at Charles Spurgeon's pace! But when we
understand all Jesus has done for us, we have the greatest motivation
for diligent, faithful living. And we find our strength through the
resources God has given us to live for and serve Him. God through
His Spirit can empower us in our efforts—big and small—to do so.

ALYSON KIEDA

How are you making every effort to grow more like Christ?
What will help you in this endeavour?

Loving God, help me to be diligent to live for You in
all I do and say. Thank You for enabling me to do so
through Your Spirit inside me.

Every word of God is flawless; he is a
shield to those who take refuge in him.
[PROVERBS 30:5]

LIES WITH TRUTH

I set my Bible on the podium and stared at the eager faces waiting for me to begin the message. I'd prayed and prepared. Why
couldn't I speak?

*You're worthless. No one will ever listen to you, especially if they
know your past. And God would never use you.* Seared into my heart
and mind, these words spoken in various ways over my life ignited a
decade-long war against the lies I so easily believed. Though I knew
the words weren't true, I couldn't seem to escape my insecurities
and fears. So I opened my Bible.

Turning to Proverbs 30:5, I inhaled and exhaled slowly before
reading out loud. "Every word of God is flawless," I read, "he is a
shield to those who take refuge in him." I closed my eyes as peace
overwhelmed me, and I began to share my testimony with the crowd.

Many of us have experienced the paralysing power of negative
words or opinions others have of us. However, God's words are
"flawless," perfect and absolutely sound. When we're tempted to
believe spirit-crushing ideas about our value or our purpose as God's
children, God's enduring and infallible truth protects our minds and
our hearts. We can echo the psalmist who wrote: "I remember,
LORD, your ancient laws, and I find comfort in them" (PSALM 119:52).

Let's combat lies we've accepted about God, ourselves, and others
by replacing negative-speak with Scripture.   *XOCHITL DIXON*

What lies have you believed? What verses in the Bible
have helped you see God, yourself and others through
the truth of Scripture?

Loving Father, please help me to prayerfully study Scripture
as You help me view life through the lens of Your truth.

We do not want you to be uninformed about those who sleep in death, so that you do not grieve like the rest of mankind, who have no hope. [1 THESSALONIANS 4:13]

HOPE IN GRIEF

As the taxi driver drove us to London's Heathrow Airport, he told us his story. He had come alone to the United Kingdom at fifteen, seeking to escape war and deprivation. Now, eleven years later, he has a family of his own and is able to provide for them in ways unavailable in his native land. But he laments that he's still separated from his parents and siblings. He told us that he has had a hard journey that won't be complete until he's reunited with his family.

Being separated from our loved ones in this life is hard, but losing a loved one in death is much harder and creates a sense of loss that won't be made right until we're reunited with them. When the new believers at Thessalonica wondered about such losses, Paul wrote, "Brothers and sisters, we do not want you to be uninformed about those who sleep in death, so that you do not grieve like the rest of mankind, who have no hope" (1 THESSALONIANS 4:13). He explained that as believers in Jesus, we can live in expectation of a wonderful reunion—together forever in the presence of Christ (V. 17).

Few experiences mark us as deeply as the separations we endure, but in Jesus we have hope of being reunited. And in the midst of grief and loss we can find the comfort we need in that enduring promise (V. 18).   *BILL CROWDER*

How has loss marked your own life? How does Jesus provide the help and hope you need?

Father, there's nothing on earth that can fill the places in my heart made empty through loss. Draw me to You and comfort me with Your love and grace.

The LORD God made garments of skin for
Adam and his wife and clothed them.
[GENESIS 3:21]

JESUS RESTORES US

Although Sam had done nothing wrong, he lost his job on the assembly line. Carelessness in another division led to problems in cars they built. After several crashes made the news, wary customers stopped buying their brand. The company had to downsize, leaving Sam out of work. He's collateral damage, and it isn't fair. It never is.

History's first collateral damage occurred immediately after the first sin. Adam and Eve were ashamed of their nakedness, so God graciously clothed them with "garments of skin" (GENESIS 3:21). It's painful to imagine, but one or more animals that had always been safe in the garden were now slaughtered and skinned.

There was more to come. God told Israel, "Every day you are to provide a year-old lamb without defect for a burnt offering to the LORD; morning by morning you shall provide it" (EZEKIEL 46:13). *Every. Single. Day.* How many thousands of animals have been sacrificed because of human sin?

Their death was necessary to cover our sin until Jesus, the Lamb of God, came to remove it (JOHN 1:29). Call this 'collateral repair'. As Adam's sin kills us, so the Last Adam's (Christ's) obedience restores all who believe in Him (ROMANS 5:17–19). Collateral repair isn't fair—it cost Jesus' life—but it's free. Reach out to Jesus in belief and receive the salvation He offers, and His righteous life will count for you.

MIKE WITTMER

***When have you suffered for someone else's mistake?
When have you benefited from someone's success,
and how should you think about both situations?***

Jesus, I believe in You, and I know Your life counts for me.

Even if your exiled people are at the furthest
horizon, I will gather them from there and
bring them to the place I have chosen.
[NEHEMIAH 1:9]

LONGING FOR GOD

When Conner and Sarah Smith moved five miles up the road, their cat Charlie expressed his displeasure by running away. One day Sarah saw a current photo of their old farmhouse on social media. There was Charlie in the picture!

Happily, the Smiths went to retrieve him. Charlie ran away again. Guess where he went? This time, the family that had purchased their house agreed to keep Charlie too. The Smiths couldn't stop the inevitable; Charlie would always return 'home'.

Nehemiah served in a prestigious position in the king's court in Susa, but his heart was elsewhere. He had just heard news of the sad condition of "the city where my ancestors are buried" (NEHEMIAH 2:3). And so he prayed, "Remember the instruction you gave your servant Moses, . . . 'if you return to me and obey my commands, then even if your exiled people are at the furthest horizon, I will gather them from there and bring them to the place I have chosen as a dwelling for my Name' " (1:8–9).

Home is where the heart is, they say. In Nehemiah's case, longing for home was more than being tied to the land. It was communion with God that he most desired. Jerusalem was "the place I have chosen as a dwelling for my Name."

The dissatisfaction we sense deep down is actually a longing for God. We're yearning to be home with Him.   *TIM GUSTAFSON*

**What's your idea of home and why? In what ways do you
sense yourself longing for God?**

*Father, help me understand that only You can satisfy my
longings. Help me be at home with You, no matter where I am.*

🌱 JAMES 1:19-27   FRIDAY | 14 JULY

Let the wise listen and add to their learning.
[PROVERBS 1:5]

LISTEN AND LEARN

Someone who read one of my articles in *Our Daily Bread* dis-
agreed with something I said. So she wrote and asked for an
explanation.

After receiving my letter, she responded, "Thank you for your
answer. It was information that I didn't know. I just took for granted what I had learned in childhood. But it is a poor day when one
doesn't learn something new—so at eighty-four, I am still learning!"

A willingness to learn is a mark of growth and wisdom. Proverbs 1:5 states, "let the wise listen and add to their learning, and
let the discerning get guidance." The Hebrew word for learning in
this verse means "a taking in".

If we desire to grow in our knowledge of God and learn to please
Him, we need not fear discarding old ideas and taking in new ones
that more adequately explain the Scriptures. People who are seeking
wisdom will welcome new ideas. They will test them by the truths of
the Bible, either to confirm what they already believe or to enlarge
their knowledge and understanding.

Someone once said, "Learning requires listening." We must be open
to God's truth as He teaches us through His Word and the people
around us. Are we listening, testing and learning? *DENNIS J. DEHAAN*

How does God want you to put James 1 into practice?
Who might you need to listen to and hear?

You know me, God. I can be opinionated sometimes.
Help me to be quick to listen and slow to speak.

Which of you fathers, if your son asks
for a fish, will give him a snake instead?
[LUKE 11:11]

CONFIDENT PRAYER

Having tried for years to have a child, Richard and Susan were
elated when Susan became pregnant. Her health problems,
however, posed a risk to the baby, and so Richard lay awake
each night praying for his wife and child. One night, Richard sensed
he didn't need to pray so hard, that God had promised to take care
of things. But a week later Susan miscarried. Richard was devastated. He wondered, *Had they lost the baby because he hadn't prayed
hard enough?*

On first reading, we might think today's parable suggests so. In
the story, a neighbour (sometimes thought to represent God) only
gets out of bed to help the friend because of the friend's annoying
persistence (LUKE 11:5–8). Read this way, the parable suggests that
God will give us what we need only if we badger Him. And if we
don't pray hard enough, maybe God won't help us.

But biblical commentators like Klyne Snodgrass believe this mis-
understands the parable—its real point being that if neighbours
might help us for selfish reasons, how much *more* will our *un*selfish
Father. We can therefore ask confidently (VV. 9–10), knowing that
God is greater than flawed human beings (VV. 11–13). He isn't the
neighbour in the parable, but the opposite of him.

"I don't know why you lost your baby," I told Richard, "but I know
it wasn't because you didn't pray 'hard' enough. God isn't like that."

SHERIDAN VOYSEY

*If the neighbour in the parable represents God, what does it
suggest God is like? If verses 11–13 clarify the parable, what
then is God like?*

*Father, today I bring You my needs and the needs of others,
confident that You'll hear and answer, and grateful that it's
Your goodness and not my words that count.*

Send me your light and your faithful care,
let them lead me. [PSALM 43:3]

NAVIGATING THE STORMS OF LIFE

On July 16, 1999, the small plane piloted by John F. Kennedy Jr. crashed into the Atlantic Ocean. Investigators determined the cause of the accident to be a common error known as spatial disorientation. This phenomenon occurs when, due to poor visibility, pilots become disoriented and forget to rely on their instruments to help them successfully reach their destination.

As we navigate life, there are often times when life gets so overwhelming we feel disoriented. A cancer diagnosis, the death of a loved one, a job loss, a betrayal by a friend—life's unexpected tragedies can easily leave us feeling lost and confused.

When we find ourselves in these kinds of situations, we might try offering the prayer of Psalm 43. In this psalm, the psalmist is overwhelmed and feeling lost because he feels surrounded by evil and injustice. In despair, the psalmist pleads with God to provide His sure guidance to help him safely navigate through the situation to his desired destination, God's presence (VV. 3–4). In God's presence the psalmist knows he'll find renewed hope and joy.

What are the tools the psalmist requests for guidance? The light of truth and the assurance of God's presence by His Holy Spirit.

When you're feeling disoriented and lost, God's faithful guidance through His Spirit and loving presence can comfort you and light your way.   LISA M. SAMRA

What disorienting circumstances are you experiencing?
How might you ask God to help guide you today?

Heavenly Father, thank You that You've not left me alone in the challenging and disorienting circumstances of life. Please help me to rely on You to guide my steps today.

I now realise how true it is that God does not show favouritism. [ACTS 10:34]

PREJUDICE AND FORGIVENESS

After hearing a message about correcting injustice, a church member approached the pastor weeping, asking for forgiveness and confessing that he hadn't voted in favour of calling the black minister to be pastor of their church because of his own prejudice. "I really need you to forgive me. I don't want the junk of prejudice and racism spilling over into my kids' lives. I didn't vote for you, and I was wrong." His tears and confession were met with the tears and forgiveness of the minister. A week later, the entire church rejoiced upon hearing the man's testimony of how God had worked in his heart.

Even Peter, a disciple of Jesus and a chief leader in the early church, had to be corrected because of his ill-conceived notions about non-Jewish people. Eating and drinking with gentiles (who were considered unclean), was a violation of social and religious protocol. Peter said, "You are well aware that it is against our law for a Jew to associate with or visit a Gentile" (ACTS 10:28). It took nothing less than the supernatural activity of God (VV. 9–23) to convince him that he "should not call anyone impure or unclean" (V. 28).

Through the preaching of Scripture, the conviction of the Spirit and life experiences, God continues to work in human hearts to correct our misguided perspectives about others. He helps us to see that "God does not show favouritism" (V. 34).   *ARTHUR JACKSON*

What experiences or people has God used to help you see that He doesn't show favouritism? What are the things in your life that may have blinded you to His acceptance of all people?

Dear God, search my heart and show me where I need to change.

People will dwell again in his shade; they will flourish
like the grain, they will blossom like the vine.
[HOSEA 14:7]

GOD'S RESTORING WAYS

One of the most moving songs in the musical *The Greatest
Showman* is "From Now On." Sung after the main character
comes to some painful self-realisations about the ways he's
wounded family and friends, the song celebrates the joy of coming
back home and finding that what we already have is more than enough.

The book of Hosea concludes with a similar tone—one of breathless joy and gratitude at the restoration God makes possible for
those who return to Him. Much of the book, which compares the
relationship between God and His people to a relationship with an
unfaithful spouse, grieves Israel's failures to love Him and live for Him.

But in chapter 14, Hosea lifts up the promise of God's boundless
love, grace and restoration—freely available to those who return to
Him heartbroken over the ways they've abandoned Him (VV. 1–3). "I
will heal their waywardness," God promises, "and love them freely"
(V. 4). And what had seemed broken beyond repair will once more
find wholeness and abundance, as God's grace, like dew, causes His
people to "blossom like a lily" and "flourish like the grain" (VV. 5–7).

When we've hurt others or taken for granted God's goodness
in our life, it's easy to assume we've forever marred the good gifts
we've been given. But when we humbly turn to Him, we find His
love is always reaching to embrace and restore.   *MONICA LA ROSE*

> **When have you experienced or witnessed restoration
> beyond what seemed possible? In what areas of your life do
> you need reassurance of God's promise to heal and restore?**

> *Loving God and Creator of Life, teach me to trust in Your
> goodness—not just when I'm good, but all the time.*

Daniel . . . still pray[ed] three times a day.
[DANIEL 6:13]

FIRM REFUSAL

When the Nazis drafted Franz Jägerstätter during World War II, he completed military basic training but refused to take the required pledge of personal loyalty to Adolf Hitler. Authorities allowed Franz to return to his farm, but they later summoned him to active duty. After seeing Nazi ideology up close and learning of the Jewish genocide, however, Jägerstätter decided his loyalty to God meant he could never fight for the Nazis. He was arrested and sentenced to execution, leaving behind his wife and three daughters.

Over the years, many believers in Jesus—under peril of death— have offered a firm refusal when commanded to disobey God. The story of Daniel is one such story. When a royal edict threatened that anyone "who pray[ed] to any god or human being except [the king]" (DANIEL 6:12) would be thrown into the lions' den, Daniel discarded safety and remained faithful. "Three times a day he got down on his knees and prayed, giving thanks to his God, just as he had done before" (V. 10). The prophet would bend his knee to God—and only God—no matter the cost.

Sometimes, our choice is clear. Though everyone around us implores us to go along with prevailing opinion—though our own reputation or wellbeing may be at risk—may we never turn from our obedience to God. Sometimes, even at great cost, all we can offer is a firm refusal.

WINN COLLIER

> **Where are you sensing that obedience to God will require your firm refusal? What might this refusal cost you? What will you gain?**

> *God, I know my loyalty to You will at times mean saying no to others' expectations or demands. It may cost me dearly. Give me courage.*

What is the way to the place where the
lightning is dispersed, or the place where
the east winds are scattered over the earth?
[JOB 38:24]

GOD'S POWER ON DISPLAY

t was a lightning storm, and my six-year-old daughter and I were
on the floor watching the dazzling display through the glass door.
She kept repeating, "Wow! God is so big." I felt the same way. It
was obvious to both of us how small we were, and how powerful
God must be. Lines from the book of Job flashed through my mind,
"What is the way to the place where the lightning is dispersed, or the
place where the east winds are scattered over the earth?" (JOB 38:24)

Job needed to be reminded of God's power (VV. 34–41). His life had
fallen apart. His children were dead. He was broke. He was sick. His
friends offered no empathy. His wife encouraged him to abandon
his faith (2:9). Eventually, Job asked God, "Why?" (CH. 24) and He
responded out of a storm (CH. 38).

God reminded Job of His control over the physical attributes of
the world (CH. 38). This comforted him and he responded, "My ears
had heard of you, but now my eyes have seen you" (42:5). In other
words, "Now I get it, God! I see that you don't fit into my box."

When life falls apart, sometimes the most comforting thing we can
do is to lie on the floor and watch the lightning—to be reminded that
the God who created the world is big enough and loving enough to
take care of us too. We may even start singing our favourite worship
songs that tell of the might and greatness of our God. *DANIEL RYAN DAY*

When was the last time you saw God's power on display?
What went through your mind as you witnessed His bigness?

God, help me see how big You are and to stop trying to fit You into small
boxes. Help me to trust that if You're big enough to create and control
lightning, You're big enough to help me through life's challenges.

Rejoice and be glad, because great is your
reward in heaven. [MATTHEW 5:12]

AUTHENTIC CHRISTIANITY

I applied for a position in a Christian organisation years ago and
was presented with a list of legalistic rules having to do with
the use of alcohol, tobacco and certain forms of entertainment.
"We expect Christian behaviour from our employees" was the explanation. I could agree with this list because I, for reasons mostly
unrelated to my faith, didn't do those things. But my argumentative
side thought, *Why don't they have a list about not being arrogant,
insensitive, harsh, spiritually indifferent and critical? None of these
were addressed.*

Following Jesus can't be defined by a list of rules. It's a subtle
quality of life that's difficult to quantify but can best be described
as "beautiful".

The Beatitudes in Matthew 5:3–10 sum up that beauty: those
who are indwelt by and dependent on the Spirit of Jesus are humble
and self-effacing. They're deeply touched by the suffering of others.
They're gentle and kind. They long for goodness in themselves and
in others. They're merciful to those who struggle and fail. They're
single-minded in their love for Jesus. They're peaceful and leave
behind a legacy of peace. They're kind to those who misuse them,
returning good for evil. And they're *blessed,* a word that means
"happy" in the deepest sense.

This kind of life attracts the attention of others and belongs to
those who come to Jesus and ask Him for it.   *DAVID H. ROPER*

**Which of the attributes from Matthew 5 do you
especially need in your life? How can you grow in this?**

*Spirit of God, please produce these characteristics from
the Beatitudes in my life.*

We will stand in your presence . . . and will cry
out to you in our distress. [2 CHRONICLES 20:9]

SEEKING GOD'S HELP

For five years in the late 1800s, grasshoppers descended on
Minnesota in America, destroying the crops. Farmers tried
trapping the grasshoppers in tar and burning their fields to kill
the eggs. Feeling desperate, and on the brink of starvation, many
people sought to have a day of prayer, yearning to seek God's help
together. The 26 April was set aside for everyone to pray.

In the days after the collective prayer, the weather warmed and
the eggs started to come to life. But then four days later a drop in
temperature surprised and delighted many, for the freezing tem-
peratures killed the larvae. The farmers once again would harvest
their crops of corn, wheat and oats.

Prayer was also behind the saving of God's people during the
reign of King Jehoshaphat. When the king learned that a vast army
was coming against him, he called God's people to pray and fast.
The people reminded God how He'd saved them in times past. And
Jehoshaphat said that if calamity came upon them, "whether the
sword of judgement, or plague or famine," they would cry out to
God knowing that He would hear and save them (2 CHRONICLES 20:9).

God rescued His people from the invading armies, and He hears
us when we cry out to Him in distress. Whatever your concern—
whether a relationship issue or something threatening from the
natural world—lift it to God in prayer. Nothing is too hard for Him.

AMY BOUCHER PYE

**How has God answered your prayers? What situations in
your life or in the world could you commit to Him today?**

*Creator God, You made the world and all that's in it. Please
restore order and save Your people, whom You love.*

We were all baptised by one Spirit so as to
form one body. [1 CORINTHIANS 12:13]

THE GREATEST SYMPHONY

When *BBC Music Magazine* asked 151 of the world's leading conductors to list what they believed to be the greatest symphonies ever written, Beethoven's Third, *Eroica*, came out on top. The work, whose title means "heroic," was written during the turmoil of the French Revolution. But it also came out of Beethoven's own struggle as he slowly lost his hearing. The music evokes extreme swings of emotion that express what it means to be human and alive while facing challenges. Through wild swings of happiness, sadness and eventual triumph Beethoven's Third Symphony is regarded as a timeless tribute to the human spirit.

Paul's first letter to the Corinthians deserves our attention for similar reasons. Through inspired words rather than musical scores, it rises in blessing (1:4–9), falls in the sadness of soul-crushing conflict (11:17–22) and rises again in the unison of gifted people working together for one another and for the glory of God (12:6–7).

The difference is that here we see the triumph of our human spirit as a tribute to the Spirit of God. As Paul urges us to experience together the inexpressible love of Christ, he helps us see ourselves as called together by our Father, led by His Son and inspired by His Spirit—not for noise, but for our contribution to the greatest symphony of all. *MART DEHAAN*

> ***Where do you hear the dissonance of conflict in your own
> life? Where do you see the symphonic harmonies of love?***
>
> *Father, please enable me to see what I can be with others, with
> my eyes on Your Son, with reliance on Your Spirit, with a growing
> awareness of what You can do with a noisemaker like me.*

There you saw how the LORD your God carried you,
as a father carries his son, all the way you went
until you reached this place. [DEUTERONOMY 1:31]

GOD CARRIES US

In 2019, Hurricane Dorian overwhelmed the islands of the Bahamas with intense rain, wind and flooding—the worst natural disaster in the country's history. As he sheltered at home with his adult son who has cerebral palsy, Brent knew they needed to leave. Even though Brent is blind, he had to save his son. Tenderly, he placed him over his shoulders and stepped into chin-deep water to carry him to safety.

If an earthly father facing a great obstacle is eager to help his son, think of how much more our heavenly Father is concerned about His children. In the Old Testament, Moses recalled how God carried His people even as they experienced the danger of faltering faith. He reminded the Israelites of how God had delivered them, providing food and water in the desert, fighting against their enemies and guiding the Israelites with pillars of cloud and fire. Meditating on the many ways God acted on their behalf, Moses said, "There you saw how the LORD your God carried you, as a father carries his son" (DEUTERONOMY 1:31).

The Israelites' journey through the wilderness wasn't easy, and their faith waned at times. But it was full of evidence of God's protection and provision. The image of a father carrying a son—tenderly, courageously, confidently—is a wonderful picture of how God cared for Israel. Even when we face challenges that test our faith, we can remember that God's there carrying us through them. *KAREN PIMPO*

In what ways have you seen God's provision and protection in your life? How can you face difficulties knowing that God carries you tenderly and confidently?

Loving God, help me remember that You carry me, even when I don't feel it. Thank You for Your strength and compassion.

Look up at the sky and count the stars.
[GENESIS 15:5]

OF PRAYER AND DUST AND STARS

ara and Dave desperately wanted a baby, but the doctor told them they were unable to have one. Lara confided to a friend: "I found myself having some very honest talks with God." But it was after one of those 'talks' that she and Dave spoke to their pastor, who told them about an adoption ministry at their church. A year later they were blessed with an adopted baby boy.

In Genesis 15, the Bible tells of another honest conversation—this one between Abram and God. God had told him, "Do not be afraid, Abram. I am . . . your very great reward" (v. 1). But Abram, uncertain of God's promises about his future, answered candidly: "Sovereign LORD, what can you give me since I remain childless?" (v. 2).

Earlier God had promised Abram, "I will make your offspring like the dust of the earth" (13:16). Now Abram—in a very human moment—reminded God of that. But note God's response: He assured Abram by telling him to look up and "count the stars—if indeed you can," indicating his descendants would be beyond numbering (15:5).

How good is God, not only to allow such candid prayer but also to gently reassure Abram! Later, God would change his name to Abraham ("father of many"). Like Abraham, you and I can openly share our hearts with Him and know that we can trust Him to do what's best for us and others.　　　　　　　　　　　*JAMES BANKS*

> **How do you think Abraham felt when God encouraged Him in such a difficult moment? What candid conversation do you need to have with God today?**

> *Loving heavenly Father, thank You for caring about even the most intimate details of my life. Help me to stay close to You in prayer today.*

A new command I give you: love one another.
As I have loved you, so you must love one
another. [JOHN 13:34]

BLOOMING FOR JESUS

I wasn't truthful about the tulips. A gift from my younger daughter,
the packaged bulbs travelled home with her from Amsterdam
after she visited there. So I made a show of accepting the bulbs
with great excitement, as excited as I was to reunite with her. But
tulips are my least favourite flower. Many bloom early and fade
fast. The July weather, meantime, made it too hot to plant them.

Finally, however, in late September, I planted 'my daughter's'
bulbs—thinking of her and thus planting them with love. With each
turn of the rocky soil, my concern for the bulbs grew. Giving their
plant bed a final pat, I offered the bulbs a blessing, "sleep well,"
hoping to see blooming tulips in the spring.

My little project became a humble reminder of God's call for us to
love one another, even if we're not each other's 'favourites'. Looking
past each other's faulty 'weeds', we're enabled by God to extend love
to others, even in temperamental seasons. Then, over time, mutual
love blooms in spite of ourselves. "By this," Jesus said, "everyone
will know that you are my disciples, if you love one another" (V. 35).
Pruned by Him, we're blessed then to bloom, as my tulips did the
next spring—on the same weekend my daughter arrived for a short
visit. "Look what's blooming!" I said. Finally, me.   PATRICIA RAYBON

*Who is God asking you to love, even if that person
isn't your 'favourite'? What can you do to show that
person more of the love of Christ?*

*Dear Jesus, prune my heart so I can learn to love
others in Christ.*

🌻 **PROVERBS 15:13–15, 30** THURSDAY | 27 JULY

A cheerful heart is good medicine.
[PROVERBS 17:22]

THE JOY GOD PROVIDES

When Marcia's out in public, she always tries to smile at others. It's her way of reaching out to people who might need to see a friendly face. Most of the time, she gets a genuine smile in return. But when Marcia was mandated to wear a facemask because of COVID-19, she realised that people could no longer see her mouth, thus no one could see her smile. *It's sad,* she thought, *but I'm not going to stop. Maybe they'll see in my eyes that I'm smiling.*

There's actually a bit of science behind that idea. The muscles for the corners of the mouth and the ones that make the eyes crinkle can work in tandem. It's called a Duchenne smile and it has been described as "smiling with the eyes."

Proverbs reminds us that "a cheerful look brings joy to the heart" and "a cheerful heart is good medicine" (15:30 NLT; 17:22). Quite often, the smiles of God's children stem from the supernatural joy we possess. It's a gift from God that regularly spills out into our lives, as we encourage people who are carrying heavy burdens or share with those who are looking for answers to life's questions. Even when we experience suffering, our joy can still shine through.

When life seems dark, choose joy. Let your smile be a window of hope reflecting God's love and the light of His presence in your life.

CINDY HESS KASPER

What else does the Bible teach us about the joy found in God? How does inner joy contribute to a healthy mind, body and spirit?

*The joy You provide is my strength, dear God.
Help me to be a messenger of Your love to others.*

BIBLE IN A YEAR | PSALMS 43–45; ACTS 27:27–44   217

Love is as strong as death.
[SONG OF SONGS 8:6]

GOD'S LOVE IS STRONGER

In 2020, Alyssa Mendoza received a surprising email from her father in the middle of the night. The message had instructions about what to do for her mother on her parents' twenty-fifth anniversary. Why was this shocking? Alyssa's father had passed away ten months earlier. She discovered that he'd written and scheduled the email while he was sick, knowing he might not be there. He'd also arranged and paid for flowers to be sent to his wife for upcoming years on her birthday, future anniversaries and Valentine's Day.

This story could stand as an example of the kind of love that's described in detail in Song of Songs. "Love is as strong as death, its jealousy unyielding as the grave" (8:6). Comparing graves and death to love seems odd, but they're strong because they don't give up their captives. However, neither will true love give up the loved one. The book reaches its peak in verses 6–7, describing marital love as one so strong that "many waters cannot quench [it]" (V. 7).

Throughout the Bible, the love of a husband and wife is compared to God's love (ISAIAH 54:5; EPHESIANS 5:25; REVELATION 21:2). Jesus is the groom and the church is His bride. God showed His love for us by sending Christ to face death so we wouldn't have to die for our sins (JOHN 3:16). Whether we're married or single, we can remember that God's love is stronger than anything we could imagine.
                                                            JULIE SCHWAB

How do you feel knowing how much God loves you?
What reminds you of His love for you?

Dear Jesus, thank You for loving me so much! Remind me of Your love each day and give me glimpses of it.

For he himself is our peace, who has made the
two groups one and has destroyed the barrier,
the dividing wall of hostility. [EPHESIANS 2:14]

JESUS IS OUR PEACE

A monk named Telemachus lived a quiet life, but his death at the
end of the fourth century changed the world. Visiting Rome
from the East, Telemachus intervened in the blood sport of
the gladiatorial arena. He jumped over the stadium wall and tried to
stop the gladiators from killing each other. But the outraged crowd
stoned the monk to death. The emperor Honorius, however, was
moved by Telemachus' act and decreed the end of the 500-year
practice of gladiator games.

When Paul calls Jesus "our peace," he refers to the end of hostility between Jews and gentiles (EPHESIANS 2:14). God's chosen
people Israel were distinct from the nations and enjoyed certain
privileges. For instance, while gentiles were allowed to worship at
the Jerusalem temple, a dividing wall restricted them to the outer
court—on punishment of death. Jews regarded gentiles unclean,
and they experienced mutual hostility. But now, because of Jesus'
death and resurrection for all, both Jew and gentile can worship
God freely through faith in Him (VV. 18–22). There's no dividing wall.
There's no privilege of one group over the other. Both are equal in
their standing before God.

Just as Telemachus brought peace to warriors through his death,
so Jesus makes peace and reconciliation possible for all who believe
in Him through His death and resurrection. So, if Jesus is our peace,
let's not let our differences divide us. He's made us one by His blood.

CON CAMPBELL

How do you reveal you're at peace with all people?
What issues—such as race, status or privilege—
sometimes get in the way? Why?

Dear God of peace, You've made us one in Jesus.
Help me to know it and live it.

Saul has slain his thousands, and David his
tens of thousands. [1 SAMUEL 18:7]

OVERCOMING ENVY

In the film *Amadeus,* ageing composer Antonio Salieri plays some
of his music on the piano for a visiting priest. The embarrassed
priest confesses he doesn't recognise the tunes. "What about this
one?" Salieri says, playing an instantly familiar melody. "I didn't know
you wrote *that*," the priest says. "I didn't," Salieri replies. "That was
Mozart!" As viewers discover, Mozart's success had caused deep
envy in Salieri—even leading him to play a part in Mozart's death.

A song lies at the heart of another envy story. After David's victory
over Goliath, the Israelites heartily sing, "Saul has slain his thousands,
and David his tens of thousands" (1 SAMUEL 18:7). The comparison
doesn't sit well with King Saul. Envious of David's success and afraid
of losing his throne (VV. 8–9), Saul begins a prolonged pursuit of David,
trying to take his life.

Like Salieri with music or Saul with power, we're usually tempted
to envy those with similar but greater gifts than we possess. And
whether it's picking fault with their work or belittling their success,
we too can seek to damage our 'rivals'.

Saul had been divinely chosen for his task (10:6–7, 24), a status
that should've fostered security in him rather than envy. Since we
each have unique callings too (EPHESIANS 2:10), maybe the best way
to overcome envy is to quit comparing ourselves. Let's celebrate
each other's successes instead.   *SHERIDAN VOYSEY*

Who are you most tempted to envy?
How can you celebrate their success?

Loving God, I thank You for my friends'
and colleagues' successes.

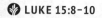

There is rejoicing in the presence of the
angels of God over one sinner who repents.
[LUKE 15:10]

PRICELESS LIVES IN CHRIST

Tears streamed down my cheeks during a frantic search for my lost wedding and anniversary rings. After an hour of lifting couch cushions and scouring every nook and cranny of our home, Alan said, "I'm sorry. We'll replace them."

"Thanks," I responded. "But their sentimental value surpasses their material worth. They're irreplaceable." Praying, I continued hunting for the jewellery. "Please, God. Help me find them."

Later, while reaching into the pocket of a sweater worn earlier in the week, I found the priceless jewels. "Thank You, Jesus!" I exclaimed. As my husband and I rejoiced, I slipped on the rings and recalled the parable of the woman who lost a coin (LUKE 15:8–10). Like the woman who searched for her lost silver coin, I knew the worth of what had been lost. Neither of us was wrong for wanting to find our valuables. Jesus simply used that story to emphasise His desire to save every person He created. One sinner repenting results in a celebration in heaven.

What a gift it would be to become a person who prays as passionately for others as we pray for lost treasures to be found. What a privilege it is to celebrate when someone repents and surrenders their lives to Christ. If we've placed our trust in Jesus, we can be thankful we've experienced the joy of being loved by Someone who never gave up because He thought we were worth finding.

XOCHITL DIXON

Whose salvation will you commit to praying for today?
Who can you share your testimony with?

*Father, thank You for reminding me that every person
You create is a priceless life worth saving.*

FELLOW CITIZENS

I didn't attend her memorial service because of the coronavirus regulations that limited the number of visitors to thirty people. But as I watched online, I thought of those around the world who were also giving thanks for what a vibrant, loving and funny person Pamela was—including her family members in Malawi, where she was buried.

She was one of many in our church in North London who came from a different country, like me, and whom I counted as a sister in Christ. After all, God's family transcends associations of tribe, race and other divisions because we have the same heavenly Father. In Christ, God brings us together.

The apostle Paul stressed our family connections when he wrote to the church at Ephesus. He was concerned over divisions between Jewish and gentile believers, saying, "You are no longer foreigners and strangers, but fellow citizens with God's people and also members of his household, built on the foundation of the apostles and prophets, with Christ Jesus himself as the chief cornerstone" (EPHESIANS 2:19–20). Paul knew that God's people are joined together as a family, "built together to become a dwelling in which God lives by his Spirit" (V. 22).

No matter our differences, believers in Jesus can look to God to help us unite with each other. Through His Spirit, He'll not only smooth over our idiosyncrasies but will help us work out our deepest differences. What unites us—God the Father, Son, and Holy Spirit—is more than what divides us.

Amy Boucher Pye, Our Daily Bread *author*

★ The topic of the **FAMILY OF GOD** is addressed in the devotions for **August 1, 9, 16** and **23**. We hope these articles will encourage you as you live and worship with other believers in Jesus.

In Christ Jesus you are all children of God through faith. [GALATIANS 3:26]

THE BEAUTY OF ADOPTION

The 2009 film *The Blind Side* depicts the true story of Michael Oher, a homeless teenager. A family takes him in and helps him overcome learning difficulties and achieve excellence in American football. In one scene, the family talks with Michael about the possibility of adopting him after he'd been living with them for several months. In a sweet and tender reply, Michael exclaims that he thought he already was a part of the family!

It's a beautiful moment, just as adoption is a beautiful thing. Love is extended and full inclusion is offered as a family opens its arms to a new member. Adoption changes lives, just as it profoundly changed Michael's life.

In Jesus, believers are made "children of God" through faith in Him (GALATIANS 3:26). We're adopted by God and become His sons and daughters (4:5). As God's adopted children, we receive the Spirit of His Son, we call God "Father" (V. 6), and we become His heirs (V. 7) and coheirs with Christ (ROMANS 8:17). We become full members of His family.

When Michael Oher was adopted, it changed his life, his identity and his future. How much more for us who are adopted by God! Our life changes as we know Him as Father. Our identity changes as we belong to Him. And our future changes as we're promised a glorious, eternal inheritance.

CON CAMPBELL

How does being a child of God affect your self-identity?
In what ways does this change the way you view yourself?

Thank You, Father, for making me Yours. Help me
to understand my identity as Your child.

Ahikam son of Shaphan supported Jeremiah, and so he was not handed over to the people to be put to death. [JEREMIAH 26:24]

WHO NEEDS YOUR SUPPORT?

Clifford Williams was sentenced to die for a murder he didn't commit. From death row he vainly filed motions to reconsider the evidence against him. Each petition was denied—for forty-two years. Then attorney Shelley Thibodeau learned of his case. She found that not only was there no evidence to convict Williams, but that another man had confessed to the crime. At the age of seventy-six, Williams was finally exonerated and released.

The prophets Jeremiah and Uriah were also in deep trouble. They had told Judah that God promised to judge His people if they didn't repent (JEREMIAH 26:12–13, 20). This message angered the people and officials of Judah, who sought to kill both prophets. They succeeded with Uriah. He fled to Egypt, but was brought back to face the king, who "had him struck down with a sword" (V. 23). Why didn't they kill Jeremiah? In part because Ahikam "stood up for Jeremiah" (NLT), "and so he was not handed over to the people to be put to death" (V. 24).

We may not know anyone facing death, but we probably know someone who could use our support. Whose rights are trampled? Whose talents are dismissed? Whose voice isn't heard? It may be risky to step out like Thibodeau or Ahikam, but it's so right. Who needs us to stand up for them as God guides us?   *MIKE WITTMER*

Whom can you stand with? If you voice your support, what do you think might happen to them, to you and to others?

Loving God, help me to love others as You've loved me.

Therefore, since we are surrounded by such
a great cloud of witnesses, let us throw off
everything that hinders and the sin that so
easily entangles. [HEBREWS 12:1]

WALKING WITH JESUS

Lean food rations, waterproof boots and a map are some of the
essentials carried by hikers on the John Muir Trail. The John Muir
Trail is a 211-mile path in the western United States that winds
across creeks, around lakes and woods, and up and over mountains,
encompassing 47,000 feet of elevation gain. Because traversing this
trail takes about three weeks, carrying the right amount of supplies
is critical. Too much and you will run out of strength to carry it all;
too little and you won't have what you need for the journey.

Finishing well on our journey as believers in Jesus also requires
careful consideration of what we bring. In Hebrews 12, we're told
to "throw off everything that hinders and the sin that so easily entangles." The author compares our lives to a "race marked out for
us," one in which we must "not grow weary and lose heart" (VV. 1, 3).
To become overburdened with sin or distracted by things outside of
God's purpose for us is to carry an unnecessary weight.

Just as there are packing lists for the John Muir Trail, God has provided directions for following Jesus in the Bible. We can know what
habits, dreams and desires are worth bringing along by examining
them in light of the Scriptures. When we travel light, we're able to
finish well.

KAREN PIMPO

What's hindering you in following Jesus? What would it look like to 'throw it off'?

*Jesus, help me travel lightly according to
Your wisdom and to finish well.*

I will not forget you! [ISAIAH 49:15]

NOT FORGOTTEN

"**U**ncle Arthur, do you remember the day you took me to the barbershop and the supermarket? I was wearing tan khakis, a blue-plaid oxford shirt, a navy-blue cardigan, brown socks and brown Rockport shoes. The date was Thursday, 20 October, 2016." My nephew Jared's autism-related challenges are offset by his phenomenal memory that can recall details like days and dates and the clothes he was wearing years after an event took place.

Because of the way he's wired, Jared possesses the kind of memory that reminds me of the all-knowing, loving God—the Keeper of time and eternity. He knows the facts and won't forget His promises or His people. Have you had moments when you've questioned whether or not you've been forgotten by God? When others appear to be healthier or happier or more successful or otherwise better off?

Ancient Israel's less-than-ideal situation caused her to say, "The LORD has forsaken me, the Lord has forgotten me" (ISAIAH 49:14). But that wasn't the case. God's compassion and care exceeded the natural bonds of affection that mothers have for their children (V. 15). Before embracing labels like "forsaken" or "forgotten", think again of what God has done in and through His Son, Jesus. In the gospel that brings forgiveness, God has clearly said, "I will not forget you!" (V. 15).

ARTHUR JACKSON

When have you felt alone, forsaken and forgotten by God? How does processing the love of God expressed by sending Jesus to die for your sins help to counter feelings of being forgotten by Him?

Father, when I'm tempted to feel neglected, forgotten and abandoned, help me to ponder again the love You demonstrated by sending Jesus to die for me.

Anyone who wants to be first must be the
very last, and the servant of all. [MARK 9:35]

GREATNESS

Cuthbert is a well-known figure in parts of northern England.
Responsible for evangelising much of the area in the seventh
century, Cuthbert counselled monarchs and influenced state
affairs; and after his death, the city of Durham was built in his honour.
But Cuthbert's legacy is great in more ways than these.

After a plague ravaged the region, Cuthbert once toured affected
towns offering solace. Readying to leave one village, he checked if
there was anyone left to pray for. There was—a woman, clutching
a child. She had already lost one son, and the child she held was
nearing death too. Cuthbert took the fevered boy in his arms, prayed
for him and kissed his forehead. "Do not fear," he told her, "for no
one else of your household will die." The boy reportedly lived.

Jesus once took a small boy into his arms to give a lesson on
greatness, saying, "Whoever welcomes one of these little children
in my name welcomes me" (MARK 9:37). To "welcome" someone in
Jewish culture meant to serve them, the way a host welcomes a
guest. Since children were to serve adults and not *be* served, the
idea must've been shocking. Jesus' point? True greatness resides
in serving the smallest and lowliest (V. 35).

A counsellor to monarchs. An influencer of history. A city built in
his honour. But perhaps heaven records Cuthbert's legacy more like
this: A mother noticed. A forehead kissed. A humble life reflecting
his Master.   *SHERIDAN VOYSEY*

> **When you think of a 'great' person in history, what
> image comes to mind? How can you pursue Jesus'
> kind of greatness today?**
>
> *Dear God, help me to humbly serve others.*

Though the righteous fall seven times,
they rise again. [PROVERBS 24:16]

RISE AGAIN

Olympic runner Ryan Hall is the US record-holder for the half marathon. He completed the event distance of 13.1 miles (21 kilometres) in a remarkable time of fifty-nine minutes and forty-three seconds, making him the first US athlete to run the race in under one hour. While Hall has celebrated record-setting victories, he has also known the disappointment of not being able to finish a race.

Having tasted both success and failure, Hall credits his faith in Jesus for sustaining him. One of his favourite Bible verses is an encouraging reminder from the book of Proverbs that "though the righteous fall seven times, they rise again" (24:16). This proverb reminds us that the righteous, those who trust in and have a right relationship with God, will still experience difficulties and hardships. However, as they continue to seek Him even in the midst of difficulty, God is faithful to give them the strength to rise again.

Have you recently experienced a devastating disappointment or failure and feel like you will never recover? Scripture encourages us not to rely on our strength but to continue to put our confidence in God and His promises. As we trust Him, God's Spirit gives us strength for every difficulty we encounter in this life, from seemingly mundane to significant struggles (2 CORINTHIANS 12:9). *LISA M. SAMRA*

> *How has God strengthened you after a difficult disappointment? How does that give you encouragement for the struggles you face today?*
>
> *Heavenly Father, thank You that in every trial and disappointment You're always close, offering comfort and strength to help me rise again.*

Esau ran to meet Jacob and embraced him.
[GENESIS 33:4]

FIRST FORGIVE

We called ourselves "sisters in Christ", but my white friend and I had begun to act like enemies. Over a café breakfast one morning, we argued unkindly over our differing racial views. Then we parted, with me vowing not to see her again. One year later, however, we were hired by the same ministry—working in the same department, unable *not* to reconnect. Awkwardly at first, we talked over conflicts. Then, over time, God helped us to apologise to each other and to heal and to give the ministry our best.

God also healed the bitter division between Esau and his twin brother, Jacob, and blessed both their lives. A one-time schemer, Jacob had robbed Esau of their father's blessing. But twenty years later, God called Jacob to return to their homeland. So, Jacob sent ahead bountiful gifts to appease Esau. "But Esau ran to meet Jacob and embraced him; he threw his arms around his neck and kissed him. And they wept" (GENESIS 33:4).

Their reunion stands as a classic example of God's urging to settle anger with a brother or sister before offering our gifts—talents or treasures—to Him (MATTHEW 5:23–24). "First go and be reconciled to them; then come and offer your gift" (V. 24). Jacob obeyed God by reconciling with Esau, and later setting up an altar to the Lord (GENESIS 33:20). What a beautiful order: first strive for forgiveness and reconciliation. Then, at His altar, He receives us.   *PATRICIA RAYBON*

> ***Against whom do you hold a grudge or grievance?***
> ***What steps can you take to reconcile?***
>
> *Dear God, when I hold onto hard feelings against another*
> *believer, inspire me on the way to Your altar to first forgive.*

Let justice roll on like a river, righteousness
like a never-failing stream! [AMOS 5:24]

GOOD TROUBLE

When John Lewis, an American politician died in 2020,
people from many political persuasions mourned. In
1965, Lewis marched with Martin Luther King Jr. to secure
voting rights for black citizens. During the march, Lewis suffered a
cracked skull, causing scars he carried the rest of his life. "When
you see something that is not right, not just, not fair," Lewis said,
"you have a moral obligation to say something. To do something."
He also said, "Never, ever, be afraid to make some noise and get in
good, necessary trouble."

Lewis learned early that doing what was right, to be faithful to
the truth, required making "good" trouble. He would need to say
things that were unpopular. The prophet Amos knew this too. Seeing
Israel's sin and injustice, he couldn't keep quiet. Amos denounced
how the powerful were oppressing "the innocent and tak[ing] bribes
and depriv[ing] the poor of justice in the courts," while building
"stone mansions" with "lush vineyards" (AMOS 5:11–12). Rather than
maintaining his own safety and comfort by staying out of the fray,
Amos named the evil. The prophet made good, necessary trouble.

But this trouble aimed at something good—justice for all. "Let
justice roll on like a river!" Amos exclaimed (V. 24). When we get
into *good* trouble (the kind of righteous, non-violent trouble justice
requires), the goal is always goodness and healing.　　*WINN COLLIER*

*Where do you sense the Holy Spirit might be prompting
you to make some good trouble? How can you discern
the godly way to do just that?*

*Heavenly Father, if I'm left to myself, I'll probably play it safe,
stay comfortable, keep quiet. But I know that You might ask
something different. Help me discern what to do to honour You.*

We know that we have passed from death to life, because we love each other. Anyone who does not love remains in death. [1 JOHN 3:14]

FEARLESS LOVE

There are some images so powerful they can never be forgotten. That was my experience when I viewed a famous photograph of the late Princess Diana of Wales. At first glance, the captured scene looks mundane: smiling warmly, the princess is shaking the hand of an unidentified man. But it's the photograph's story that makes it remarkable.

On 19 April, 1987, when Princess Diana visited London Middlesex Hospital, the United Kingdom was engulfed in a wave of panic as it confronted the AIDS epidemic. Not knowing how the disease—which often killed with terrifying speed—was spread, the public at times treated AIDS victims like social pariahs.

So it was a stunning moment when Diana, with ungloved hands and a genuine smile, calmly shook an AIDS patient's hand that day. That image of respect and kindness would move the world to treat victims of the disease with similar mercy and compassion.

The picture reminds me of something I often forget: freely and generously offering the love of Jesus to others is worth it. John reminded early believers in Christ that to let love wither or hide in the face of our fear is really to live "in death" (1 JOHN 3:14). And to love freely and unafraid, filled and empowered with the Spirit's self-giving love, is to experience resurrection life in all its fullness (VV. 14, 16).

MONICA LA ROSE

> **When are you most prone to let fear stifle your love for others? How can you grow in experiencing and sharing the Spirit's boundless love within those fearful places?**
>
> *God of love, You are love, and to live in love is to live in You. I long to live with that kind of fearless, joyous love. Fill me with Your Spirit, and carry me ever deeper into Your love, until fear dissolves and Your love flows freely through me.*

BIBLE IN A YEAR | PSALMS 77–78; ROMANS 10   231

Do not despise the LORD's discipline.
[PROVERBS 3:11]

LOVE THAT DISCIPLINES

When I took a family studies class in college, we were asked to write a "family history"—a record of the key events that make up one's childhood. This included the patterns that characterised typical family life and the methods of discipline we experienced. We all had at least one instance of a parent misapplying discipline and leaving an emotional or physical scar. Understandably, traumatic experiences like these may affect the way we interpret our heavenly Father's discipline.

In Proverbs 3:11–12, the wise teacher invites readers to accept God's discipline. The word *discipline* could be translated "correction". As a good and loving Father, God speaks through His Spirit and the Scriptures to correct self-destructive behaviour. God's discipline is relational—rooted in His love and His desire for what's best for us. Sometimes it looks like consequences. Sometimes God prompts someone to point out our blind spots. Often, it's uncomfortable, but God's discipline is a gift.

But we don't always see it that way. The wise man cautioned, "Do not despise the LORD's discipline" (V. 11). Sometimes we fear God's discipline. At other times we misinterpret bad things in our lives as God's discipline. This is far from the heart of a loving Father who disciplines because He delights in us and corrects because He loves us.

Instead of fearing God's discipline, may we learn to accept it. When we hear God's voice of correction in our hearts or experience conviction when reading Scripture, may we thank God that He delights in us enough to lead us to what's best. *DANIEL RYAN DAY*

> *How do you recognise God's discipline? How do you*
> *sense the love of God in the midst of it?*
>
> *God, help me to recognise Your discipline so that I can*
> *discover the freedom You offer.*

Small is the gate and narrow the road
that leads to life, and only a few find it.
[MATTHEW 7:14]

ACCESSIBLE TO ALL

From a manmade bridge on the small Caribbean island of Eleuthera, visitors can admire the stark contrast between the roiling dark blue waters of the Atlantic and the calm turquoise waters of the Caribbean Sea. Over time, storms washed away the original strip of land once marked by a natural stone arch. The glass window bridge that now serves as a tourist attraction on Eleuthera is known as "the narrowest place on earth."

The Bible describes the road that leads to eternal life as narrow "and only a few find it" (MATTHEW 7:14). The gate is considered small because God the Son is the only bridge that can reconcile fallen man and God the Father through the power of the Holy Spirit (VV. 13–14; SEE JOHN 10:7–9; 16:13). However, Scripture also says that believers from every people, nation and societal rank can enter heaven and will bow before the King of Kings and worship together around His throne (REVELATION 5:9). This phenomenal image of contrast and unity includes all of God's beautifully diverse people.

Though we are separated from God by our sin, every person God created is invited to enter eternity in heaven by walking this narrow path of reconciliation through a personal relationship with Christ. His sacrifice on the cross, resurrection from the tomb and ascension to heaven is the good news, accessible to all and worth sharing today and every day.

XOCHITL DIXON

How did you respond after hearing the good news?
How can you be more intentional about sharing it
with others?

God the Father, please empower me through Your Holy
Spirit so I can show others the accessible path that
leads to Your approachable Son, Jesus.

BIBLE IN A YEAR | PSALMS 81-83; ROMANS 11:19-36

I will listen to what God the LORD says.
[PSALM 85:8]

LISTENING MATTERS

"Come at once. We have struck a berg." Those were the first words Harold Cottam, the wireless operator on the RMS *Carpathia*, received from the sinking RMS *Titanic* at 12:25 a.m. on April 15, 1912. The *Carpathia* would be the first ship to the disaster scene, saving 706 lives.

In the US Senate hearings days later, the *Carpathia*'s captain Arthur Rostron testified, "The whole thing was absolutely providential. . . . The wireless operator was in his cabin at the time, not on official business at all, but just simply listening as he was undressing. . . . In ten minutes maybe he would have been in bed, and we would not have heard the message."

Listening matters—especially listening to God. The writers of Psalm 85, the sons of Korah, urged attentive obedience when they wrote, "I will listen to what God the LORD says; he promises peace to his people, his faithful servants—but let them not turn to folly. Surely his salvation is near those who fear him" (VV. 8–9). Their admonition is especially poignant because their ancestor Korah had rebelled against God and had perished in the wilderness (NUMBERS 16:1–35).

The night the *Titanic* sank, another ship was much closer, but its wireless operator had gone to bed. Had he heard the distress signal, perhaps more lives would have been saved. When we listen to God by obeying His teaching, He'll help us navigate even life's most troubled waters.

JAMES BANKS

In what ways will you stay attentive to God and the Scriptures today? How can doing so help you to help others?

Father, help me to stay close to You in my thoughts, words, and actions. Please use me as Your servant to bring Your hope to others.

They gave as much as they were able.
[2 CORINTHIANS 8:3]

THE TRUE NATURE OF LOVE

During the pandemic's first lockdown, Jerry was forced to close his fitness centre and had no income for months. One day he received a text from a friend asking to meet him at his facility at 6:00 p.m. Jerry wasn't sure why but made his way there. Soon cars started streaming into the car park. The driver in the first car placed a basket on the pavement near the building. Then car after car (maybe fifty of them) came by. Those inside waved at Jerry or hollered out a hello, stopped at the basket, and dropped in a card or cash. Some sacrificed their money; all gave their time to encourage him.

The true nature of love is sacrificial, according to the apostle Paul. He explained to the Corinthians that the Macedonians gave "even beyond their ability" so they could meet the needs of the apostles and others (2 CORINTHIANS 8:3). They even "pleaded" with Paul for the opportunity to give to them and to God's people. The basis for their giving was the sacrificial heart of Jesus Himself. He left the riches of heaven to come to earth to be a servant and to give His very life. "Though he was rich, yet for [our] sake he became poor" (V. 9).

May we too plead with God so that we might "excel in this grace of giving" (V. 7) in order to lovingly meet the needs of others.

ANNE CETAS

How might sacrificial service or giving fit into your life this week? Who needs your encouragement?

Loving God, You are so good. Please give me opportunities to bless others for You in Your power and wisdom.

In all this, Job did not sin in what he said.
[JOB 2:10]

WHEN WE DON'T UNDERSTAND

66 I don't understand His plan. I turned my whole life over to Him. And this happens!" Such was the message of a son to his mother when his dream to succeed as a professional athlete was temporarily derailed. Who among us hasn't had some kind of unexpected, disappointing experience that sends our minds into overdrive with exclamations and questions? A family member cuts off communication without explanation; health gains are reversed; a company relocates unexpectedly; a life-altering accident happens.

Job 1–2 records a series of tragedies and setbacks in Job's life. Humanly speaking, if there was anyone who qualified for a life free from trouble, it was Job. "This man was blameless and upright; he feared God and shunned evil" (JOB 1:1). But life doesn't always work out the way we'd like it to—it didn't for Job, and it doesn't for us. When his wife counselled him to "curse God and die!" (2:9), Job's words to her were wise, instructive and fitting for us as well when things happen—big or small—that we'd rather not face. " 'Shall we accept good from God, and not trouble?' In all this, Job did not sin in what he said" (V. 10).

By God's strength, may our trust in and reverence for Him remain even when we can't understand how He's at work during life's difficult days.
ARTHUR JACKSON

When has your faith in God been tested? What has He used during tough circumstances to help your reverence for Him to remain intact?

Father, help me to trust You and honour You when I can't see Your hand or understand Your plan.

God's grace was so powerfully at work in
them all that there were no needy persons
among them. [ACTS 4:33–34]

EXTENDING GRACE TO OTHERS

Our son spent the early years of his life in a children's home prior
to our adopting him. Before leaving the building together to go
home, we asked to collect his belongings. Sadly, he had none.
We exchanged the clothes he was wearing for the new items we'd
brought for him and also left some clothing for the other children.
Even though I was grieved by how little he had, I rejoiced that we
could now help meet his physical and emotional needs.

A few years later, we saw a person asking for donations for families
in need. My son was eager to donate his stuffed animals and a few
coins to help them. Given his background, he might have (understandably) been more inclined to hold tightly to his belongings.

I'd like to think the reason for his generous response was the
same as that of the early church: "God's grace was so powerfully at
work in them all" that nobody in their midst had need (ACTS 4:33–34).
The people willingly sold their own possessions to provide for one
another's needs.

When we become aware of the needs of others, whether material
or intangible, may God's grace be so powerfully at work in us that
we respond as they did, willingly giving from our hearts to those
in need. This makes us vessels of God's grace as fellow believers in
Jesus, "one in heart and mind" (V. 32).   *KIRSTEN HOLMBERG*

*How is God's grace at work in you? What could you share
with others as a manifestation of His grace?*

*Thank you, God, for all You've given to me, including Your
grace. Help me to extend Your grace to others.*

Religion that God our Father accepts as pure
and faultless is this: to look after orphans and
widows in their distress. [JAMES 1:27]

ACTIVE FAITH

Sam's father had to flee for his life during a military coup. With the sudden loss of income, the family could no longer afford the crucial medicine that kept Sam's brother alive. Seething at God, Sam thought, *What have we done to deserve this?*

A follower of Jesus heard about the family's troubles. Finding he had enough money to cover the medicine, he bought a supply and took it to them. The life-saving gift from a stranger had a profound impact. "This Sunday, we will go to this man's church," his mother declared. Sam's anger began to subside. And eventually, one by one, each member of the family put their faith in Jesus.

When James wrote about the necessity of a lifestyle of integrity accompanying a profession of faith in Christ, he singled out the need to care for others. "Suppose a brother or a sister is without clothes and daily food," James wrote. "If one of you says to them, 'Go in peace; keep warm and well fed,' but does nothing about their physical needs, what good is it?" (2:15–16).

Our actions demonstrate the genuineness of our faith. Significantly, those actions can influence the faith-choices of others. In Sam's case, he became a pastor and church-planter. Eventually he would call the man who helped his family "Papa Mapes." He now knew him as his spiritual father—the one who showed them the love of Jesus. *TIM GUSTAFSON*

> **How have you experienced the love of Jesus extended to you? What can you do to help someone in need?**
>
> *Faithful God, help me to live out my faith in You.
> I want the way I serve others to honour You.*

When your words came, I ate them.
[JEREMIAH 15:16]

TRUSTING THE BIBLE

Billy Graham, the renowned American evangelist, once described his struggle to accept the Bible as completely true. One night as he walked alone in the moonlight at a retreat centre, he dropped to his knees and placed his Bible on a tree stump, able only to 'stutter' a prayer: "Oh, God! There are many things in this book I do not understand."

By confessing his confusion, Graham said the Holy Spirit finally "freed me to say it. 'Father, I am going to accept this as thy Word—by faith!'" When he stood up, he still had questions, but he said, "I knew a spiritual battle in my soul had been fought and won."

The young prophet Jeremiah fought spiritual battles too. Yet he consistently sought answers in Scripture. "When your words came, I ate them; they were my joy and my heart's delight" (JEREMIAH 15:16). He declared, "The word of the LORD . . . is in my heart like a fire, a fire shut up in my bones" (20:8–9). Nineteenth-century evangelist Charles Spurgeon wrote, "[Jeremiah] lets us into a secret. His outer life, especially his faithful ministry, was due to his inward love of the Word which he preached."

We too can shape our life through the wisdom of Scripture despite our struggles. We can keep studying, as always, by faith.

PATRICIA RAYBON

> **How has your life been shaped by Scripture?**
> **As you accept it by faith, how do you expect**
> **your life to change?**
>
> *Heavenly Father, show me new things about*
> *You as I read the Bible. Teach me Your ways.*
> *Show me Your love.*

Search me, God, and know my heart;
test me and know my anxious thoughts.
[PSALM 139:23]

GOD KNOWS YOUR STORY

As I drove home after lunch with my best friend, I thanked God out loud for her. She knows me and loves me in spite of things I don't love about myself. She's one of a small circle of people who accept me as I am—my quirks, habits and mistakes. Still, there are parts of my story I resist sharing even with her and others that I love—times where I've clearly not been the hero, times I've been judgemental or unkind or unloving.

But God *does* know my whole story. He's the One I can freely talk to even if I'm reluctant to talk with others.

The familiar words of Psalm 139 describe the intimacy we enjoy with our Sovereign King. He knows us completely! (V. 1). He's "familiar with all [our] ways" (V. 3). He invites us to come to Him with our confusion, our anxious thoughts and our struggles with temptation. When we're willing to yield completely to Him, He reaches out to restore and rewrite the parts of our story that make us sad because we've wandered from Him.

God knows us better than anyone else ever can, and *still* . . . He loves us! When we daily surrender ourselves to Him and seek to know Him more fully, He can change our story for His glory. He's the Author who's continuing to write it.   *CINDY HESS KASPER*

What assurance do you have that God will always love you unconditionally? How can you make yielding to Him a daily practice?

Precious Father, thank You for loving me as Your child despite the times I've disappointed You. Help me to yield all of myself to You in full assurance that You're faithfully walking beside me.

[Jesus] took bread, gave thanks and broke it,
and gave it to them, saying, "This is my body
given for you; do this in remembrance of me."
[LUKE 22:19]

REMEMBER AND CELEBRATE

O
n 6 December, 1907, explosions rocked a small community in the
US state of West Virginia, producing one of the worst disasters
in the history of the coal-mining industry in America. Some 360
miners were killed, and it's been estimated that this horrific tragedy left
behind about 250 widows and 1,000 children without fathers. Historians
maintain that the memorial service became the seedbed from which the
celebration of Father's Day in the US would eventually grow. Out of great
loss came remembrance and—eventually—celebration.

The greatest tragedy in human history occurred when human
beings crucified their Creator. Yet, that dark moment also produced
both remembrance and celebration. The night before He would
go to the cross, Jesus took the elements of Israel's Passover and
created His own memorial celebration. Luke's record describes the
scene this way: "And he took bread, gave thanks and broke it, and
gave it to them, saying, 'This is my body given for you; do this in
remembrance of me'" (LUKE 22:19).

Still today, whenever we take communion, we honour His great,
unflinching love for us—remembering the cost of our rescue and
celebrating the gift of life His sacrifice produced. As Charles Wesley
said in his great hymn, "Amazing love! How can it be that Thou, my
God, shouldst die for me?"
BILL CROWDER

> ***How often do you find yourself just going through the motions
> when taking communion? What are some ways to keep your
> focus on the cross?***

> *Father, when I come to the memorial table, help me to
> remember why my forgiveness was so costly, and help me to
> celebrate Your great, awesome love.*

[Our] help comes from the LORD, the Maker of heaven and earth. [PSALM 121:2]

PEACE IN THE CHAOS

Something that sounded like firecrackers roused Joanne from sleep. Glass shattered. Wishing she didn't live alone, she got up to see what was going on. The dark streets were empty and the house seemed to be okay—then she saw the broken mirror.

Investigators found a bullet only a half-inch from the gas line. If it had struck the line, she probably wouldn't have made it out alive. Later they discovered it was a stray bullet from a nearby flat, but now Joanne was afraid to be at home. She prayed for peace, and once the glass was cleaned up, her heart calmed.

Psalm 121 is a reminder for us to look to God in times of trouble. Here, we see that we can have peace and calm because our "help comes from the LORD, the Maker of heaven and earth" (V. 2). The God who created the universe helps and watches over us (V. 3)—even while we sleep—but He Himself never sleeps (V. 4). He watches over us day and night (V. 6), "both now and forevermore" (V. 8).

No matter what kind of situations we find ourselves in, God sees. And He's waiting for us to turn to Him. When we do, our circumstances may not always change, but He's promised His peace in the midst of it all.

JULIE SCHWAB

When have you experienced God's peace in a troubling situation? How have you seen Him help others?

Loving God, thank You for Your peace. Please continue to calm my heart in the areas of my life that feel chaotic.

He stilled the storm to a whisper; the waves of
the sea were hushed. [PSALM 107:29]

CARRIED THROUGH THE STORM

During Scottish missionary Alexander Duff's first voyage to
India in 1830, he was shipwrecked in a storm off the coast of
South Africa. He and his fellow passengers made it to a small,
desolate island; and a short time later, one of the crew found a copy
of a Bible belonging to Duff washed ashore on the beach. When the
book dried, Duff read Psalm 107 to his fellow survivors, and they
took courage. Finally, after a rescue and yet another shipwreck,
Duff arrived in India.

Psalm 107 lists some of the ways God delivered the Israelites. Duff
and his shipmates no doubt identified with and took comfort in the
words: "He stilled the storm to a whisper; the waves of the sea were
hushed. They were glad when it grew calm, and he guided them to
their desired haven" (VV. 29–30). And, like the Israelites, they too
"[gave] thanks to the LORD for his unfailing love and his wonderful
deeds for mankind" (V. 31).

We see a parallel to Psalm 107:28–30 in the New Testament
(MATTHEW 8:23–27; MARK 4:35–41). Jesus and His disciples were in a
boat at sea when a violent storm began. His disciples cried out in
fear, and Jesus—God in flesh—calmed the sea. We too can take
courage! Our powerful God and Saviour hears and responds to our
cries and comforts us in the midst of our storms.   *ALYSON KIEDA*

> **When have you cried out to God in a 'storm'?
> What was the result?**
>
> *Thank You, God, for not leaving me to face the
> storms on my own. I need You!*

[Saul said], "The LORD delivered me into your hands, but you did not kill me."
[1 SAMUEL 24:18]

NOT SEEKING REVENGE

The farmer climbed into his tractor and began his morning inspection of the crops. On reaching the furthest edge of the property, his blood began to boil. Someone had used the farm's seclusion to illegally dump their rubbish—again.

As he filled the trailer with the bags of food scraps, the farmer found an envelope. On it was printed the offender's address. Here was an opportunity too good to ignore. That night he drove to the offender's house and filled his garden with not just the dumped rubbish, but his own!

Revenge is sweet, some say, but is it right? In 1 Samuel 24, David and his men were hiding in a cave to escape a murderous King Saul. When Saul wandered into the same cave to relieve himself, David's men saw a too-good-to-ignore opportunity for David to get revenge (VV. 3–4). But David went against this desire to get even. "The LORD forbid that I should do such a thing to my master," he said (V. 6). When Saul discovered that David chose to spare his life, he was incredulous. "You are more righteous than I," he exclaimed (VV. 17–18).

As we or our loved ones face injustice, opportunities to take revenge on offenders may well come. Will we give in to these desires, as the farmer did, or go against them, like David? Will we choose righteousness over revenge?　　　　　　　　　*SHERIDAN VOYSEY*

> **When have you most felt like getting even with someone?
> How can David's response guide you as you seek justice
> for yourself and others?**
>
> *Jesus, lover of our enemies, may I seek justice Your way.*

You will be my witnesses in Jerusalem, and in
all Judea and Samaria. [ACTS 1:8]

LOVING YOUR ENEMY

ducked into a room before she saw me. I was ashamed of hiding,
but I didn't want to deal with her right then—or *ever*. I longed to
tell her off, to put her in her place. Though I'd been annoyed by
her past behaviour, it's likely I had irritated her even more!

The Jews and Samaritans also shared a mutually irritating relationship. Being a people of mixed origin and worshipping their
own gods, the Samaritans—in the eyes of the Jews—had spoiled
the Jewish bloodline and faith, erecting a rival religion on Mount
Gerazim (JOHN 4:20). In fact, the Jews so despised Samaritans they
walked the long way around rather than take the direct route
through their country.

Jesus revealed a better way. He brought salvation for all people,
including Samaritans. So He ventured into the heart of Samaria to
bring living water to a sinful woman and her town (VV. 4–42). His last
words to His disciples were to follow His example. They must share
His good news with everyone, beginning in Jerusalem and dispersing
through Samaria until they reached "the ends of the earth" (ACTS 1:8).
Samaria was more than the next geographical sequence. It was the
most painful part of the mission. The disciples had to overcome
lifetimes of prejudice to love people they didn't like.

Does Jesus matter more to us than our grievances? There's only
one way to be sure. Love your 'Samaritan'.   *MIKE WITTMER*

> **How can you begin to show love to those who aren't
> very loving? When have you been loving to a difficult
> person and then found them softening?**
>
> *Father, may the waves of Your love crash over me,
> producing a torrent that streams to others through me.*

See how the flowers of the field grow.
. . . Will he not much more clothe you?
[MATTHEW 6:28, 30]

GOD'S PROVISION

We trekked deeper and deeper into the forest, venturing further and further away from the village at Yunnan Province, China. After an hour or so, we heard the deafening roar of the water. Quickening our steps, we soon reached a clearing and were greeted by a beautiful view of a curtain of white water cascading over the grey rocks. *Spectacular!*

Our hiking companions, who lived in the village we had left an hour earlier, decided that we should have a picnic. Great idea, but where was the food? We hadn't brought any. My friends disappeared into the surrounding forest and returned with an assortment of fruits and vegetables and even some fish. The *shuixiangcai* looked strange with its small purple flowers, but tasted heavenly!

I was reminded that creation declares God's extravagant provision. We can see proof of His generosity in "all sorts of seed-bearing plants, and trees with seed-bearing fruit" (GENESIS 1:12 NLT). God has made and given us for food "every seed-bearing plant . . . and every tree that has fruit with seed in it" (V. 29).

Do you sometimes find it hard to trust God to meet your needs? Why not take a walk in nature? Let what you see remind you of Jesus' assuring words: "Do not worry, saying, 'What shall we eat?' or 'What shall we drink?' . . . Your heavenly Father knows that you need [all these things]" (MATTHEW 6:31–32).   *POH FANG CHIA*

How has God provided for you in the past? How can you continue to lean on His provision in the present?

*Loving Father, You're a generous provider.
Help me to trust You to meet my needs.*

Put [your] religion into practice by caring for
[your] own family. [1 TIMOTHY 5:4]

A GOOD REASON

The two women occupied the aisle seats across from each other. The flight was two hours, so I couldn't help but see some of their interactions. It was clear they knew each other, might even be related. The younger of the two (probably in her sixties) kept reaching in her bag to hand the older (I'd guess in her nineties) fresh apple slices, then homemade finger sandwiches, then some wipes to clean up, and finally a crisp copy of a newspaper. Each hand-off was done with such tenderness, such dignity. As we stood to exit the plane, I told the younger woman, "I noticed the way you cared for her. It was beautiful." She replied, "She's my best friend. She's my mother."

Wouldn't it be great if we could all say something like that? Some parents are like best friends. Some parents are nothing like that. The truth is those relationships are always complicated at best. While Paul's letter to Timothy doesn't ignore that complexity, it still calls us to put our "religion into practice" by taking care of parents and grandparents—our "relatives," our "own household" (1 TIMOTHY 5:4, 8).

We all too often practise such care only if family members were or are good to us. In other words, if they deserve it. But Paul offers up a more beautiful reason to repay them. Take care of them because "this is pleasing to God" (V. 4).   *JOHN BLASE*

*If your parents are still living, how would you describe
your relationship with them? Regardless of what kind
of job they did as parents, what are some ways you can
take care of them right now?*

*Father, give me grace and mercy as I seek to care for
those who cared for me. And help me to remember the
reason I'm doing it.*

Whoever disowns me before others, I
will disown before my Father in heaven.
[MATTHEW 10:33]

HEEDING THE WARNINGS

When a pickpocket tried to pilfer my property while I was
on holiday in another country, it wasn't a surprise. I'd read
warnings about the danger of subway thieves, so I knew
what to do to protect my wallet. But I never expected it to happen.

Fortunately, the young man who grabbed my wallet had slippery
fingers, so it fell to the floor where I could retrieve it. But the incident
reminded me that I should have heeded the warnings.

We don't like to dwell on warnings because we think they'll get in
the way of enjoying life, but it's imperative to pay attention to them.
For instance, Jesus gave us a clear warning while sending out His
disciples to proclaim God's coming kingdom (MATTHEW 10:7). He said,
"Whoever acknowledges me before others, I will also acknowledge
before my Father in heaven. But whoever disowns me before others,
I will disown before my Father in heaven" (VV. 32–33).

We have a choice. In love, God provided a Saviour and a plan
for us to be in His presence for eternity. But if we turn away from
God and choose to reject His message of salvation and the real life
He offers for both now and forever, we lose out on the opportunity
to be with Him.

May we trust in Jesus, the One who chose to save us from being
eternally separated from the One who loves and made us.

DAVE BRANON

> ***Why is rejecting Jesus such a serious thing?***
> ***How have you chosen to respond to His call?***
>
> *Heavenly Father, thank You for providing salvation*
> *through Jesus. And thank You for sending warnings to*
> *remind me of the importance of putting my faith in Him.*

[Hezekiah] broke into pieces the bronze snake
Moses had made. [2 KINGS 18:4]

THE ULTIMATE HEALER

When a medical treatment began to provide relief for a family member's severe food allergies, I became so excited that I talked about it all the time. I described the intense process and extolled the doctor who had created the programme. Finally, some friends commented, "We think God should always get the credit for healing." Their statement made me pause. Had I taken my eyes off the Ultimate Healer and made the healing into an idol?

The nation of Israel fell into a similar trap when they began to burn incense to a bronze snake which God had used to heal them. They'd been performing this act of worship until Hezekiah identified it as idolatry and "broke into pieces the bronze snake Moses had made" (2 KINGS 18:4).

Several centuries earlier, a group of venomous snakes had invaded the Israelite camp. The snakes bit the people and many died (NUMBERS 21:6). Although spiritual rebellion had caused the problem, the people cried out to God for help. Showing mercy, He directed Moses to sculpt a bronze snake, fasten it to a pole, and hold it up for everyone to see. When the people looked at it, they were healed (VV. 4–9).

Think of God's gifts to you. Have any of them become objects of praise instead of evidence of His mercy and grace? Only our holy God—the source of every good gift (JAMES 1:17)—is worthy of worship.

JENNIFER BENSON SCHULDT

> ***How has God shown you His goodness through other
> people? Why is it so easy to give people credit for
> what God has done in your life?***
>
> *Dear God, I worship You as the all-powerful God who
> hears my prayers. Thank You for sustaining my life and
> caring for me.*

Look, I am coming soon! My reward is with
me, and I will give to each person according to
what they have done. [REVELATION 22:12]

A GREAT ENDING

My husband and son surfed television channels looking for a
movie to watch and discovered that their favourite movies
were already in progress. As they enjoyed watching the final
scenes, the search became a game. They managed to find eight of
their favourite flicks. Frustrated, I asked why they wouldn't just
choose a movie to watch from the beginning. My husband laughed.
"Who doesn't love a great ending?"

I had to admit I too look forward to the endings of my favourite
books or movies. I've even skimmed through my Bible and focused
on my favourite parts or the stories that seem more palatable and
easier to understand. But the Holy Spirit uses all of God's reliable
and life-applicable words to transform us and affirm that His story
will end well for believers in Jesus.

Christ declares Himself to be "the Alpha and the Omega, the
First and the Last, the Beginning and the End" (REVELATION 22:13). He
proclaims that His people will inherit eternal life (V. 14) and warns
those who dare to add or subtract from "the words of the prophecy
of this scroll" (VV. 18–19).

We may not know or understand everything in the Bible, but we
do know Jesus is coming again. He'll keep His word. He'll demolish
sin, right every wrong, make all things new, and reign as our loving
King forever. Now, that's a great ending that leads to our new beginning!   XOCHITL DIXON

> **How does the certainty of knowing Jesus is coming again
> help you live for Him today? What excites you the most
> about Christ's promised return?**
>
> *Come, Lord Jesus! Come!*

I am so eager to preach the gospel also to you
who are in Rome. [ROMANS 1:15]

THE POWER OF THE GOSPEL

ncient Rome had its own version of 'the gospel'—the good
news. According to the poet Virgil, Zeus, king of the gods, had
decreed for the Romans a kingdom without end or boundaries.
The gods had chosen Augustus as divine son and saviour of the world
by ushering in a golden age of peace and prosperity.

This, however, wasn't everyone's idea of good news. For many it
was an unwelcome reality enforced by the heavy hand of the emperor's army and executioners. The glory of the empire was built on
the backs of enslaved people who served without legal personhood
or property at the pleasure of masters who ruled over them.

This was the world in which Paul introduced himself as a servant
of Christ (ROMANS 1:1). Jesus—how Paul had once hated that name.
And how Jesus Himself had suffered for admitting to being the King
of the Jews and Saviour of the world.

This was the good news Paul would explain in the rest of his letter
to the Romans. This gospel was "the power of God that brings salvation to everyone who believes" (V. 16). Oh, how it was needed by
those who suffered under Caesar! Here was the news of a crucified
and resurrected Saviour—the liberator who conquered His enemies
by showing how much He loved them.   *MART DEHAAN*

*As you read Paul's opening words to the Romans, what
phrases describe the good news to you? (1:1–7). Why
would Paul, who had once hated Jesus so much, now
want everyone to believe in Him? (see Acts 26).*

*Good news is known best by those who know
how much they need it.*

[Josiah] began to seek the God of his father
David. [2 CHRONICLES 34:3]

MERCY AND GRACE

A stately sunflower stood on its own in the centre of a lonely stretch of dual carriageway, just a few feet from the road's surface. As I drove past, I wondered how it had grown there with no other sunflowers visible for miles. Only God could create a plant so hardy it could thrive so close to the roadway in the grey gravel lining the middle barrier. There it was, thriving, swaying gently in the breeze and cheerfully greeting travellers as they hurried by.

The Old Testament tells the story of a faithful king of Judah who also showed up unexpectedly. His father and grandfather had enthusiastically served other gods; but after Josiah had been in power for eight years, "while he was still young, he began to seek the God of his father David" (2 CHRONICLES 34:3). He sent workmen to "repair the temple of the LORD" (V. 8), and as they did they discovered the Book of the Law (the first five books of the Old Testament; v. 14). God then inspired Josiah to lead the entire nation of Judah to return to the faith of their ancestors, and they served the Lord "as long as [Josiah] lived" (V. 33).

Our God is the master of unanticipated mercies. He's able to cause great good to spring up unexpectedly out of the hard gravel of life's most unfavourable circumstances. Watch Him closely. He may do it again today.   *JAMES BANKS*

*What mercies have you seen from God that you never
anticipated? How does the thought that He's able to bring
about unexpected good give you hope today?*

*Heavenly Father, I praise You for never changing.
Your mercies are "new every morning!" (Lamentations 3:23).
Help me to look forward to what You have for me today.*

Give praise to the LORD, proclaim his name; make known among the nations what he has done. [ISAIAH 12:4]

SHARING JESUS

Shortly after Dwight Moody (1837–99) came to faith in Christ, the evangelist resolved not to let a day pass without sharing God's good news with at least one person. On busy days, he'd sometimes forget his resolution until late. One night, he was in bed before he remembered. As he stepped outside, he thought, *No one will be out in this pouring rain.* Just then he saw a man walking down the street. Moody rushed over and asked to stand under his umbrella to avoid the rain. When granted permission, he asked, "Have you any shelter in the time of storm? Could I tell you about Jesus?"

Moody embodied a readiness to share how God saves us from the consequences of our sins. He obeyed God's instructions to the Israelites to proclaim His name and "make known among the nations what he has done" (ISAIAH 12:4). Not only were God's people called to "proclaim that his name is exalted" (V. 4), but they were also to share how He had "become [their] salvation" (V. 2). Centuries later, our call remains to tell the wonders of Jesus becoming a man, dying on the cross, and rising again.

Perhaps we heard about God's love when, as Moody did, someone left their comfort zone to talk with us about Jesus. And we too, each in our own way, can let someone know about the One who saves.

AMY BOUCHER PYE

What has God done in your life that you can share with another? How has He equipped you to present the good news?

*Jesus, thank You for setting me free from my sins.
Help me to be ready to tell others of Your good news.*

HOPE DEEPER THAN DEATH

I've been hearing conversations lately by church leaders realising the need for the church to regain a central focus on the cross and resurrection of Christ—the story of God's cosmic defeat of the principalities and powers of death and evil—for truly sustaining hope. Sadly, some faith communities have lost this emphasis in exchange for a primarily individualistic emphasis of a personal experience of forgiveness merged with positive advice for a happy life.

But during the pandemic, church leaders began to realise that for those grieving the loss of loved ones or those weighed down by the suffering around them, messages focused on individual happiness were ringing hollow.

We need hope that truly reckons with the full weight of sin and death's wounding of our world—hope that's deeper than death.

The gospel is the story of God's redemption of a wounded cosmos through the cross and resurrection of Jesus—an event that has changed the fabric of reality. One that, in God's grace, we've been invited to share with the world.

Only when we fully reckon with the bad news—the depth of sin and death's stranglehold over creation—can we grasp the wonder of the good news, that "creation itself will be liberated from its bondage to decay and brought into the freedom and glory of the children of God" (ROMANS 8:21).

Even as we lament honestly the "groaning" of creation (V. 22), we can experience the good news that Jesus is alive! Working through communities of people filled with the Spirit and with hope. Carrying us from death into glorious resurrection life.

Monica La Rose, Our Daily Bread *author*

★ A **BIBLICAL THEOLOGY OF MISSION** is explored in the above feature article and the devotions for **September 1, 9, 23** and **26.** We trust these articles will enhance your understanding of what it means to live in God's kingdom and share the good news of salvation in Christ with others.

All Scripture is God-breathed and is useful for teaching, rebuking, correcting and training in righteousness. [2 TIMOTHY 3:16]

THE BIG STORY OF THE BIBLE

When Colin opened the box of stained-glass pieces he'd purchased, instead of finding the fragments he'd ordered for a project, he discovered intact, whole windows. He sleuthed out the windows' origin and learned they'd been removed from a church to protect them from World War II bombings. Colin marvelled at the quality of work and how the 'fragments' formed a beautiful picture.

If I'm honest, there are times when I open particular passages of the Bible—such as chapters containing lists of genealogies—and I don't immediately see how they fit within the bigger picture of Scripture. Such is the case with Genesis 11—a chapter that contains a repetitive cadence of unfamiliar names and their families, such as Shem, Shelah, Eber, Nahor and Terah (VV. 10–32). I'm often tempted to gloss over these sections and skip to a part that contains something that feels familiar and fits more easily into my 'window' of understanding of the Bible's narrative.

Since "all Scripture is God-breathed and is useful" (2 TIMOTHY 3:16), the Holy Spirit can help us better understand how a fragment fits into the whole, opening our eyes to see, for example, how Shelah is related to Abram (GENESIS 11:12–26), the ancestor of David and—more importantly—Jesus (MATTHEW 1:2, 6, 16). He delights in surprising us with the treasure of a perfectly intact window where even the smaller parts reveal the story of God's mission throughout the Bible.   *KIRSTEN HOLMBERG*

Why is it important to recognise each portion of Scripture as a fragment of God's bigger story?

Father God, please help me to see You and Your work more clearly.

Be made new in the attitude of your minds.
[EPHESIANS 4:23]

FIX UP TIME

I t was time to give the inside of our home a fresh, new look. But just as I'd begun prepping a room for painting, many home improvement shops announced they were going to temporarily close due to the COVID-19 pandemic. As soon as I heard the announcement, I rushed to my local shop and purchased the essential materials before they shut. You simply can't remodel without the proper supplies.

Paul had a bit of a remodelling project in mind when he wrote Ephesians 4. But the changes he was talking about went far beyond superficial alterations. Even though trusting Jesus as our Saviour makes us a new creation, there's still some ongoing work the Spirit needs to do. And it takes time and work for Him to accomplish "true righteousness and holiness" (EPHESIANS 4:24).

The presence of the Spirit makes needed changes on the inside that can help us reflect Jesus in our words and actions. He helps us replace lying with speaking "truthfully" (V. 25). He guides us to avoid sin in regard to anger (V. 26). And He directs us to speak words that are "helpful for building others up" (V. 29). These Spirit-controlled actions are part of the internal change that's manifested in things like kindness, compassion and forgiveness (V. 32). The Spirit works in us to enable us to imitate Jesus Himself and reflect the heart of our heavenly Father (V. 24; 5:1).   *DAVE BRANON*

> **What areas of real, heart-based improvement do
> you need the Holy Spirit to make in you through His
> leading and strength? How will you get started?**
>
> *Loving God, thank You for making me a new creation
> in Christ. Help my actions, through Your guidance,
> to reflect the change You've made in me.*

His father saw him and was filled with compassion for him. [LUKE 15:20]

EMPTY HANDS

Robert was embarrassed when he showed up for a breakfast meeting and realised he'd forgotten his wallet. It bothered him to the point that he pondered whether he should eat at all or simply get something to drink. After some convincing from his friend, he relaxed his resistance. He and his friend enjoyed their food, and his friend gladly paid the bill.

Perhaps you can identify with this dilemma or some other situation that puts you on the receiving end. Wanting to pay our own way is normal, but there are occasions when we must humbly receive what's graciously being given.

Some kind of payback may have been what the younger son had in mind in Luke 15:17–24 as he contemplated what he would say to his father. "I am no longer worthy to be called your son; make me like one of your hired servants" (V. 19). *Hired servant?* His father would have no such thing! In his father's eyes, he was a much-loved son who'd come home. As such he was met with a father's embrace and an affectionate kiss (V. 20). What a grand gospel picture! It reminds us that by Jesus' death He revealed a loving Father who welcomes empty-handed children with open arms. One hymn writer expressed it like this: "Nothing in my hand I bring, simply to thy cross I cling."

ARTHUR JACKSON

How does it make you feel that because Jesus has paid your sin debt, you can receive forgiveness for all your sins? If you've never received this forgiveness, what's keeping you from accepting this gift through Jesus?

God of heaven, help me to receive and enjoy the forgiveness You've provided through Your Son, Jesus.

Pray continually, give thanks in all circumstances;
for this is God's will for you in Christ Jesus.
[1 THESSALONIANS 5:17–18]

MAN OF PRAYER

My family remembers my Grandpa Dierking as a man of strong faith and prayer. But it wasn't always so. My aunt recalls the first time her father announced to the family, "We're going to start giving thanks to God before we eat." His first prayer was far from eloquent, but Grandpa continued the practice of prayer for the next fifty years, praying often throughout each day. When he died, my husband gave my grandmother a 'praying hands' plant, saying, "Grandpa was a man of prayer." His decision to follow God and talk to Him each day changed him into a faithful servant of Christ.

The Bible has a lot to say about prayer. In Matthew 6:9–13, Jesus gave a pattern for prayer to His followers, teaching them to approach God with sincere praise for who He is. As we bring our requests to God, we trust Him to provide "our daily bread" (V. 11). As we confess our sins, we ask Him for forgiveness and for help to avoid temptation (VV. 12–13).

But we aren't limited to praying the "Lord's Prayer." God wants us to pray "all kinds of prayers" on "all occasions" (EPHESIANS 6:18). Praying is vital for our spiritual growth, and it gives us the opportunity to be in continual conversation with Him every day (1 THESSALONIANS 5:17–18).

As we approach God with humble hearts that yearn to talk with Him, may He help us know and love Him better.   *CINDY HESS KASPER*

> *How does God view the humble prayers of His children*
> *that may be less than eloquent? How can you make*
> *prayer a part of your daily life?*
>
> *Father, thank You for the blessing of prayer and Your*
> *acceptance whenever I call on You.*

Return, faithless people. I will cure you
of backsliding. [JEREMIAH 3:22]

HELP FROM THE HOLY SPIRIT

While my classmates and I used to skip the occasional lecture in university, everyone always made sure to attend Professor Chris' lecture the week before the year-end exams. That was when he would unfailingly drop big hints about the exam questions he'd set.

I always wondered why he did that, until I realised that Prof Chris genuinely wanted us to do well. He had high standards, but he would help us meet them. All we had to do was show up and listen so we could prepare properly.

It struck me that God is like that too. God can't compromise His standards, but because He deeply desires us to be like He is, He's given us the Holy Spirit to help us meet those standards.

In Jeremiah 3:11–14, God urged unfaithful Israel to acknowledge their guilt and return to Him. But knowing how stubborn and weak they were, He would help them. He promised to cure their backsliding ways (V. 22), and He sent shepherds to teach and guide them (V. 15).

How comforting it is to know that no matter how big the sin we're trapped in or how far we've turned from God, He's ready to heal us of our faithlessness! All we need to do is to acknowledge our wrong ways and allow His Holy Spirit to begin changing our hearts.

LESLIE KOH

***Where do you struggle to follow God faithfully and
obediently? How can you ask God to heal you and help you?***

*Loving God, thank You for Your merciful love that enables me
to be holy like You are. Please help me to let Your Spirit heal
me of my faithlessness and transform my heart.*

Let the beloved of the LORD rest secure
in him, for he shields him all day long.
[DEUTERONOMY 33:12]

RESTING SECURE IN GOD

I wrote a letter to our children as each became a teenager. In one I talked about our identity in Christ, remembering that when I was a teenager, I felt unsure of myself, lacking confidence. I had to learn that I was God's beloved—His child. I said in the letter, "Knowing who you are comes down to knowing Whose you are." For when we understand that God has created us and we commit to following Him, we can be at peace with who He's made us to be. And we also know that He changes us to be more like Him each day.

A foundational passage from Scripture about our identity as God's children is Deuteronomy 33:12: "Let the beloved of the LORD rest secure in him, for he shields him all day long, and the one the LORD loves rests between his shoulders." Just before Moses died, he proclaimed this blessing over the tribe of Benjamin as God's people prepared to enter the land He'd promised them. God wanted them to always remember that they were His beloved and to rest secure in their identity as His children.

Knowing our identity as God's children is equally important for everyone—teenagers, those in the middle of life and those who have lived a long time. When we understand that God created us and watches over us, we can find security, hope, and love.

AMY BOUCHER PYE

How does knowing that you can "rest between his shoulders" increase your love for God? How does this deepen your understanding of who you are?

Loving Father, You created me and You hold me close. Let my identity as Your child permeate my thoughts and actions.

So you also are complete through your union
with Christ. [COLOSSIANS 2:10 NLT]

COMPLETE IN CHRIST

In a popular film, an actor plays a success-driven sports agent whose marriage begins to crumble. Attempting to win back his wife, Dorothy, he looks into her eyes and says, "You complete me." It's a heart-warming message that echoes a tale in Greek philosophy. According to that myth, each of us is a 'half' that must find our 'other half' to become whole.

The belief that a romantic partner 'completes' us is now part of popular culture. But is it true? I talk to many married couples who still feel incomplete because they haven't been able to have children and others who've had kids but feel something else is missing. Ultimately, no human can fully complete us.

The apostle Paul gives another solution. "For in Christ lives all the fullness of God in a human body. So you also are complete through your union with Christ" (COLOSSIANS 2:9–10 NLT). Jesus doesn't just forgive us and liberate us, He also completes us by bringing the life of God into our lives (VV. 13–15).

Marriage is good, but it can't make us whole. Only Jesus can do that. Instead of expecting a person, career, or anything else to complete us, let's accept God's invitation to let His fullness fill our lives more and more.   *SHERIDAN VOYSEY*

> *How have you sought spiritual fulfilment through people instead of God? How does Jesus completing you change your view of marriage and singleness?*

> *Jesus, thank You for making me complete through Your death, resurrection, forgiveness and restoration.*

Then I heard the voice of the Lord saying,
"Whom shall I send? . . . I said, "Here am I.
Send me!" [ISAIAH 6:8]

SEND ME

When Swedish missionary Eric Lund felt called by God to go to Spain to do mission work in the late 1890s, he immediately obeyed. He saw little success there, but persevered in his conviction of God's calling. One day, he met a Filipino man, Braulio Manikan, and shared the gospel with him. Together, Lund and Manikan translated the Bible into a local Philippine language, and later they started the first Baptist mission station in the Philippines. Many would turn to Jesus—all because Lund, like the prophet Isaiah, responded to God's call.

In Isaiah 6:8, God asked for a willing person to go to Israel to declare His judgement for the present and hope for the future. Isaiah volunteered boldly: "Here am I. Send me!" He didn't think he was qualified, for he'd confessed earlier: "I am a man of unclean lips" (V. 5). But he responded willingly because he'd witnessed God's holiness, recognised his own sinfulness and received His cleansing (VV. 1–7).

Is God calling you to do something for Him? Are you holding back? If so, remember all God has done through Jesus' death and resurrection. He's given us the Holy Spirit to help and guide us (JOHN 14:26; 15:26–27), and He'll prepare us to answer His call. Like Isaiah, may we respond, "Send me!"   *FRANCIS NEIL G. JALANDO-ON*

**Is God calling you to do something for Him?
What's hindering you from responding?**

*Jesus, thank You for calling and enabling me to
serve You. Help me to see this as a privilege and
to serve You willingly.*

Christ's love compels us, because we are
convinced that one died for all . . . . From now on
we regard no one from a worldly point of view.
[2 CORINTHIANS 5:14, 16]

HOTEL CORONA

The Dan Hotel in Jerusalem became known by a different name
in 2020—"Hotel Corona." The government dedicated the hotel
to patients recovering from COVID-19, and the hotel became
known as a rare site of joy and unity during a difficult time. Since
the residents already had the virus, they were free to sing, dance
and laugh together. And they did! In a country where tensions between different political and religious groups run high, the shared
crisis created a space where people could learn to see each other
as human beings first—and even become friends.

It's natural, normal even, for us to be drawn towards those we see
as similar to us, people we suspect share similar experiences and
values to our own. But as the apostle Paul often emphasised, the
gospel is a challenge to any barriers between human beings that we
see as "normal" (2 CORINTHIANS 5:15). Through the lens of the gospel,
we see a bigger picture than our differences—a shared brokenness
and a shared longing and need to experience healing in God's love.

If we believe that "one died for all," then we can also no longer
be content with surface-level assumptions about others. Instead,
"Christ's love compels us" (V. 14) to share His love and mission with
those God loves more than we can imagine—*all* of us.

MONICA LA ROSE

***When do you find yourself most prone to forget the 'bigger
picture' of your shared humanity with others? What helps
remind you of our equal brokenness and need for Jesus' love?***

*In hard times, Jesus, thank You for those moments when I see
a glimmer of breath-taking beauty through the love and joy
of others. Help me to live each day this way, regarding
"no one from a worldly point of view."*

BIBLE IN A YEAR | PROVERBS 6–7; 2 CORINTHIANS 2

Make my joy complete by being like-minded, having the same love, being one in spirit and of one mind. [PHILIPPIANS 2:2]

LIKE A SYMPHONY

surprised my wife with concert tickets to listen to a performer she'd always wanted to see. The gifted singer was accompanied by a symphony orchestra, and the setting was an open-air amphitheatre built between two 300-foot rock formations at more than 6,000 feet above sea level. The orchestra played a number of well-loved classical songs and folk tunes. Their final number was a fresh treatment of the classic hymn "Amazing Grace." The beautiful, harmonised arrangement took our breath away!

There's something beautiful about harmony—individual instruments playing together in a way that creates a bigger and more layered sonic landscape. The apostle Paul pointed to the beauty of harmony when he told the Philippians to be "like-minded," have "the same love," and be "one in spirit and . . . mind" (PHILIPPIANS 2:2). He wasn't asking them to become identical but to embrace the humble attitude and self-giving love of Jesus. The gospel, as Paul well knew and taught, doesn't erase our distinctions, but it can eliminate our divisions.

It's also interesting that many scholars believe Paul's words here (VV. 6–11) are a prelude to an early hymn. Here's the point: when we allow the Holy Spirit to work through our distinct lives and contexts, making us more like Jesus, together we become a symphony that reverberates with a humble Christ-like love. *GLENN PACKIAM*

Who could use some encouragement from you today? How could you put the interests of others above your own, just as Jesus did for us?

Dear Jesus, thank You for saving me. May Your Spirit transform me into Your image. In my attitude and actions, help me to take on Your humility and sacrificial love. May it result in a greater unity with other believers in my life.

[Wisdom] will guide you down delightful paths. [PROVERBS 3:17 NLT]

FROM WISDOM TO JOY

The phone rang and I picked it up without delay. Calling was the oldest member of our church family—a vibrant, hard-working woman who was nearly one hundred years old. Putting the final touches on her latest book, she asked me some writing questions to help her cross the finish line. As always, however, I soon was asking *her* questions—about life, work, love, family. Her many lessons from a long life sparkled with wisdom. She told me, "Pace yourself." And soon we were laughing about times she'd forgotten to do that—her wonderful stories all seasoned with true joy.

Wisdom leads to joy, the Bible teaches. "Joyful is the person who finds wisdom, the one who gains understanding" (PROVERBS 3:13 NLT). We find that this path—from wisdom to joy—is a biblical virtue, indeed. "For wisdom will enter your heart, and knowledge will fill you with joy" (PROVERBS 2:10 NLT). "God gives wisdom, knowledge, and joy to those who please him" (ECCLESIASTES 2:26 NLT). Wisdom "will guide you down delightful paths," adds Proverbs 3:17 (NLT).

Reflecting on the matters of life, author C. S. Lewis declared that "joy is the serious business of heaven." The path there, however, is paved with wisdom. My church friend, who lived to be 107, would agree. She walked a wise, joyful pace to the King.　*PATRICIA RAYBON*

**What paths have you taken in trying to find joy?
How can wisdom lead you to joy?**

*When I might take a rocky road, loving God, please
point me back to Your path of wisdom and joy.*

Consequently, just as one trespass resulted in condemnation for all people, so also one righteous act resulted in justification and life for all people.
[ROMANS 5:18]

A GREAT ACT OF LOVE

In Oregon's Malheur National Forest, a fungus popularly known as the honey mushroom spreads through tree roots across 2,200 acres, making it the largest living organism ever found. It's been "weaving its black shoestring filaments" through the forest for more than two millennia, killing trees as it grows. Its shoestring filaments, called "rhizomorphs", tunnel as deep as ten feet into the soil. And although the organism is incredibly large, it began with a single microscopic spore!

The Bible tells us of a single act of disobedience that caused widespread condemnation and a single act of obedience that reversed it. The apostle Paul contrasted two individuals—Adam and Jesus (ROMANS 5:14-15). Adam's sin brought condemnation and death "to all people" (V. 12). Through one act of disobedience, all people were made sinners and stood condemned before God (V. 17). But He had a means of dealing with humanity's sin problem. Through the righteous act of Jesus on the cross, God provides eternal life and a right standing before Him. Christ's act of love and obedience was powerful enough to overcome Adam's one act of disobedience—providing "life for all people" (V. 18).

Through His death on the cross, Jesus offers eternal life to anyone who puts their faith in Him. If you haven't received His forgiveness and salvation, may you do so today. If you're already a believer, praise Him for what He's done by His great act of love!   MARVIN WILLIAMS

What do the single acts of Adam and Jesus tell you about the impact of sin? How does Jesus' sacrifice ignite or renew your desire to live a life that honours Him?

God, thank You for providing salvation and eternal life through Jesus! Help me to reveal Your saving ways to others.

Blessed is the one . . . whose delight is in the
law of the LORD, and who meditates on his law
day and night. [PSALM 1:1-2]

A LIVING DOCUMENT

In memorialising his grandfather's work, Peter Croft wrote, "It is my deepest desire for the person who picks up their Bible, whatever version they use, to not only understand but *experience* the scriptures as *living* documents, just as relevant, dangerous and exciting now as they were those thousands of years ago." Peter's grandfather was J.B. Phillips, a youth minister who undertook a new paraphrase of the Bible in English during World War II in order to make it come alive to students at his church.

Like Phillips' students, we face barriers to reading and experiencing Scripture, and not necessarily because of our Bible translation. We may lack time, discipline or the right tools for understanding. But Psalm 1 tells us that "Blessed is the one . . . whose delight is in the law of the LORD" (VV. 1-2). Meditating on Scripture daily allows us to "prosper" in all seasons, no matter what hardship we're facing.

How do you view your Bible? It's still relevant with insight for living today, still dangerous in its call to believe and follow Jesus, still exciting in the intimate knowledge of God and humanity that it imparts. It's like a stream of water (V. 3) that provides the sustenance we need daily. Today, let's lean in—make time, get the right tools, and ask God to help us experience Scripture as a living document.

KAREN PIMPO

What barriers do you face when reading the Bible?
How can you make space to listen to God's voice?

*God, help me experience Scripture as a living
document today.*

Jesus also suffered outside the city gate to make the people holy through his own blood.
[HEBREWS 13:12]

OUTSIDE THE CAMP

Friday was market day in the rural town in Ghana where I grew up. After all these years, I still recall one particular vendor. Her fingers and toes eroded by Hansen's disease (leprosy), she would crouch on her mat and scoop her produce with a hollowed-out gourd. Some avoided her. My mother made it a point to buy from her regularly. I saw her only on market days. Then she would disappear outside the town.

In the time of the ancient Israelites, diseases like leprosy meant living 'outside the camp'. It was a forlorn existence. Israelite law said of such people, "They must live alone" (LEVITICUS 13:46). Outside the camp was also where the carcasses of the sacrificial bulls were burned (4:12). Outside the camp was not where you wanted to be.

This harsh reality breathes life into the statement about Jesus in Hebrews 13: "Let us, then, go to him outside the camp, bearing the disgrace he bore" (V. 13). Jesus was crucified outside the gates of Jerusalem, a significant point when we study the Hebrew sacrificial system.

We want to be popular, to be honoured, to live comfortable lives. But God calls us to go "outside the camp"—where the disgrace is. That's where we'll find the vendor with Hansen's disease. That's where we'll find people the world has rejected. That's where we'll find Jesus. *TIM GUSTAFSON*

How do you initially react to outsiders and misfits? In what practical way might you go to Jesus 'outside the camp'?

Thank You, Jesus, that You don't show any favouritism. Thank You for going outside the camp for me.

We are the clay, you are the potter; we are all
the work of your hand. [ISAIAH 64:8]

GOD'S MOULDED INSTRUMENTS

Considered one of the greatest video games ever made, Nintendo's *The Legend of Zelda: Ocarina of Time* has sold more than seven million copies worldwide. It's also popularised the ocarina, a tiny, ancient, potato-shaped musical instrument made of clay.

The ocarina doesn't look like much of a musical instrument. However, when it's played—by blowing into its mouthpiece and covering various holes around its misshapen body—it produces a strikingly serene and hauntingly hopeful sound.

The ocarina's maker took a lump of clay, applied pressure and heat to it, and transformed it into an amazing musical instrument. I see a picture of God and us here. Isaiah 64:6, 8–9 tells us: "All of us have become like one who is unclean. . . . Yet you, LORD, are our Father. We are the clay, you are the potter. . . . Do not be angry beyond measure." The prophet was saying: *God, You're in charge. We're all sinful. Shape us into beautiful instruments for You*.

That's exactly what God does! In His mercy, He sent His Son, Jesus, to die for our sin, and now He's shaping and transforming us as we walk in step with His Spirit every day. Just as the ocarina maker's breath flows through the instrument to produce beautiful music, God works through us—His moulded instruments—to accomplish His beautiful will: to be more and more like Jesus (ROMANS 8:29).

RUTH WAN-LAU

*How can knowing that you're a recipient of God's mercy
affect what you think, say and do today? How can you
submit yourself to His transformation?*

*Father, thank You for saving me and transforming me so that
I'll become more like Your Son Jesus. Teach me to submit to
Your Spirit's work of transforming me.*

Tell them how much the Lord has done for
you, and how he has had mercy on you.
[MARK 5:19]

FROM MESS TO MESSAGE

Darryl was a sporting legend who nearly destroyed his life with drugs. But Jesus set him free, and he's been clean for years. Today he helps others struggling with addiction and points them to faith. Looking back, he affirms that God turned his mess into a message.

Nothing is too hard for God. When Jesus came ashore near a cemetery after a stormy night on the Sea of Galilee with His disciples, a man possessed by darkness immediately approached Him. Jesus spoke to the demons inside him, drove them away and set him free.

When Jesus left, the man begged to go along. But Jesus didn't allow it, because He had work for him to do: "Go home to your own people and tell them how much the Lord has done for you" (MARK 5:19).

We never see the man again, but Scripture shows us something intriguing. The people of that region had fearfully pleaded with Jesus "to leave" (V. 17), but the next time He returned there, a large crowd gathered (8:1). Could the crowd have resulted from Jesus sending the man? Could it be that he, once dominated by darkness, became one of the first missionaries, effectively communicating Jesus' power to save?

We'll never know this side of heaven, but this much is clear: when God sets us free to serve Him, He can turn even a messy past into a message of hope and love.   *JAMES BANKS*

What has Jesus set you free from? How can you share with others what He's done for you?

Beautiful Saviour, I praise You for Your amazing power! No darkness can stand against You! Help me to walk in Your light today.

See, I am doing a new thing!
[ISAIAH 43:19]

MOVE YOUR FENCE

The village vicar couldn't sleep. As World War II raged, he'd told a small group of soldiers they couldn't bury their fallen comrade inside the fenced cemetery next to his church. Only burials for church members were allowed. So the men buried their beloved friend just outside the fence.

The next morning, however, the soldiers couldn't find the grave. "What happened? The grave is gone," one soldier told the reverend. "Oh, it's still there," he told him. The soldier was confused, but the churchman explained. "I regretted telling you no. So, last night, I got up—and I moved the fence."

God may give fresh perspective for our life challenges too—if we look for it. That was the prophet Isaiah's message to the downtrodden people of Israel. Instead of looking back with longing at their Red Sea rescue, they needed to shift their sight, seeing God doing new miracles, blazing new paths. "Do not dwell on the past," He urged them. "See, I am doing a new thing!" (ISAIAH 43:18–19). He's our source of hope during doubts and battles. "I provide water in the wilderness and streams in the wasteland, [providing] drink to my people, my chosen [people]" (V. 20).

Refreshed with new vision, we too can see God's fresh direction in our lives. May we look with new eyes to see His new paths. Then, with courage, may we step onto new ground, bravely following Him.

PATRICIA RAYBON

> **What new thing would God like to accomplish in your life? What new ground has God led you to and what will you do with it?**
>
> *Merciful God, thank You for providing fresh perspective for my life in You. Refresh my sight to see new ground to walk with You.*

We are to God the pleasing aroma of
Christ among those who are being saved
and among those who are perishing.
[2 CORINTHIANS 2:15]

THE SWEET AROMA OF CHRIST

I knew a farmer who lived near my home. His two grandsons were my best friends. We would go into town with him and follow him around while he shopped and chatted with the folks he knew. He knew them all by name and he knew their stories. He'd stop here and there and ask about a sick child or a difficult marriage, and he'd offer a word of encouragement or two. He would share Scripture and pray if it seemed the right thing to do. I'll never forget the man. He was something special. He didn't force his faith on anyone, but he always seemed to leave it behind.

The elderly farmer had about him what Paul would call the sweet "aroma of Christ" (2 CORINTHIANS 2:15). God used him to "spread the aroma of the knowledge of [Christ]" (V. 14). He's gone to be with God now, but his fragrance lingers on.

C. S. Lewis wrote, "There are no ordinary people. You have never talked with a mere mortal." Put another way, every human contact has eternal consequences. Every day we have opportunities to make a difference in the lives of people around us through the quiet witness of a faithful and gentle life or through encouraging words to a weary soul. Never underestimate the effect a Christ-like life can have on others.
DAVID H. ROPER

What do you think about the statement, "There are no neutral contacts"? What difference could it make in the way you view every contact and conversation throughout the day?

Fill me, Holy Spirit, with love, gentleness and kindness towards others.

"Do not be afraid of them, for I am with you and will rescue you," declares the LORD.
[JEREMIAH 1:8]

UNBREAKABLE IN JESUS

L ouis Zamperini's military plane crashed at sea during the war, killing eight of eleven men on board. "Louie" and two others clambered into life rafts. They drifted for two months, fending off sharks, riding out storms, ducking bullets from an enemy plane, and catching and eating raw fish and birds. They finally drifted onto an island and were immediately captured. For two years Louie was beaten, tortured and worked mercilessly as a prisoner of war. His remarkable story is told in the book *Unbroken*.

Jeremiah is one of the Bible's unbreakable characters. He endured enemy plots (JEREMIAH 11:18), was whipped and put in stocks (20:2), flogged and bound in a dungeon (37:15–16) and lowered by ropes into the deep mire of a cistern (38:6). He survived because God had promised to stay with him and rescue him (1:8). God makes a similar promise to us: "Never will I leave you; never will I forsake you" (HEBREWS 13:5). God didn't promise to save Jeremiah or us *from* trouble, but He has promised to carry us *through* trouble.

Louie recognised God's protection, and after the war he gave his life to Jesus. He forgave his captors and led some to Christ. Louie realised that while we can't avoid all problems, we need not suffer them alone. When we face them with Jesus, we become unbreakable.   *MIKE WITTMER*

What problem is causing you stress? Tell Jesus that you believe His promise to stay with you through this trial. Let Him carry you.

Jesus, You're stronger than any storm. Please carry me through the one I'm facing!

[Jesus said], "Zacchaeus, come down
immediately. I must stay at your house today."
[LUKE 19:5]

AN UNEXPECTED GUEST

Zach was a lonely guy. When he walked down the city streets,
he could feel the hostile glares. But then his life took a turn.
Clement of Alexandria, one of the church fathers, says that
Zach became a very prominent Christian leader and a pastor of the
church in Caesarea. Yes, we're talking about Zacchaeus, the chief
tax collector who climbed a sycamore tree to see Jesus (LUKE 19:1–10).

What prompted him to climb the tree? Tax collectors were perceived as traitors because they heavily taxed their own people to
serve the Roman Empire. Yet Jesus had a reputation for accepting
them. Zacchaeus might have wondered if Jesus would accept him
too. Being short in stature, however, he couldn't see over the crowd
(V. 3). Perhaps he climbed a tree to seek Him out.

And Jesus was *seeking* Zacchaeus too. When Christ reached the
tree where he was perched, He looked up and said, "Zacchaeus,
come down immediately. I *must* stay at your house today" (V. 5).
Jesus considered it absolutely necessary that He be a guest in this
outcast's home. Imagine that! The Saviour of the world wanting to
spend time with a social reject.

Whether it's our hearts, relationships or lives that need mending,
like Zacchaeus we can have hope. Jesus will never reject us when
we turn to Him. He can restore what's been lost and broken and
give our lives new meaning and purpose.　　　*POH FANG CHIA*

What relationships in your life can Jesus help restore?
What will it mean for you to be restored by Him?

Jesus, thank You for seeking me when I was lost in sin
and for redeeming my messed-up life.

These are the very Scriptures that testify
about me. [JOHN 5:39]

THE AUTHOR OF EVERYTHING

Listening to BBC Radio 4, I was struck by something comedian Lee Mack said: "It's quite odd that people like myself, in their forties, [are] happy to dismiss the Bible, but I've never read it. I always think that if an alien came down and you were the only person they met, and they said, 'What's life about? What's earth about? Tell us everything,' and you said, 'Well, there's a book here that purports to tell you everything.' . . . And you go, '. . . I've never read it.' It would be an odd thing wouldn't it?"

Indeed, the Bible tells the story of our world, from the very beginning (GENESIS 1:1) right through to the dramatic and triumphant end to come (REVELATION 21). Yet God's Word actually does much more than just retell everything; it introduces the Author of everything.

That's what Jesus wanted the Jewish leaders to realise. They thought they were righteous simply because they knew the Scriptures. But Jesus observed: "These are the very Scriptures that testify about me, yet you refuse to come to me to have life" (JOHN 5:39–40).

To know the Bible's story is to know the One it is about. As we seek to embrace the love of Jesus Christ and to understand His character, we'll increasingly make sense of every passage, event and promise in the Bible. And we'll find our place with Him within His story.　　　　　　　　　　　　　　　　　　　*CHRIS WALE*

> **How have you glimpsed Jesus throughout the Bible's story?**
> **How might your studies and reflections deepen by asking of**
> **each passage: "What does this show me about Jesus?"**

Heavenly Father, thank You for Your Word and for speaking faithfully to me through it by Your Spirit. When the world doesn't make sense, help me see more clearly through reflecting on Jesus.

We know that in all things God works for the good of those who love him. [ROMANS 8:28]

NO MISUNDERSTANDING

Alexa, Siri and other voice assistants embedded in smart devices in our homes occasionally misunderstand what we're saying. A six-year-old talked to her family's new device about biscuits and a dollhouse. Later her mum received an email saying that an order of three kilos of biscuits and a £120 dollhouse were on their way to her home. Even a talking parrot in London, whose owner had never bought anything online, somehow ordered a package of golden gift boxes without her knowledge. One person asked their device to "turn on the living room lights," and it replied, "There is no pudding room."

There's no such misunderstanding on God's part when we talk with Him. He's never confused, because He knows our hearts better than we do. The Spirit both searches our hearts and understands God's will. The apostle Paul told the churches in Rome that God promises He'll accomplish His good purpose of maturing us and making us more like His Son (ROMANS 8:28-29). Even when because of "our weakness" we don't know what we need in order to grow, the Spirit prays according to God's will for us (VV. 26–27).

Troubled about how to express yourself to God? Not understanding what or how to pray? Say what you can from the heart. The Spirit will understand and accomplish God's purpose.   *ANNE CETAS*

> **What's on your mind right now that you should share with God? How are you encouraged by the truth that He knows and understands what you're facing?**

> *Thank You, God, that You know my heart. I love You for that and many other reasons. Help me to express my thoughts to You and to trust You to understand.*

You will go out and frolic like well-fed calves.
[MALACHI 4:2]

FROLICKING IN FREEDOM

A third-generation farmer, Jim was so moved when he read "You who revere my name . . . will go out and frolic like well-fed calves" (MALACHI 4:2) that he prayed to receive Jesus' offer of eternal life. Vividly recalling his own calves' leaps of excitement after exiting their confined stalls at high speed, Jim finally understood God's promise of true freedom.

Jim's daughter told me this story because we'd been discussing the imagery in Malachi 4, where the prophet made a distinction between those who revered God's name, or remained faithful to Him, and those who only trusted in themselves (4:1–2). The prophet was encouraging the Israelites to follow God at a time when so many, including the religious leaders, disregarded God and His standards for faithful living (1:12–14; 3:5–9). Malachi called the people to live faithfully because of a coming time when God would make the final distinction between these two groups. In this context, Malachi used the unexpected imagery of a frolicking calf to describe the unspeakable joy that the faithful group will experience when "the sun of righteousness will rise with healing in its rays" (4:2).

Jesus is the ultimate fulfilment of this promise, bringing the good news that true freedom is available to all people (LUKE 4:16–21). And one day, in God's renewed and restored creation, we'll experience this freedom fully. What indescribable joy it will be to frolic there!

LISA M. SAMRA

> ***How have you experienced freedom in Jesus?***
> ***What other images help you to visualise joy?***
>
> *Jesus, help me to live joyfully as I remember the freedom only You provide.*

Brothers and sisters, whatever . . . is excellent
or praiseworthy—think about such things.
[PHILIPPIANS 4:8]

THE WHATEVERS

Every Friday evening, the national news my family watches concludes the broadcast by highlighting an uplifting story. In contrast to the rest of the news, it's always a breath of fresh air. A recent 'good' Friday story focused on a reporter who had suffered from COVID-19, fully recovered, and then decided to donate plasma to possibly help others in their fight against the virus. At the time, the jury was still out on how effective antibodies would be. But when many of us felt helpless and even in light of the discomfort of donating plasma (via needle), she felt it "was a small price to pay for the potential payoff."

After that Friday broadcast, my family and I felt encouraged—dare I say hope-filled. That's the power of the 'whatevers' Paul described in Philippians 4: "whatever is true, whatever is noble, whatever is right, whatever is pure, whatever is lovely, whatever is admirable" (V. 8). Did Paul have in mind plasma donation? Of course not. But did he have in mind sacrificial actions on behalf of someone in need—in other words, Christ-like behaviour? I've no doubt the answer is *yes*.

But that hopeful news wouldn't have had its full effect if it hadn't been broadcast. It's our privilege as witnesses to God's goodness to look and listen for the 'whatevers' all around us and then share that good news with others that they may be encouraged.　　*JOHN BLASE*

What's a 'whatever' story that's encouraged you lately?
Who might want or need to hear your story?

Father, I know that behind whatever is excellent and
praiseworthy is You. I love You.

By day the LORD directs his love, at night his
song is with me—a prayer to the God of my
life. [PSALM 42:8]

GOD KNOWS WE FEEL

Feeling overwhelmed, Sierra grieved her son's fight with addiction. "I feel bad," she said. "Does God think I have no faith because I can't stop crying when I'm praying?"

"I don't know what God thinks," I said. "But I know He can handle real emotions. It's not like He doesn't know how we feel." I prayed and shed tears with Sierra as we pleaded for her son's deliverance.

Scripture contains many examples of people wrestling with God while struggling. The writer of Psalm 42 expresses a deep longing to experience the peace of God's constant and powerful presence. He acknowledges his tears and his depression over the grief he's endured. His inner turmoil ebbs and flows with confident praises, as he reminds himself of God's faithfulness. Encouraging his "soul," the psalmist writes, "Put your hope in God, for I will yet praise him, my Saviour and my God" (V. 11). He's tugged back and forth between what he knows to be true about God and the undeniable reality of his overwhelming emotions.

God designed us in His image and with emotions. Our tears for others reveal deep love and compassion, not necessarily a lack of faith. We can approach God with raw wounds or old scars because He knows we feel. Each prayer, whether silent, sobbed or shouted with confidence, demonstrates our trust in His promise to hear and care for us.

XOCHITL DIXON

**What emotion have you tried to hide from God?
Why is it often hard to be honest with God about
difficult or overwhelming emotions?**

*Unchanging Father, thank You for assuring me that You know
I feel and need to process my ever-changing emotions.*

Come to me, all you who are weary
and burdened, and I will give you rest.
[MATTHEW 11:28]

REST WELL

The clock blinked 1:55 a.m. Burdened by a late-night text conversation, sleep wasn't coming. I unwound the mummy-like clutch of my tangled sheets and padded quietly to the couch. I googled what to do to fall asleep but instead found what *not* to do: don't take a nap or drink caffeine or work out late in the day. *Check.* Reading further on my tablet, I was advised not to use "screen time" late either. *Oops.* Texting hadn't been a good idea. When it comes to resting well, there are lists of what *not* to do.

In the Old Testament, God handed down rules regarding what not to do on the Sabbath in order to embrace rest. In the New Testament, Jesus offered a new way. Rather than stressing regulations, Jesus called the disciples into relationship. "Come to me, all you who are weary and burdened, and I will give you rest" (MATTHEW 11:28). In the preceding verse, Jesus pointed to His own ongoing relationship of oneness with His Father—the One He's revealed to us. The provision of ongoing help Jesus enjoyed from the Father is one we can experience as well.

While we're wise to avoid certain pastimes that can interrupt our sleep, resting well in Christ has more to do with relationship than regulation. I clicked my reader off and laid my burdened heart down on the pillow of Jesus' invitation: "Come to me . . ."   *ELISA MORGAN*

*How does viewing rest as a relationship rather than a
regulation change your view of rest? In what area of your
life is Jesus calling you to rest in relationship with Him?*

*Dear Jesus, thank You for the rest You call me to in an
ongoing relationship with You.*

The LORD is the everlasting God, the Creator of
the ends of the earth. He will not grow tired or
weary. [ISAIAH 40:28]

UNLIMITED

There I am, sitting in the shopping centre food court, my body
tense and my stomach knotted over looming work deadlines.
As I unwrap my burger and take a bite, people rush around
me, fretting over their own tasks. *How limited we all are,* I think to
myself, *limited in time, energy and capacity.*

I consider writing a new to-do list and prioritising the urgent tasks,
but as I pull out a pen another thought enters my mind: a thought
of One who is infinite and unlimited, who effortlessly accomplishes
all that He desires.

This God, Isaiah says, can measure the oceans in the hollow of
His hand and collect the dust of the earth in a basket (ISAIAH 40:12).
He names the stars of the heavens and directs their path (V. 26),
knows the rulers of the world and oversees their careers (V. 23),
considers islands mere specks of dust and the nations like drops
in the sea (V. 15). "To whom will you compare me?" He asks (V. 25).
"The LORD is the everlasting God," Isaiah replies. "He will not grow
tired or weary" (V. 28).

Stress and strain are never good for us, but on this day they deliver
a powerful lesson. The unlimited God is not like me. He accomplishes
everything He wishes. I finish my burger, and then pause once more.
And silently worship.   *SHERIDAN VOYSEY*

> ***How will you draw on God's unlimited strength today? (vv.
> 29–31). In the midst of your tasks and deadlines,
> how will you pause to worship the infinite One?***
>
> *Loving God, You're the unlimited One who'll
> accomplish all You've promised*

Paul shouted, "Don't harm yourself!
We are all here!" [ACTS 16:28]

WORKING WITHIN OUR WALLS

"You're free to go." Those words ended sixty-one days of isolation for three friends who tested positive for COVID-19 while teaching in Italy during 2020. For two months they ate, slept and exercised completely alone. One of them summed up hearing the news of their release simply: "We were ecstatic."

Imagine day after day being surrounded by the same walls, willing the phone to ring with news of your freedom. Or perhaps this feels all too familiar. Your so-called walls might be health problems, a job you dislike or family tension. You might feel as if you're waiting for God to call and say, "You're free to go."

We could have expected Paul and Silas to adopt this attitude after they were beaten and thrown in prison in Philippi (ACTS 16:23–24). But it doesn't seem as if they did. Not only did they spend their time praying to God and praising Him (V. 25), when they did receive their 'phone call'—an earthquake that opened the prison doors (V. 26)—Paul and Silas stayed put.

Perhaps they knew that God can work within walls, even using prisons for good. Because Paul and Silas stayed, salvation came to the trembling jailer when he asked, "Sirs, what must I do to be saved?" (V. 30).

If you feel trapped, remember Paul and Silas. Keep praising God and offering your prayers to Him, knowing that He can use you, even within your walls.   *CHRIS WALE*

*What situations or problems are you facing that you just wish
would disappear? How might your attitude to these things
change if you look for God to work for good within them?*

*Thank You, Jesus, for Your love. You promise rest and peace
for all who come to You. Help me to find joy in Your presence
as a willing and grateful prisoner of Your love.*

BIBLE IN A YEAR │ ISAIAH 5–6; EPHESIANS 1

Be transformed by the renewing of your mind.
[ROMANS 12:2]

JOYFUL LEARNING

I n the city of Mysore, India, there's a school made of two refurbished train cars connected end-to-end. Local educators teamed up with the South Western Railway Company to buy and remodel the discarded coaches. The units were essentially large metal boxes, unusable until workers installed stairways, fans, lights and desks. Workers also painted the walls and added colourful murals inside and out. Now, sixty students attend classes there because of the amazing transformation that took place.

Something even more amazing takes place when we follow the apostle Paul's command to "be transformed by the renewing of your mind" (ROMANS 12:2). As we allow the Holy Spirit to uncouple us from the world and its ways, our thoughts and attitudes begin to change. We become more loving, more hopeful and filled with inner peace (8:6).

Something else happens too. Although this transformation process is ongoing, and often has more stops and starts than a train ride, the process helps us understand what God wants for our lives. It takes us to a place where we "will learn to know God's will" (12:2 NLT). Learning His will may or may not involve specifics, but it always involves aligning ourselves with His character and His work in the world.

Nali Kali, the name of the transformed school in India, means "joyful learning" in English. How is God's transforming power leading you to the joyful learning of His will?   *JENNIFER BENSON SCHULDT*

> **Which areas of your thought life are most in need of
> God's transforming power? How willing are you to
> act when you clearly understand His will for your life?**
>
> *Dear God, I invite You to transform me by renewing my
> mind today. Thank You for all that's possible when I
> surrender to You.*

BIBLE IN A YEAR | ISAIAH 7-8; EPHESIANS 2

God is the strength of my heart and my
portion forever. [PSALM 73:26]

ALL THAT YOU NEED

Seated at the dining room table, I gazed at the happy chaos
around me. Aunts, uncles, cousins, nieces and nephews were
enjoying the food and being together at our family reunion. I
was enjoying it all, too. But one thought pierced my heart: *You're the
only woman here with no children, with no family to call your own.*

Many single women like me have similar experiences. In my culture,
an Asian culture where marriage and children are highly valued, not
having a family of one's own can bring a sense of incompleteness.
It can feel like you're lacking something that defines who you are
and makes you whole.

That's why the truth of God being my "portion" is so comforting to
me (PSALM 73:26). When the tribes of Israel were given their allotments
of land, the priestly tribe of Levi was assigned none. Instead, God
promised that He Himself would be their portion and inheritance
(DEUTERONOMY 10:9). They could find complete satisfaction in Him
and trust Him to supply their every need.

For some of us, the sense of lack may have nothing to do with
family. Perhaps we yearn for a better job or higher academic achievement. Regardless of our circumstances, we can embrace God as our
portion. He makes us whole. In Him, we have no lack. *KAREN HUANG*

What's one thing lacking in your life that you feel
would make you whole? How can you surrender it to
God and find satisfaction in Him as your portion?

Father, thank You for making me complete in Christ. Help
me to say along with the psalmist, "As for me, it is good
to be near God" (Psalm 73:28).

WISDOM TO LIVE BEAUTIFULLY

We all experience days when we wish we were wiser. How do I handle that tricky email at work? What should I do when my son keeps misbehaving? Whether it's making decisions at work or dealing with personal trials, time and time again, we experience the pressing need for wisdom.

So we read books, consult others or take classes, hoping to get some useful advice on how to manage our lives and relationships better. But while the acquired knowledge is helpful, often we still find something lacking. We need more than the wisdom the world offers; we need godly wisdom.

Where can we find this wisdom? Scripture tells us that it begins with the "fear of the LORD" (PSALM 111:10; PROVERBS 1:7). To fear God is to revere and honour Him for His majesty and holiness. We can understand why acquiring wisdom begins here when we discover what true wisdom looks like.

James 3:17 lists seven marks of godly wisdom: it's pure, peace-loving, considerate, submissive, full of mercy and good fruit, impartial and sincere. The wisdom that all believers in Jesus should seek is connected to a godly character—a Christ-like nature. It's the fruit of someone who walks with God, choosing to live in an upright, obedient way. In short, it's the result of someone who fears God.

Do you want to navigate through life making decisions that will bring glory to God and benefit others? James says, "If you need wisdom, ask our generous God, and he will give it to you. He will not rebuke you for asking" (JAMES 1:5 NLT). Our generous God will help you fear Him so you may gain wisdom to live life beautifully for Him.

Poh Fang Chia, Our Daily Bread *author*

★ The topic of **WISDOM** is the focus in the devotions for **October 1, 9** and **16**. We hope these readings will help you to grow in your understanding of what it means to live beautifully for Christ.

Oh, that their hearts would be inclined to
fear me and keep all my commands always.
[DEUTERONOMY 5:29]

ADOLESCENT FAITH

The teenage years are sometimes among the most agonising seasons in life—for both parent and child. In my adolescent quest to be independent from my mother, I openly rejected her values and rebelled against her rules, suspicious their purposes were merely to make me miserable. Though we've since come to agree on those matters, that time in our relationship was riddled with tension. Mum undoubtedly lamented my refusal to heed the wisdom of her instructions, knowing they would spare me unnecessary emotional and physical pain.

God had the same heart for His children, Israel. God imparted His wisdom for living in what we know as the Ten Commandments (DEUTERONOMY 5:7–21). Though they could be viewed as a list of rules, God's intention is evident in His words to Moses: "so that it might go well with them and their children forever!" (V. 29). Moses recognised God's desire, saying that obedience to the decrees would result in their enjoyment of His ongoing presence with them in the Promised Land (V. 33).

We all go through a season of 'adolescence' with God, not trusting that His guidelines for living are truly meant for our good. May we grow into the realisation that He wants what's best for us and learn to heed the wisdom He offers. His guidance is meant to lead us into spiritual maturity as we become more like Jesus (PSALM 119:97–104; EPHESIANS 4:15; 2 PETER 3:18). *KIRSTEN HOLMBERG*

> *How has God's wisdom helped you grow in your*
> *relationship with Him? In what area of your life do*
> *you need to heed His wisdom?*

> *Loving God, help me to trust that You know*
> *what's best for me.*

I will also give that person a white stone with
a new name written on it. [REVELATION 2:17]

WHAT'S YOUR NAME?

Someone said we go through life with three names: the name
our parents gave us, the name others give us (our reputation)
and the name we give ourselves (our character). The name
others give us matters, as "a good name is more desirable than great
riches; to be esteemed is better than silver or gold" (PROVERBS 22:1).
But while reputation is important, character matters more.

There's yet another name that's even more important. Jesus told
the Christians in Pergamum that though their reputation had suffered
some well-deserved hits, He had a new name reserved in heaven for
those who fight back and conquer temptation. "To the one who is
victorious, I will give . . . a white stone with a new name written on
it, known only to the one who receives it" (REVELATION 2:17).

We aren't sure why Jesus promised a white stone. Is it an award for
winning? A token for admission to the messianic banquet? Perhaps
it's similar to what jurors once used to vote for acquittal. We simply
don't know. Whatever it is, God promises our new name will wipe
away our shame (SEE ISAIAH 62:1–5).

Our reputation may be tattered, and our character may be
seemingly beyond repair. But neither name ultimately defines us.
It's not what others call you nor even what you call yourself that
matters. You are who Jesus says you are. Live into your new name.

MIKE WITTMER

How does your reputation match up against your character?
How well is your character reflecting who you are in Jesus?

Father, I believe I am who You say I am. Help me to live as Your child.

Therefore we do not lose heart. Though
outwardly we are wasting away, yet
inwardly we are being renewed day by day.
[2 CORINTHIANS 4:16]

THE DWINDLES

I t started with a tickle in my throat. *Uh oh,* I thought. That tickle
turned out to be influenza. And that was just the beginning of
bronchial affliction. Influenza morphed into whooping cough—yes,
that whooping cough—and *that* turned into pneumonia.

Eight weeks of torso-wracking coughing—it's not called *whooping
cough* for nothing—has left me humbled. I don't think of myself
as old. But I'm old enough to start thinking about heading in that
direction. A member of my small group at church has a funny name
for the health issues that assail us as we age: "the dwindles." But
there's nothing funny about dwindling's work 'in action'.

In 2 Corinthians 4, Paul too wrote—in his own way—about "the
dwindles". That chapter chronicles the persecution he and his team
endured. Fulfilling his mission had taken a heavy toll: "Outwardly we
are wasting away," he admitted. But even as his body failed—from
age, persecution and harsh conditions—Paul held tightly to his sustaining hope: "Inwardly we are being renewed day by day" (V. 16).
These "light and momentary troubles," he insisted, can't compare
to what awaits: "an eternal glory that far outweighs them all" (V. 17).

Even as I write tonight, "the dwindles" claw insistently at my chest.
But I know that in my life and that of anyone who clings to Christ,
they'll not have the last word.   *ADAM R. HOLZ*

> **What "dwindles" are affecting you or someone
> you love right now? What can help you maintain
> your faith and hope during seasons of struggle or
> discouragement with health issues?**
>
> *Father, even as our bodies "waste away," help me to
> see those physical struggles through the lens of our
> hope in Jesus and the glory He promises.*

A time is coming and has now come when the
true worshippers will worship the Father in
the Spirit and in truth, for they are the kind of
worshippers the Father seeks. [JOHN 4:23]

WHEREVER WE WORSHIP

Intense pain and a debilitating headache prevented me from attending services with my local church family . . . *again*. Grieving the loss of community worship, I watched an online sermon. At first, complaints soured my experience. The poor sound and video quality distracted me. But then a voice on the video warbled a familiar hymn. Tears flowed as I sang: "Be Thou my vision, O Lord of my heart. Naught be all else to me save that Thou art. Thou my best thought, by day or by night. Waking or sleeping, Thy presence my light." Focusing on the gift of God's constant presence, I worshipped Him while sitting in my living room.

While Scripture affirms the vital, essential nature of corporate worship (HEBREWS 10:25), God's not bound within the walls of a church building. During Jesus' chat with the Samaritan woman at the well, He defied all expectations of the Messiah (JOHN 4:9). Instead of condemnation, Jesus spoke truth and loved her as she stood next to that well (V. 10). He revealed His intimate and sovereign knowledge of His children (VV. 17–18). Proclaiming His deity, Jesus declared that the Holy Spirit evoked true worship from the hearts of God's people, not from a specific physical location (VV. 23–24).

When we focus on who God is, what He's done and all He's promised, we can rejoice in His constant presence as we worship Him with other believers, in our living rooms . . . and everywhere!

XOCHITL DIXON

Where do you enjoy worshipping God? How do you enjoy His presence and experience joy while worshipping Him?

Amazing God, please help me worship You as I rejoice in who You are, what You've done and all You promise to do.

BIBLE IN A YEAR | ISAIAH 20–22; EPHESIANS 6

I will fear no evil, for you are with me.
[PSALM 23:4]

WITH US IN THE VALLEY

As Hannah Wilberforce (aunt of British abolitionist William Wilberforce) lay dying, she wrote a letter in which she mentioned hearing about the death of a fellow believer in Jesus: "Happy is the dear man who is gone to glory, now in the presence of Jesus, whom unseen he loved. My heart seemed to jump for joy." Then she described her own situation: "Myself, better and worse; Jesus, as good as ever."

Her words make me think of Psalm 23, where David writes, "Even though I walk through the darkest valley [the valley of the shadow of death], I will fear no evil, for you are with me" (V. 4). Those words leap from the page because it's there, in the middle of the valley of the shadow of death, where David's description of God turns deeply personal. He moves from talking *about* God in the beginning of the psalm—"the LORD is my shepherd" (V. 1)—to talking *to* Him: "for *you* are *with* me" (V. 4, italics added).

How reassuring it is to know that almighty God who "brought forth the whole world" (PSALM 90:2) is so compassionate that He walks with us through even the most difficult places. Whether our situation turns better or worse, we can turn to our Shepherd, Saviour and Friend and find Him "as good as ever." So good that death itself is vanquished, and we will "dwell in the house of the LORD forever" (PSALM 23:6).   *JAMES BANKS*

How does it comfort you to know that Jesus our Shepherd is always with you? How can you share that hope with someone today?

My Shepherd, thank You for Your perfect faithfulness and kindness to me. Help me to stay near You today.

Always strive to do what is good for
each other and for everyone else.
[1 THESSALONIANS 5:15]

HELPING EACH OTHER

When playing basketball with her friends, Amber realised her community could benefit from an all-female local league. So she started a non-profit organisation to foster teamwork and impact the next generation. The leaders of Ladies Who Hoop strive to build confidence and character in the women and girls and encourage them to become meaningful contributors to their local communities. One of the original players who now mentors other girls said, "There is so much camaraderie among us. This is something I'd been missing. We support each other in so many different ways. I love seeing the girls succeed and grow."

God intends His people to team up to help each other as well. The apostle Paul urged the Thessalonians to "encourage one another and build each other up" (1 THESSALONIANS 5:11). God has put us into the family of His people for support in our lives. We need each other to keep walking the path of life in Christ. Sometimes that may mean listening to someone who's struggling, providing for a practical need, or speaking a few words of encouragement. We can celebrate successes, offer a prayer for strength in a difficulty, or challenge each other to grow in faith. And in everything, we can "always strive to do what is good for each other" (V. 15).

What camaraderie we can enjoy as we team up with other believers in Jesus to keep trusting God together!   *ANNE CETAS*

*In what ways have others encouraged you? How can you
prepare yourself to receive and give support to others?*

*I love being a part of Your family, God. Show me how I can
have a part in the lives of others.*

If on some point you think differently, that too
God will make clear to you. [PHILIPPIANS 3:15]

CURRENT BATTLES

When you plug in your toaster, you benefit from the results of a bitter feud from the late nineteenth century. Back then, inventors Thomas Edison and Nikola Tesla battled over which was the best kind of electricity for development: direct current (DC), like the current that goes from a battery to a torch; or alternating current (AC), which we get from an electrical outlet.

Eventually, Tesla's AC ideas powered through and have been used to provide electricity for homes, businesses and communities around the world. AC is much more efficient at sending electricity across great distances and proved to be the wiser choice.

Sometimes we need wisdom as we face issues of concern between believers in Jesus (SEE ROMANS 14:1–12). The apostle Paul called us to seek God's help for clarity in such matters. He said, "If on some point you think differently, that too God will make clear to you" (PHILIPPIANS 3:15). A few verses later, we see the results of two people who let a difference divide them—a conflict that grieved Paul: "I plead with Euodia and I plead with Syntyche to be of the same mind in the Lord" (4:2).

Whenever a disagreement starts to tear us apart, may we seek God's grace and wisdom in the Scriptures, the counsel of mature believers, and power of prayer. Let's strive to "be of the same mind" in Him (V. 2).   *DAVE BRANON*

*How can you apply God's grace and wisdom to a
current battle of personal preferences? Why is prayer
vital as you face this conflict?*

*Dear God, life is complicated. I have a situation, and
I'm not sure which way to go. Please help me discern,
with the help of the Holy Spirit, what to do next.*

These were all commended for their faith,
yet none of them received what had been
promised. [HEBREWS 11:39]

NO SUCH THING AS ORDINARY

When Anita passed away in her sleep on her ninetieth birthday, the quietness of her departure reflected the quietness of her life. A widow, she had been devoted to her children and grandchildren and to being a friend to younger women in the church.

Anita wasn't particularly remarkable in talent or achievement. But her deep faith in God inspired those who knew her. "When I don't know what to do about a problem," a friend of mine said, "I don't think about the words of a famous preacher or author. I think about what Anita would say."

Many of us are like Anita—ordinary people living ordinary lives. Our names will never be in the news, and we won't have monuments built in our honour. But a life lived with faith in Jesus is never ordinary. Some of the people listed in Hebrews 11 were not named (VV. 35–38); they walked the path of obscurity and did not receive the reward promised to them in this life (V. 39). Yet, because they obeyed God, their faith wasn't in vain. God used their lives in ways that went beyond their lack of notoriety (V. 40).

If you feel discouraged about the seeming ordinary state of your life, remember that a life lived by faith in God has an impact throughout eternity. Even if we're ordinary, we can have an extraordinary faith.

KAREN HUANG

In what area of your daily life might God be calling you to exercise faith in Him? How can He help you be more obedient and faithful in what you do every day?

Faithful God, please help me to trust and obey You always.

Moses listened to his father-in-law and did
everything he said. [EXODUS 18:24]

THE NEED FOR WISDOM

Growing up without a dad, Rob felt he missed out on a lot of
practical wisdom that fathers often pass on to their children.
Not wanting anyone to lack important life skills, Rob made a
series of practical "Dad, How Do I?" videos demonstrating everything
from how to put up a shelf to how to change a tyre. With his kind
compassion and warm style, Rob has become a YouTube sensation,
amassing millions of subscribers.

Many of us long for the expertise of a parental figure to teach us
valuable skills as well as help us navigate difficult situations. Moses
needed some wisdom after he and the Israelites fled captivity in
Egypt and were establishing themselves as a nation. Jethro, Moses'
father-in-law, saw the strain that settling disputes among the people
was having on Moses. So Jethro gave Moses thoughtful advice on
how to delegate responsibility in leadership (EXODUS 18:17–23). Moses
"listened to his father-in-law and did everything he said" (V. 24).

God knows we all need wisdom. Some may be blessed with godly
parents who offer wise advice, and some aren't. But God's wisdom
is available to all who ask (JAMES 1:5). He's also provided wisdom
throughout the pages of Scripture, which reminds us that when we
humbly and sincerely listen to the wise, we "will be counted among
the wise" (PROVERBS 19:20) and have wisdom to share with others.

LISA M. SAMRA

In what ways have you benefited from sage advice?
Who might you come alongside?

Heavenly Father, help me to seek out and listen to wise
counsel from the people You've put in my life.

All food is clean, but it is wrong for a person
to eat anything that causes someone else to
stumble. [ROMANS 14:20]

FOR OTHERS' SAKE

During the COVID-19 pandemic, many people in Singapore
(where I live) stayed home to avoid being infected. But I
blissfully continued swimming, believing it was safe.

My wife, however, feared that I might pick up an infection at the
public pool and pass it on to her aged mother—who, like other
seniors, was more vulnerable to the virus. "Can you just avoid
swimming for some time, for my sake?" she asked.

At first, I wanted to argue that there was little risk. Then I realised
that this mattered less than her feelings. Why would I insist on
swimming—hardly an essential thing—when it made her worry?

In Romans 14, Paul addressed issues like whether believers in
Christ should eat certain foods or celebrate certain festivals. He was
concerned that some people were imposing their views on others.

Paul reminded the church in Rome, and us, that believers in Jesus
may view situations differently. We also have diverse backgrounds
that colour our attitudes and practices. He wrote, "Let us stop
passing judgement on one another. Instead, make up your mind
not to put any stumbling block or obstacle in the way of a brother
or sister" (V. 13).

God's grace gives us great freedom even as it helps us express
His love to fellow believers. We can use that freedom to put the
spiritual needs of others above our own convictions about rules
and practices that don't contradict the essential truths found in the
gospel (V. 20).   *LESLIE KOH*

***What are some of the rules and practices you keep as a believer in
Christ? How might they affect other believers who think differently?***

*Jesus, give me the grace to give way on things that don't
contradict the gospel truth, and the love to put the feelings of
others above my own.*

So Mephibosheth ate at David's table like
one of the king's sons. [2 SAMUEL 9:11]

AT THE KING'S TABLE

"He'll live," the vet announced, "but his leg will have to be amputated." The stray mongrel my friend had brought in had been run over by a car. "Are you the owner?" There would be a hefty surgery bill, and the puppy would need care as it recovered. "I am now," my friend replied. Her kindness has given that dog a future in a loving home.

Mephibosheth saw himself as a "dead dog", unworthy of favour (2 SAMUEL 9:8). Being lame in both feet due to an accident, he was dependent on others to protect and provide for him (SEE 4:4). Furthermore, after the death of his grandfather, King Saul, he probably feared that David, the new king, would order all enemies and rivals to the throne killed, as was the common practice of the time.

Yet, out of love for his friend Jonathan, David ensured that Jonathan's son Mephibosheth would always be safe and cared for as his own son (9:7). In the same way, we who were once God's enemies, marked for death, have been saved by Jesus and given a place with Him in heaven forever. That's what it means to eat at the banquet in the kingdom of God that Luke describes in his gospel (LUKE 14:15). Here we are—the sons and daughters of a King! What extravagant, undeserved kindness we've received! Let's draw near to God in gratitude and joy.

KAREN KWEK

> **When are you likely to forget that God protects and cares for you? How could 2 Samuel 9:6–13 encourage you during such times?**
>
> *Dear Jesus, thank You for saving me and giving me a place at Your table forever. Remind me that I'm Your dear child, and help me to always praise and trust You.*

Who was it that taught [the LORD] knowledge?
[ISAIAH 40:14]

THE GREATEST TEACHER

"I don't get it!" My daughter slapped her pencil down on the desk. She was working on a maths assignment, and I'd just begun my 'job' as a home-schooling mum/teacher. We were in trouble. I couldn't recall what I'd learned thirty-five years ago about changing decimals into fractions. I couldn't teach her something I didn't already know, so we watched an online teacher explain the skill.

As human beings, we'll struggle at times with things we don't know or understand. But not God; He's the all-knowing One—the omniscient One. Isaiah wrote, "Who can . . . instruct the LORD as his counsellor? Whom did the LORD consult to enlighten him, and who taught him the right way? Who was it that taught him knowledge, or showed him the path of understanding?" (ISAIAH 40:13–14). The answer? *No one!*

Humans have intelligence because God created us in His own image. Still, our intelligence is just an inkling of His. Our knowledge is limited, but God knows everything from eternity past to eternity future (PSALM 147:5). Our knowledge is increasing today with the aid of technology, but we still get things wrong. Jesus, however, knows all things "immediately, simultaneously, exhaustively and truly," as one theologian put it.

No matter how much humans advance in knowledge, we'll never surpass Christ's all-knowing status. We'll always need Him to bless our understanding and to teach us what's good and true.

JENNIFER BENSON SCHULDT

In what types of situations are you thankful for God's omniscience? How does knowing that Jesus understands everything encourage you?

Jesus, I praise You as the One who knows everything. Teach me what You want me to learn, and help me to love You with all my mind.

This word came to Jeremiah from the LORD.
[JEREMIAH 36:1]

WORDS THAT ENDURE

I n the early nineteenth century, Thomas Carlyle gave a manuscript to philosopher John Stuart Mill to review. Somehow, whether accidentally or intentionally, the manuscript got tossed into a fire. It was Carlyle's only copy. Undaunted, he set to work rewriting the lost chapters. Mere flames couldn't stop the story, which remained intact in his mind. Out of great loss, Carlyle produced his monumental work *The French Revolution*.

In the waning days of ancient Judah's decadent kingdom, God told the prophet Jeremiah, "Take a scroll and write on it all the words I have spoken to you" (JEREMIAH 36:2). The message revealed God's tender heart, calling on His people to repent in order to avoid imminent invasion (V. 3).

Jeremiah did as he was told. The scroll soon found its way to Judah's king Jehoiakim, who methodically shredded it and threw it into the fire (VV. 23–25). The king's act of arson only made matters worse. God told Jeremiah to write another scroll with the same message. He said, "[Jehoiakim] will have no one to sit on the throne of David; his body will be thrown out and exposed to the heat by day and the frost by night" (V. 30).

It's possible to burn the words of God by tossing a book into a fire. Possible, but utterly *futile*. The Word behind the words endures forever.   *TIM GUSTAFSON*

What has caused you or those you know to ignore the words of God? Why is it vital for you to submit to and obediently follow what He's instructed?

Father, help me to take Your words to heart, even if they're difficult to hear. Please give me a heart of repentance—not defiance.

The wages of sin is death, but the gift of
God is eternal life in Christ Jesus our Lord.
[ROMANS 6:23]

A BEGINNER'S GUIDE TO LIFE

After my mother's sudden death, I was motivated to start blogging. I wanted to write posts that would inspire people to use their minutes on earth to create significant life moments. So I turned to a beginner's guide to blogging. I learned what platform to use, how to choose titles and how to craft compelling posts. And in 2016, my first blog post was born.

Paul wrote a 'beginner's guide' that explains how to obtain eternal life. In Romans 6:16–18, he contrasts the fact that we're all born in rebellion to God (sinners) with the truth that Jesus can help us be "set free from [our] sin" (V. 18). Paul then describes the difference between being a slave to sin and a slave to God and His life-giving ways (VV. 19–20). He continues by stating that "the wages of sin is death, but the gift of God is eternal life" (V. 23). Death means being separated from God forever. This is the devastating outcome we face when we reject Christ. But God has offered us a gift in Jesus—new life. It's the kind of life that begins on earth and continues forever in heaven with Him.

Paul's beginner's guide to eternal life leaves us with two choices—choosing sin, which leads to death, or choosing Jesus' gift, which leads to eternal life. May you receive His gift of life, and if you've already accepted Christ, may you share this gift with others today!

MARVIN WILLIAMS

**How would you describe what it means to receive the
free gift of eternal life through Jesus Christ? What's the
difference between being a slave to sin and a slave to
God and His life-giving ways?**

*Jesus, thank You for loving me and forgiving me. You paid a
debt I couldn't pay and gave me a gift I couldn't buy.*

Take delight in the LORD, and he will give you
the desires of your heart. [PSALM 37:4]

GOD'S PLANS FOR YOU

For six years, Agnes tried to make herself the 'perfect minister's wife', modelling herself after her adored mother-in-law (also a pastor's wife). She thought that in this role she couldn't also be a writer and painter, but in burying her creativity she became depressed and contemplated suicide. Only the help of a neighbouring pastor moved her out of the darkness as he prayed with her and assigned her two hours of writing each morning. This awakened her to what she called her "sealed orders"—the calling God had given her. She wrote, "For me to be really myself—my complete self—every . . . flow of creativity that God had given me had to find its channel."

Later, she pointed to one of David's songs that expressed how she found her calling: "Take delight in the LORD, and he will give you the desires of your heart" (PSALM 37:4). As she committed her way to God, trusting Him to lead and guide her (V. 5), He made a way for her not only to write and paint but to help others to better communicate with Him.

God has a set of "sealed orders" for each of us, not only that we'll know we're His beloved children but understand the unique ways we can serve Him through our gifts and passions. He'll lead us as we trust and delight in Him.   AMY BOUCHER PYE

How does Agnes' story of living someone else's life resonate with you? What has God put in your "sealed orders"?

Creator God, You've made me in Your image. Help me to know and embrace my calling that I might better love and serve You.

Death is the destiny of everyone; the living
should take this to heart. [ECCLESIASTES 7:2]

LIVING WELL

ree funerals for the living. That's the service offered by an
establishment in South Korea. Since it opened in 2012, more
than 25,000 people—from teenagers to retirees—have participated in mass "living funeral" services, hoping to improve their
lives by considering their deaths. Officials say "the simulated death
ceremonies are meant to give the participant a truthful sense of
their lives, inspire gratitude, and aid in forgiveness and reconnection
among family and friends."

These words echo the wisdom given by the teacher who wrote
Ecclesiastes. "Death is the destiny of everyone; the living should
take this to heart" (ECCLESIASTES 7:2). Death reminds us of the brevity
of life and that we only have a certain amount of time to live and
love well. It loosens our grip on some of God's good gifts—such as
money, relationships and pleasure—and frees us to enjoy them in
the here and now as we store up "treasures in heaven, where moths
and vermin do not destroy, and where thieves do not break in and
steal" (MATTHEW 6:20).

As we remember that death may come knocking anytime, perhaps
it'll compel us to not postpone that visit with our parents, delay our
decision to serve God in a particular way or compromise our time
with our children for our work. With God's help, we can learn to
live wisely.

POH FANG CHIA

**What changes will you make in your life today as you think
about death? How can you be more conscious about death
amid the hustle and bustle of life?**

*Loving God, help me to remember the brevity of life
and to live well today.*

When he, the Spirit of truth, comes, he will
guide you into all the truth. [JOHN 16:13]

INSIGHT FROM THE SPIRIT

As the French soldier dug in the desert sand, reinforcing the
defences of his army's encampment, he had no idea he
would make a momentous discovery. Moving another shov-
elful of sand, he saw a stone. Not just any stone. It was the Rosetta
Stone, containing laws and governance from King Ptolemy V written
in three languages. That stone (now housed in the British Museum)
would be one of the most important archaeological finds of the
nineteenth century, helping to unlock the mysteries of the ancient
Egyptian writing known as hieroglyphics.

For many of us, much of Scripture is also wrapped in deep mystery.
Still, the night before the cross, Jesus promised His followers that He
would send the Holy Spirit. He told them, "But when he, the Spirit
of truth, comes, he will guide you into all the truth. He will not speak
on his own; he will speak only what he hears, and he will tell you
what is yet to come" (JOHN 16:13). The Holy Spirit is, in a sense, our
divine Rosetta Stone, shedding light on the truth—including truths
behind the mysteries of the Bible.

While we're not promised absolute understanding of everything
given to us in the Scriptures, we can have confidence that by the
Spirit we can comprehend everything necessary for us to follow
Jesus. He will guide us into those vital truths.   *BILL CROWDER*

**What are some portions of the Bible you have found
difficult? List them and ask the Holy Spirit to guide you into
better understanding of those Scriptures.**

*God of all truth, help me to rest in the Spirit of truth that I
might better understand the wisdom You've provided.*

There is a time for everything . . . a time to be
silent and a time to speak. [ECCLESIASTES 3:1, 7]

A TIME TO SPEAK

For thirty long years, the African American woman worked
faithfully for a large global ministry. Yet when she sought to
talk with co-workers about racial injustice, she was met with
silence. Finally, however, in the spring of 2020—as open discussions
about racism expanded around the world—her ministry friends
"started having some open dialogue." With mixed feelings and pain,
she was grateful discussions began, but wondered why it took her
colleagues so long to speak up.

Silence can be a virtue in some situations. As King Solomon wrote
in the book of Ecclesiastes, "There is a time for everything, and a
season for every activity under the heavens: . . . a time to be silent
and a time to speak" (ECCLESIASTES 3:1, 7).

Silence in the face of bigotry and injustice, however, only enables
harm and hurt. Lutheran pastor Martin Niemoeller (jailed in Nazi
Germany for speaking out) confessed that in a poem he wrote after
the war. "First they came for the Communists," he wrote, "but I
didn't speak up because I wasn't a Communist." He added, "Then
they came for" the Jews, the Catholics and others, "but I didn't
speak up." Finally, "they came for me—and by that time there was
no one left to speak up."

It takes courage—and love—to speak up against injustice. Seeking God's help, however, we recognise the time to speak is now.

PATRICIA RAYBON

> *Why is it important not to be silent during discussions
> about racial injustice and other forms of injustice?
> What hinders your willingness to engage in dialogue
> about addressing racial harm?*

> *Dear God, release my tongue and heart from the
> enemy's grip. Equip me to see and feel the harm of racial
> injustice so that I may speak up for those hurt by this sin.*

BIBLE IN A YEAR | ISAIAH 53–55; 2 THESSALONIANS 1

But the fruit of the Spirit is love, joy,
peace, forbearance, kindness, goodness,
faithfulness, gentleness and self-control.
[GALATIANS 5:22–23]

WHEN TO SACRIFICE

I n February 2020, as the COVID-19 crisis was just beginning, a newspaper columnist's concerns struck me. Would we willingly self-isolate, she wondered, changing our work, travel and shopping habits so others wouldn't get sick? "This isn't just a test of clinical resources," she wrote, "but of our willingness to put ourselves out for others." Suddenly, the need for virtue was front-page news.

It can be hard to consider others' needs while we're anxious about our own. Thankfully, we're not left with willpower alone to meet the need. We can ask the Holy Spirit to give us *love* to replace our indifference, *joy* to counter sadness, *peace* to replace our anxiety, *forbearance* (patience) to push out our impulsiveness, *kindness* to care about others, *goodness* to see to their needs, *faithfulness* to keep our promises, *gentleness* instead of harshness, and *self-control* to lift us beyond self-centeredness (GALATIANS 5:22–23). While we won't be perfect at all of this, we're called to seek the Spirit's gifts of virtue regularly (EPHESIANS 5:18).

Author Richard Foster once described holiness as the ability to do what needs to be done when it needs to be done. And such holiness is needed every day, not just in a pandemic. Do we have the capacity to make sacrifices for the sake of others? Holy Spirit, fill us with the power to do what needs to be done. *SHERIDAN VOYSEY*

When have you made a sacrifice for the sake of others?
What needs around you call for the Holy Spirit's fruit today?

Holy Spirit, fill me afresh today and make me a person of virtue.

I said, "I will confess my transgressions to the
LORD." And you forgave the guilt of my sin.
[PSALM 32:5]

CRUMBLED FROM WITHIN

When I was a teenager, my mum painted a mural on our living room wall, which stayed there for several years. It showed an ancient Greek scene of a ruined temple with white columns lying on their sides, a crumbling fountain and a broken statue. As I looked at the Hellenistic architecture that had once held great beauty, I tried to imagine what had destroyed it. I was curious, especially when I began studying about the tragedy of once great and thriving civilizations that had decayed and crumbled from *within*.

The sinful depravity and wanton destruction we see around us today can be troubling. It's natural for us to try to explain it by pointing to people and nations that have rejected God. But shouldn't we be casting our gaze inwardly as well? Scripture warns us about being hypocrites when we call out others to turn from their sinful ways without also taking a deeper look inside our own hearts (MATTHEW 7:1–5).

Psalm 32 challenges us to see and confess our own sin. It's only when we recognise and confess our personal sin that we can experience freedom from guilt and the joy of true repentance (VV. 1–5). And as we rejoice in knowing that God offers us complete forgiveness, we can share that hope with others who are also struggling with sin.

CINDY HESS KASPER

What's the first step in identifying sin in your life?
Why is it vital that you confess your sin to God?

Father God, I thank You for the gift of Your forgiveness that eliminates the guilt of my sin. Help me to first examine my own heart before I concern myself with the sins of others.

[Jesus said], "These are the very Scriptures
that testify about me." [JOHN 5:39]

STUDYING THE SCRIPTURES

J. I. Packer (1926–2020), in his classic work *Knowing God,* spoke
of four well-known believers in Christ whom he called "beavers
for the Bible." Not all were trained scholars, but each one exercised great care to know God by gnawing into the Scripture, like a
beaver digs in and gnaws away at a tree. Packer further noted that
knowing God through Bible study is not just for scholars. "A simple
Bible reader and sermon hearer who is full of the Holy Spirit will
develop a far deeper acquaintance with his God and Saviour than a
more learned scholar who is content with being theologically correct."

Unfortunately, not all who study the Bible do so with humble
hearts with the goal of getting to know the Saviour better and becoming more like Him. In Jesus' day there were those who read the
Old Testament Scriptures, yet they missed the very One they spoke
of. "You study the Scriptures diligently because you think that in
them you have eternal life. These are the very Scriptures that testify
about me, yet you refuse to come to me to have life" (JOHN 5:39–40).

Do you sometimes find yourself stumped as you read the Bible?
Or have you given up studying the Scriptures altogether? Bible
'beavers' are more than Bible readers. They prayerfully and carefully
gnaw away at Scripture in ways that open their eyes and hearts to
see and love Jesus—the One revealed in it.　　　*ARTHUR JACKSON*

*What are some Old Testament Scripture passages
that you recognise as testifying about Jesus?
What better habits do you need to develop to
become a better student of the Scriptures?*

*Father, open my eyes to see Jesus in all of Scripture
so that I might love, obey and serve Him more.*

Each of you should use whatever gift you have received to serve others, as faithful stewards of God's grace in its various forms. [1 PETER 4:10]

LIVE TO SERVE

After ten-year-old Chelsea received an elaborate art set, she discovered that God used art to help her feel better when she was sad. When she found out that some kids didn't have art supplies readily available, she wanted to help them. So when it was time for her birthday party, she asked her friends *not* to bring her gifts. Instead, she invited them to donate art supplies and help fill boxes for children in need.

Later, with her family's help, she started Chelsea's Charity. She began asking more people to help her fill boxes so she could help more kids. She has even taught art tips to groups who have received her boxes. After a local newscaster interviewed Chelsea, people started donating supplies from all over the country. As Chelsea's Charity continues sending art supplies internationally, this young girl is demonstrating how God can use us when we're willing to live to serve others.

Chelsea's compassion and willingness to share reflects the heart of a faithful steward. The apostle Peter encourages all believers in Jesus to be faithful stewards as they "love each other deeply" by sharing the resources and talents God has given them (1 PETER 4:8–11).

Our small acts of love can inspire others to join us in giving. God can even rally supporters to serve alongside us. As we rely on Him, we can live to serve and give Him the glory He deserves.

XOCHITL DIXON

***How can you rely on God to help you serve others today?
In what way has God been nudging you to serve Him that
seems too big for you to handle alone?***

*Faithful Father, please give me all I need to serve You by
loving others with my words and actions today.*

BIBLE IN A YEAR | ISAIAH 65–66; 1 TIMOTHY 2

Go! I am sending you out like lambs among
wolves. Do not take a purse or bag or sandals.
[LUKE 10:3–4]

ALL WE NEED

"**A**bsolutely ridiculous," said someone on Twitter. "Pretty
sure that if you are isolated for 17 days and your kettle
packs in, you should be able to buy a new one." Kettles were
just one of many items considered non-essential during the October
2020 fire-breaker lockdown in Wales. Shops weren't allowed to sell
things that many people consider to be basic necessities, such as
clothes, toiletries and baby products.

When Jesus sent out His disciples to preach in the surrounding
towns, He also told them not to take things that, at first glance,
sound pretty essential. He said: "Go! I am sending you out like lambs
among wolves. Do not take a purse or bag or sandals" (LUKE 10:3–4).
They were embarking on a dangerous mission, yet they couldn't
take money, supplies, food or spare clothing. We might think His
instructions seem a little extreme.

In this, Jesus was teaching His disciples a key lesson that we too
will keep relearning every day. If we have Him, we have everything
we need—only Jesus is truly essential.

Jesus wants to draw our focus away from the things we think we
have to have. Instead, He wants us to put all our faith, confidence
and hope in Him. When we do, we—like those first disciples—will
find Him to be utterly and wonderfully faithful. He is all we need.

CHRIS WALE

What competes with Jesus as being essential in your life?
What do you think Paul meant when he called everything in
his life rubbish compared to Jesus (see Philippians 3:8)?

Thank You, Jesus, that I have You. Be my strength,
my life and my hope today.

The Spirit you received does not make you
slaves, so that you live in fear. [ROMANS 8:15]

TALK, TRUST, FEEL

"Don't talk, don't trust, don't feel was the law we lived by,"
says Frederick Buechner in his powerful memoir *Telling
Secrets*, "and woe to the one who broke it." Buechner
is describing his experience of what he calls the "unwritten law of
families who for one reason or another have gone out of whack."
In his own family, that "law" meant Buechner was not allowed to
talk about or grieve his father's suicide, leaving him with no one he
could trust with his pain.

Can you relate? Many of us in one way or another have learned
to live with a warped version of love, one that demands dishonesty
or silence about what's harmed us. That kind of 'love' relies on fear
for control—and is a kind of slavery.

We can't afford to forget just how different Jesus' invitation to
love is from the kind of conditional love we often experience—a kind
of love we're always afraid we could lose. As Paul explains, through
Christ's love we can finally understand what it means to not live
in fear (ROMANS 8:15) and start to understand the kind of glorious
freedom (V. 21) that's possible when we know we're deeply, truly and
unconditionally loved. We're free to talk, to trust and to feel once
more—to learn what it means to live unafraid.   *MONICA LA ROSE*

> ***Are there any unspoken 'rules' you've learned as conditions
> for acceptance and love? How might you live differently if you
> believed you didn't have to follow those rules to be loved?***
>
> *Loving God, at times I'm afraid to live honestly with myself
> and with others—thinking that by doing so I'll no longer be
> loved. Heal my heart, and help me believe in and live for the
> glory, freedom and joy Your love makes possible.*

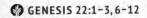

Some time later God tested Abraham.
[GENESIS 22:1]

THE TESTING

The first time I took my sons to hike up a mountain with an elevation of a least 14,000 feet, they were nervous. *Could they make it? Were they up to the challenge?* My youngest stopped on the trail for extended breaks. "Dad, I can't go any more," he said repeatedly. But I believed this test would be good for them, and I wanted them to trust me. A mile from the peak, my son who'd insisted he could go no further caught his second wind and beat us to the summit. He was so glad he trusted me, even amid his fears.

I marvel at the trust Isaac had in his father as they climbed their mountain. Far more, I'm undone by the trust Abraham had in God as he raised his knife over his son (GENESIS 22:10). Even with his confused and wrenching heart, Abraham obeyed. Mercifully, an angel stopped him. "Do not lay a hand on the boy," God's messenger declared (V. 12). God never intended for Isaac to die.

As we draw parallels from this unique story to our own with caution, it's crucial to note the opening line: "God tested Abraham" (V. 1). Through his test, Abraham learned how much he trusted God. He discovered His loving heart and profound provision.

In our confusion, darkness and testing, we learn truths about ourselves and about God. And we may even find that our testing leads to a deeper trust in Him.   *WINN COLLIER*

> *How do you believe you've been tested by God?*
> *What was that experience like, and what did you*
> *take away from it?*
>
> *God, I don't know if what I'm experiencing is Your*
> *testing or not, but either way, I want to trust You.*
> *I give my future to You.*

Paul was . . . set apart for the gospel of God.
[ROMANS 1:1]

SET APART

The three-wheeled taxis of Sri Lanka, known as "tuk tuks", are a convenient and delightful mode of transport for many. Lorraine, a resident of the capital of Colombo, also realised that they're a mission field. Hopping onto a *tuk tuk* one day, she found the friendly driver more than happy to engage in conversation about religion. The next time, she told herself, she would talk to the driver about the good news.

The book of Romans starts with Paul declaring himself as "set apart for the gospel of God" (ROMANS 1:1). The Greek word for "gospel" is *evangelion,* which means "good news". Paul was essentially saying that his main purpose was to tell God's good news.

What is this good news? Romans 1:3 says that the gospel of God is "regarding his Son." The good news is Jesus! It's *God* who wants to tell the world that Jesus came to save us from sin and death, and He's chosen us to be His mode of communication. What a humbling fact!

Sharing the good news is a privilege all believers in Jesus have been given. We've "received grace" to call others to this faith (VV. 5–6). God has set us apart to carry the exciting news of the gospel to those around us, whether on tuk tuks or wherever we are. May we, like Lorraine, look for opportunities in our daily life to tell others the good news that is Jesus.   *ASIRI FERNANDO*

What barriers do you experience in sharing your faith? What talents or interests can you use to present the good news?

Jesus, thank You for making me Your mouthpiece for Your good news. May Your Spirit give me the courage and love to share about You today.

I am angry with you and your two friends,
because you have not spoken the truth about
me, as my servant Job has. [JOB 42:7]

A PURPOSE IN SUFFERING

"So what you're saying is, it may not be my fault." The woman's words took me by surprise. Having been a guest speaker at her church, we were now discussing what I'd shared that morning. "I have a chronic illness," she explained, "and I have prayed, fasted, confessed my sins and done everything else I was told to do to be healed. But I'm still sick, so I thought I was to blame."

I felt sad at the woman's confession. Having been given a spiritual 'formula' to fix her problem, she had blamed herself when the formula hadn't worked. Even worse, this formulaic approach to suffering was disproved generations ago.

Simply put, this old formula says that if you're suffering, you must have sinned. When Job tragically lost his livestock, children and health, his friends used the formula on him. "Who, being innocent, has ever perished?" Eliphaz said, suspecting Job's guilt (JOB 4:7). Bildad even told Job that his children only died because they had sinned (8:4). Ignorant of the real cause of Job's calamities (1:6–2:10), they tormented him with simplistic reasons for his pain, later receiving God's rebuke (42:7).

Suffering is a part of living in a fallen world. Like Job, it can happen for reasons we may never know. But God has a purpose for you that goes beyond the pain you endure. Don't get discouraged by falling for simplistic formulas.   *SHERIDAN VOYSEY*

*How else do you see the 'suffering = sin' formula
being used? Why do you think it's still so prevalent?*

*Great Doctor, give me words to heal, not hurt,
in times of pain.*

If we ask anything according to his will, he
hears us. [1 JOHN 5:14]

IS GOD LISTENING?

When I served on my church's pastoral care team, one of
my duties was to pray over the requests penciled on
pew cards during the services. For an aunt's health. For
a couple's finances. For a grandson's discovery of God. Rarely did I
hear the results of these prayers. Most were anonymous, and I had
no way of knowing how God had responded. I confess that at times
I wondered, *Was He really listening? Was anything happening as
a result of my prayers?*

Over our lifetimes, most of us question, "Does God hear me?" I
remember my own Hannah-like pleas for a child that went unan-
swered for years. And there were my pleas that my father would
come to faith in Christ, yet he died without any apparent confession.

Etched across the millennia are myriad instances of God's ear
bending to listen: to Israel's groans under slavery (EXODUS 2:24);
to Moses on Mount Sinai (DEUTERONOMY 9:19); to Joshua at Gilgal
(JOSHUA 10:14); to Hannah's prayers for a child (1 SAMUEL 1:10–17); to
David crying out for deliverance from Saul (2 SAMUEL 22:7).

Then we read this promise in 1 John 5:14, "If we ask anything
according to his will, he hears us." The word for "hears" means "to
pay attention" and to respond on the basis of having heard.

As we go to God today, may we have the confidence of His listening ear spanning the history of His people. He hears our pleas.

ELISA MORGAN

> ***Pause to consider what you've most recently
> asked of God. What motivated you to ask?
> How can you know that God hears you?***
>
> *Father, I come asking and trusting You to hear
> me because You say that You do.*

[God] will rejoice over you with singing.
[ZEPHANIAH 3:17]

GOD SINGS OVER YOU

Seventeen months after our first child—a boy—was born, along came a little girl. I was overjoyed at the thought of having a daughter, but I was also a bit uneasy because while I knew a few things about little boys, this was uncharted territory. We named her Sarah, and one of my privileges was rocking her to sleep so my wife could rest. I'm not sure why, but I started trying to sing her to sleep, and the song of choice was "You Are My Sunshine." Whether holding her in my arms or standing above her in her crib, I quite literally sang over her, and loved every minute of it. She's in her twenties now, and I still call her *Sunshine*.

We usually think about angels singing. But when was the last time you thought about God singing? That's right—*God* singing. And furthermore, when was the last time you thought about Him singing over you? Zephaniah is clear in his message to Jerusalem, "The LORD your God" takes great delight in you, so much so that He "rejoice[s] over you with singing" (3:17). Although this message speaks directly to Jerusalem, it's likely God sings over us—those who have received Jesus as Saviour—too! What song does He sing? Well, Scripture's not clear on that. But the song is born out of His love, so we can trust it's true and noble and right and pure and lovely and admirable (PHILIPPIANS 4:8).   *JOHN BLASE*

> **What feelings are stirred when you consider God singing over you? Is that something unbelievable or something comforting? Why?**

> *Good Father, the thought that You would sing over me in joy is such an assurance and comfort. Thank You.*

He has saved us and called us to a holy life.
[2 TIMOTHY 1:9]

A NEW CALLING

Teenage gang leader Casey and his followers broke into homes and cars, robbed corner shops and fought other gangs. Eventually, Casey was arrested and sentenced. In prison, he became a "shot caller", someone who handed out homemade knives during riots.

Sometime later, he was placed in solitary confinement. While daydreaming in his cell, Casey experienced a 'movie' of sorts replaying key events of his life—and of Jesus, being led to and nailed to the cross and telling him, "I'm doing this for you." Casey fell to the floor weeping and confessed his sins. Later, he shared his experience with a chaplain, who explained more about Jesus and gave him a Bible. "That was the start of my journey of faith," Casey said. Eventually, he was released into the mainline prison population, where he was mistreated for his faith. But he felt at peace, because "[he] had found a new calling: telling other inmates about Jesus."

In his letter to Timothy, the apostle Paul talks about the power of Christ to change lives: God calls us from lives of wrongdoing to follow and serve Jesus (2 TIMOTHY 1:9). When we receive Him by faith, we desire to be a living witness of Christ's love. The Holy Spirit enables us to do so, even when suffering, in our quest to share the good news (v. 8). Like Casey, let's live out our new calling.   *ALYSON KIEDA*

> **When have you shared the gospel with someone, and what was the result? Did it ever lead to suffering? What happened?**

> *Dear God, thank You for offering me a new calling through Your Son. And thank You for giving me the Spirit to live inside me to guide and empower me to serve You.*

He made the moon to mark the seasons.
[PSALM 104:19]

REDEEMING THE SEASON

eisa wanted a way to redeem the season. So many of the decorations she saw put up in people's homes during October seemed to celebrate death, sometimes in gruesome and macabre ways. Determined to counter the darkness in some small way, Leisa began to write things she was grateful for with a permanent marker on a large pumpkin. "Sunshine" was the first item. Soon visitors were adding to her list. Some entries were whimsical: "doodling", for instance. Others were practical: "a warm house"; "a working car". Still others were poignant, like the name of a departed loved one. A chain of gratitude began to wind its way around the pumpkin.

Psalm 104 offers a litany of praise to God for things we easily overlook. "[God] makes springs pour water into the ravines," sang the poet (V. 10). "He makes grass grow for the cattle, and plants for people to cultivate" (V. 14). Even the night is seen as good and fitting. "You bring darkness, it becomes night, and all the beasts of the forest prowl" (V. 20). But then, "The sun rises . . . . People go out to their work, to their labour until evening" (VV. 22–23). For all these things, the psalmist concluded, "I will sing praise to my God as long as I live" (V. 33).

In a world that doesn't know how to deal with death, even the smallest offering of praise to our Creator can become a shining contrast of hope.   *TIM GUSTAFSON*

How do you and your friends deal with the idea of death?
What are some ways you might make the world curious
about the hope you have in Jesus?

Thank You, Father, for the multiple good things You've placed on
this earth. Make my life a grateful offering of praise to You.

FOLLOWING JESUS TOGETHER

Anew believer in Jesus asked Barb, "Would you disciple me?" Barb was uncertain about how to proceed. Should they have a study together? And if so, what topic would be best? Barb prayerfully picked out a resource to look at together and is finding joy in helping her new friend grow in her understanding of Christ.

New immigrants moved into Sue's neighbourhood. She befriended the young family of seven and invited the kids over to play with her children. Sue began talking with the mum about her Saviour and friend, Jesus, and invited the family to church.

Whenever he can, Jerry brings up his faith in Christ when talking with his co-workers. He never pushes his beliefs but shares if someone seems curious. He even started a small discussion group during lunchtime for those wanting to know more about Jesus.

These individuals are following the example of Christ, who said about Himself: "The Son of Man came to seek and to save the lost" (LUKE 19:10). When Jesus met a woman at a well, their conversation prompted her to believe Jesus could be the Messiah (JOHN 4:4–26). And then she ran back to her village to tell others about Him (V. 29). As a result, "many Samaritans from that town believed in him" (V. 39).

Jesus pursued us in love. Now we have the privilege of continuing His mission of carrying His good news into the world (MATTHEW 28:19–20). We don't need to worry about whether we'll do a perfect job. God will help us to walk with others to discover more of Him. It's what He's called us to do.

Anne Cetas, Our Daily Bread *author*

★ The topic of **DISCIPLE-MAKING** is discussed in the above feature article. Read more about sharing the good news with others in the devotions for **November 1, 9, 16** and **23**.

Go and make disciples of all nations.
[MATTHEW 28:19]

REACHING OTHERS FOR JESUS

A decade ago, they didn't know the name of Jesus. Hidden in the mountains of Mindanao in the Philippines, the Banwaon people had little contact with the outside world. A trip for supplies could take two days, requiring an arduous hike over rugged terrain. The world took no notice of them.

Then a mission group reached out, shuttling people in and out of the region via helicopter. This gained the Banwaon access to needed supplies, crucial medical help and an awareness of the larger world. It also introduced them to Jesus. Now, instead of singing to the spirits, they chant their traditional tribal songs with new words that praise the one true God. Mission Aviation established the critical link.

When Jesus returned to His heavenly Father, He gave His disciples these instructions: "Go and make disciples of all nations, baptising them in the name of the Father and of the Son and of the Holy Spirit" (MATTHEW 28:19). That command still stands.

Unreached people groups aren't limited to exotic locales we haven't heard of. Often, they live among us. Reaching the Banwaon people took creativity and resourcefulness, and it inspires us to find creative ways to overcome the barriers in our communities. That might include an 'inaccessible' group you haven't even considered—someone right in your neighbourhood. How might God use you to reach others for Jesus?   *TIM GUSTAFSON*

***Who are the hardest to reach people in your community?
In what ways can you tell them about Jesus?***

*Father, please use me as You see fit in order that _____
might turn to You in faith.*

Shout to God with cries of joy.
[PSALM 47:1]

RING THE BELL

After an astounding thirty rounds of radiation treatments, Darla was finally pronounced cancer-free. As part of hospital tradition, she was eager to ring the "cancer-free bell" that marked the end of her treatment and celebrated her clean bill of health. Darla was so enthusiastic and vigorous in her celebratory ringing that the rope actually detached from the bell! Peals of joyous laughter ensued.

Darla's story brings a smile to my face and gives me a sense of what the psalmist might have envisioned when he invited the Israelites to celebrate God's work in their lives. The writer encouraged them to "clap [their] hands," "shout to God" and "sing praises" because God had routed their enemies and chosen the Israelites as His beloved people (PSALM 47:1, 6).

God doesn't always grant us victory over our struggles in this life, whether health-related or financial or relational. He's worthy of our worship and praise in even those circumstances because we can trust that He's still "seated on his holy throne" (V. 8). When He does bring us to a place of healing—at least in a way we recognise in this earthly life—it's cause for great celebration. We may not have a physical bell to ring, but we can joyfully celebrate His goodness to us with the same kind of exuberance Darla showed. *KIRSTEN HOLMBERG*

***How do you show your gratitude to God? What good work
has He done in your life recently that merits celebration?***

*Thank You, God, for Your many gifts to me. I shout my praises to
You and clap my hands in celebration of Your work in my life.*

We can comfort those in any trouble with
the comfort we ourselves receive from God.
[2 CORINTHIANS 1:4]

COMFORT SHARED

When my daughter Hayley came to visit me, I saw her three-year-old son, Callum, wearing a strange piece of clothing. Called a ScratchMeNot, it's a long-sleeved top with mittens attached to the sleeves. My grandson Callum suffers from chronic eczema, a skin disease that makes his skin itch, making it rough and sore. "The ScratchMeNot prevents Callum from scratching and injuring his skin," Hayley explained.

Seven months later, Hayley's skin flared up and she couldn't stop scratching. "I now understand what Callum endures," Hayley confessed to me. "Maybe I should wear a ScratchMeNot!"

Hayley's situation reminded me of 2 Corinthians 1:3–5, in which Paul says that our God is "the God of all comfort, who comforts us in all our troubles, so that we can comfort those in any trouble with the comfort we ourselves receive from God. For just as we share abundantly in the sufferings of Christ, so also our comfort abounds through Christ."

Sometimes God allows us to go through trying times such as an illness, loss or crisis. He teaches us through our suffering to appreciate the greatest suffering that Christ went through on our behalf on the cross. In turn, when we rely on Him for comfort and strength, we're able to comfort and encourage others in their suffering. Let's reflect on who we can extend comfort because of what God has brought us through.   *GOH BEE LEE*

> **Who has God helped you to comfort through your own experiences of suffering? What can you do to help them appreciate Christ's suffering on the cross through their pain?**

God, help me to experience Your comfort in my sufferings and to become a source of comfort to others.

A generous person will prosper; whoever
refreshes others will be refreshed.
[PROVERBS 11:25]

RAINY DAYS

When small businesses in one small town were abruptly closed in an attempt to stop the spread of COVID-19, shop owners worried about how to care for their employees, how to pay their rent and how to simply survive the crisis. In response to their concerns, the pastor of a local church started an initiative to supply cash to struggling business owners.

"We don't feel like we can sit on a rainy-day fund when somebody else is going through a rainy day," the pastor explained, as he encouraged other churches in the area to join the effort.

A rainy-day fund is money that's put aside in case normal income is decreased for a time while regular operations need to continue. While it's natural for us to look out for ourselves first, Scripture encourages us to always look beyond our own needs, to find ways to serve others and to practise generosity. Proverbs 11 reminds us, "One person gives freely, yet gains even more," "a generous person will prosper" and "whoever refreshes others will be refreshed" (VV. 24–25).

Is the sun shining extra bright in your life today? Look around to see if there's torrential rain in someone else's world. The blessings God has graciously given you are multiplied when you freely share them with others. Being generous and open-handed is a wonderful way to give hope to others and to remind hurting people that God loves them.   *CINDY HESS KASPER*

> **When has someone been open-handed with their time
> or resources with you? How could you do the same for
> someone in need today?**
>
> *Gracious God, help me to be tender-hearted towards the
> needs of others and show me how I can share Your love and
> generosity with them.*

BIBLE IN A YEAR | JEREMIAH 32–33; HEBREWS 1

When I surveyed all that my hands had done and what I had toiled to achieve, everything was meaningless, a chasing after the wind.
[ECCLESIASTES 2:11]

FINDING JOY IN THE MEANINGLESS

In 2010, James Ward, the creator of the blog "I like Boring Things," launched a conference called the "Boring Conference." It's a one-day celebration of the mundane, the ordinary and the overlooked. In the past, speakers have addressed seemingly meaningless topics like sneezing, sounds that vending machines make and inkjet printers of 1999. Ward knows the topics may be boring, but the speakers can take a mundane subject and make it interesting, meaningful and even joyful.

Several millennia ago, Solomon, the wisest of kings, launched his own search for joy in the meaningless and mundane. He pursued work, bought flocks, built wealth, acquired singers and constructed buildings (ECCLESIASTES 2:4–9). Some of these pursuits were honourable and some were not. Ultimately, in his pursuit of meaning, the king found nothing but boredom (V. 11). Solomon maintained a worldview that didn't press beyond the limits of human experience to include God. Ultimately, however, he realised that he'd find joy in the mundane only when he remembered and worshipped God (12:1–7).

When we find ourselves in the whirlwind of tedium, let's launch our own daily mini-conference, as we "remember [our] Creator" (V. 1)—the God who fills the mundane with meaning. As we remember and worship Him, we'll find wonder in the ordinary, gratitude in the mundane and joy in the seemingly meaningless things of life.

MARVIN WILLIAMS

Why is it so hard to find meaning in things that can never satisfy? How do you need to reprioritise your commitment to and worship of God so you can find your meaning in Him?

God, take the unremarkable moments of my life and infuse them with Your joy and wonder.

Jesus called out with a loud voice, "Father,
into your hands I commit my spirit."
[LUKE 23:46]

A GLOSSARY FOR GRIEF

When Hugh and DeeDee released their only child to heaven, they struggled with what to call themselves in the aftermath. There is no specific word in the English language to describe a parent who has lost a child. A wife without her husband is a widow. A husband without his wife is a widower. A child bereft of parents is an orphan. A parent whose child has died is an undefined hollow of hurt.

Miscarriage. Sudden infant death. Suicide. Illness. Accident. Death steals a child from this world and then robs the surviving parents of an expressed identity.

Yet God Himself understands such devastating grief as His only Son, Jesus, called to Him while dying on the cross, "Father, into your hands I commit my spirit" (LUKE 23:46). God was Father before Jesus' earthly birth and remained Father when Jesus released His final breath. God continued as Father when the still body of His Son was laid in a tomb. God lives on today as Father of a risen Son who brings every parent the hope that a child can live again.

What do you call a heavenly Father who sacrifices His Son for the universe? For you and for me? Father. Still, Father. When there are no words in the glossary of grief to describe the pain of loss, God is our Father and calls us His children (1 JOHN 3:1). *ELISA MORGAN*

> **How does it shape your heart to realise that God remains
> your Father and calls you His child—always? How might this
> thought comfort you?**
>
> *Dear heavenly Father, thank You for being my Father
> and claiming me as Your child.*

Whatever you do, whether in word or deed,
do it all in the name of the Lord Jesus.
[COLOSSIANS 3:17]

THE JESUS LABEL

"Son, I don't have much to give you. But I do have a good name, so don't mess it up." Those wise, weighty words were uttered by Johnnie Bettis as his son Jerome left home for college. Jerome quoted his father in a speech he later made. These sage words that Jerome has carried with him throughout his life have been so influential that he closed his riveting speech with similar words to his own son. "Son, there's not much that I can give you that's more important than our good name."

A good name is vital for believers in Jesus. Paul's words in Colossians 3:12–17 remind us about who it is that we represent (V. 17). Character is like the clothing that we wear; and this passage puts the 'Jesus label' of clothing on display: "As God's chosen people . . . clothe yourselves with compassion, kindness, humility, gentleness and patience. Bear with each other and forgive one another. . . . And over all these virtues put on love" (VV. 12–14). These aren't just our 'Sunday clothes'. We're to wear them everywhere, all the time, as God works in us to reflect Him. When our lives are characterised by these qualities, we demonstrate that we have His name.

May we prayerfully and carefully represent Him as He provides what we need.   *ARTHUR JACKSON*

> *As you evaluate your wardrobe, how 'well dressed' with Jesus' character are you? How can you seek His wisdom, power and guidance to reflect Him even more clearly?*

> *Father, forgive me when I don't represent Jesus well. Give me strength and courage to be better dressed for Your glory and Christ's name's sake.*

Give praise to the LORD, proclaim his name;
make known among the nations what he has
done. [1 CHRONICLES 16:8]

SING PRAISE TO GOD

The heat and humidity of the summer closed in on us all week at the discipleship conference, but on the last day we welcomed a front of cooler air. Giving thanks for the break in weather and the amazing work God had done, hundreds joined voices to worship God. Many felt liberated to sing wholeheartedly before God, offering hearts, souls, bodies and minds to Him. As I think back to that day decades later, I'm reminded of the pure wonder and joy of praising God.

King David knew how to wholeheartedly worship God. He rejoiced when the ark of the covenant, which signified God's presence, was placed in Jerusalem—by dancing, leaping and celebrating (1 CHRONICLES 15:29). Even though his wife Michal observed his abandon and "despised him in her heart" (V. 29), David didn't let her criticism stop him from worshipping the one true God. Even if he appeared undignified, he wanted to give thanks to God for choosing him to lead the nation (SEE 2 SAMUEL 6:21–22).

David "appointed Asaph and his associates to give praise to the LORD in this manner: Give praise to the LORD, proclaim his name; make known among the nations what he has done. Sing to him, sing praise to him; tell of all his wonderful acts" (1 CHRONICLES 16:7–9). May we too give ourselves fully to worshipping God by pouring out our praise and adoration.   *AMY BOUCHER PYE*

When have you felt free to worship God wholeheartedly?
What led you to that sense of freedom and release?

Creator God, we proclaim Your name above all others.
You're worthy to be praised! We worship You!

I am the vine; you are the branches.
[JOHN 15:5]

A TRUE DISCIPLE OF JESUS

When Christian Mustad showed his Van Gogh landscape to art collector Auguste Pellerin, Pellerin took one look and said it wasn't authentic. Mustad hid the painting in his attic, where it remained for fifty years. Mustad died, and the painting was evaluated off and on over the next four decades. Each time it was determined to be a fake—until 2012, when an expert used a computer to count the thread separations in the painting's canvas. He discovered it had been cut from the same canvas as another work of Van Gogh. Mustad had owned a real Van Gogh all along.

Do you feel like a fake? Do you fear that if people examined you, they'd see how little you pray, give and serve? Are you tempted to hide in the attic, away from prying eyes?

Look deeper, beneath the colours and contours of your life. If you've turned from your own ways and put your faith in Jesus, then you and He belong to the same canvas. To use Jesus' picture, "I am the vine; you are the branches" (JOHN 15:5). Jesus and you form a seamless whole.

Resting in Jesus makes you a true disciple of His. It's also the only way to improve your picture. He said, "If you remain in me and I in you, you will bear much fruit; apart from me you can do nothing" (V. 5).　　　　　　　　　　　　　　　　　　　　*MIKE WITTMER*

> **What things cause you to wonder if you're a true disciple of Jesus? How might this fear drive you to Him?**
>
> *Jesus, I rest in You like a branch clings to its vine.*

I reserve seven thousand in Israel—all
whose knees have not bowed down to Baal.
[1 KINGS 19:18]

YOU'RE NOT ALONE

"**S**o great to see you!" "You, too!" "So glad you're here!"
The greetings were warm and welcoming. Members of a
church gathered online before their evening programme.
As their speaker, I watched silently as the others gathered on the
video call. As an introvert and not knowing anyone, I felt like a social
outsider. Then suddenly, a screen opened and there was my pastor.
Then another screen opened. A old church friend was joining the
call, too. Seeing them, I no longer felt alone. God, it seemed, had
sent support.

Elijah wasn't alone either, despite feeling like "the only [prophet]
left" after fleeing the wrath of Jezebel and Ahab (1 KINGS 19:10). Jour-
neying through desert wilderness for forty days and forty nights, Elijah
hid in a cave on Mount Horeb. But God called him back into service,
telling him, "Go back the way you came, and go to the Desert of
Damascus. When you get there, anoint Hazael king over Aram. Also,
anoint Jehu son of Nimshi king over Israel, and anoint Elisha son of
Shaphat from Abel Meholah to succeed you as prophet" (VV. 15-16).

God then assured him, "Yet I reserve seven thousand in Israel—all
whose knees have not bowed down to Baal and whose mouths have
not kissed him" (V. 18). As Elijah learned, while serving God we don't
serve alone. As God brings help, we'll serve together.

PATRICIA RAYBON

**What support has God recently sent when you were serving
Him? Whom could you invite to serve with you to grow your
ministry impact for God?**

*Dear God, when I feel alone while serving You, remind me
that others are with me as we joyfully serve.*

We tell you the good news: What God
promised our ancestors he has fulfilled for us.
[ACTS 13:32–33]

GOOD NEWS

n 1941, as Hitler's reign was expanding across Europe, novelist
John Steinbeck was asked to help with the war effort. He wasn't
asked to fight or visit troops on the frontline, but to instead write
a story. The result was *The Moon Is Down*, a novel about a peaceful
land that gets invaded by an evil regime. Printed on underground
presses and secretly distributed throughout occupied countries, the
novel sent a message: the Allies were coming, and by imitating the
novel's characters, readers could help secure their freedom. Through
The Moon Is Down, Steinbeck brought good news to people under
Nazi rule—their liberation was near.

Like the characters in Steinbeck's story, Jews in the first century
were an occupied people under brutal Roman rule. But centuries
before, God had promised to send an Ally to liberate them and bring
peace to the world (ISAIAH 11). Joy erupted when that Ally arrived!
"We tell you the good news," Paul said. "What God promised our
ancestors he has fulfilled for us . . . by raising up Jesus" (ACTS 13:32–33).
Through Jesus' resurrection and offer of forgiveness, the world's
restoration had begun (VV. 38–39; ROMANS 8:21).

Since then, *this* story has spread throughout the globe, bringing
peace and freedom wherever it's embraced. Jesus has been raised
from the dead. Our liberation from sin and evil has begun. In Him
we're free!   *SHERIDAN VOYSEY*

***Compared to other rulers, how does Jesus bring peace to
the world? How can you join Him in this work?***

Jesus, my ultimate Ally, I surrender to Your rightful rule.

Before a word is on my tongue you, LORD,
know it completely. [PSALM 139:4]

BEFORE YOU EVEN SAY IT

They were a master and a slave in ancient Rome. Yet surviving correspondence tells the story of a deep friendship and mutual respect that went beyond social rank. "Your services to me are beyond count," Cicero wrote to Tiro in 50 BC, "in my home and out of it, in Rome and abroad, in private affairs and public, in my studies and literary work."

Many historians believe that Marcus Tiro could write down the orator Cicero's words as fast as he spoke them. He created his own shorthand system to transcribe senate meetings quickly and accurately, which became an essential part of Cicero's political career.

On average we can speak around 130 words a minute, so Tiro's ability to hear, absorb and note them down at the same speed is incredible. Yet he's got nothing on God.

What could be better than someone hanging onto our every word? How about the One who perceives our thoughts from afar: "Before a word is on my tongue you, LORD, know it completely" (PSALM 139:4). The attention Tiro paid to his master's words was impressive, but the attention God gives to us is divine. God doesn't just hear us as we speak; amazingly, He's already at work answering our needs.

Today, may we give our words and our worries to the One who already knows them perfectly and whose hand is ready to guide us through them all (V. 10). *CHRIS WALE*

When do you struggle to believe that God hears your prayers? How does it encourage you that God listens to your heart, even before you give Him your words?

Thank You, Father, for Your loving attention towards me. I praise You because my prayers are precious to You, and because You promise Your answer is on the way, even before I speak!

Who shall separate us from the love of Christ?
Shall trouble or hardship or persecution or
famine or nakedness or danger or sword?
[ROMANS 8:35]

NOTHING CAN SEPARATE

When Pris' father, a pastor, answered God's call to pioneer a mission on a small island in Indonesia, Pris' family found themselves living in a rundown shack once used to house animals. Pris remembers the family celebrating Christmas sitting on the floor and singing praises while rainwater dripped through the thatched roof. But her father reminded her, "Pris, just because we are poor doesn't mean God doesn't love us."

Some may see a life blessed by God as one that's filled with riches, health and longevity. So in times of hardship, they may wonder if they're still loved by Him. But in Romans 8:31–39, Paul reminds us that nothing can separate us from Jesus' love—including trouble, hardship, persecution and famine (V. 35). This is the foundation for a truly blessed life: God showed His love for us by sending His Son Jesus to die for our sins (V. 32). Christ rose from death and is now sitting "at the right hand" of the Father, interceding for us (V. 34).

In times of suffering, we can hold fast to the comforting truth that our life is rooted in what Christ has done for us. Nothing—"neither death nor life . . . nor anything else in all creation" (VV. 38–39)—can separate us from His love. Whatever our circumstance, whatever our hardship, may we be reminded that God is with us and that nothing can separate us from Him.   *YOHANNA ANG*

> *How can you remind yourself that nothing can separate you from Jesus' love? How can knowing this truth change the way you respond to life's challenges?*

> *Heavenly Father, open my eyes and heart to understand more of Your love, and help me realise that Your love is enough for my life.*

You came near and stood at the foot of the mountain while it blazed with fire to the very heavens, with black clouds and deep darkness. [DEUTERONOMY 4:11]

POWERFUL AND LOVING

I n 2020, the Ecuadorian volcano Sangay erupted. The BBC described the "dark ash plume which reached a height of more than 12,000m." The discharge covered four provinces (about 198,000 acres) in grey ash and grimy soot. The sky turned dingy and grim, and the air was thick—making it difficult to breathe. Farmer Feliciano Inga described the unnerving scene to *El Comercio* newspaper: "We didn't know where all this dust was coming from. . . . We saw the sky go dark and grew afraid."

The Israelites experienced a similar fear at the base of Mount Sinai, as they "stood at the foot of the mountain while it blazed with fire . . . with black clouds and deep darkness" (DEUTERONOMY 4:11). God's voice thundered, and the people trembled. It was terrifying. It's an awesome, knee-buckling experience to encounter the living God.

"Then the LORD spoke," and they "heard the sound of words but saw no form" (V. 12). The voice that rattled their bones provided life and hope. God gave Israel the Ten Commandments and renewed His covenant with them. The voice from the dark cloud caused them to quake, but also wooed and loved them with tenacity (EXODUS 34:6–7).

God is powerful, beyond our reach, even startling. And yet He's also full of love, always reaching out to us. A God both powerful and loving—this is who we desperately need.   *WINN COLLIER*

***When has an encounter with God made you tremble?
How did He also communicate love?***

*God, at times I've approached You too casually, assumed
too much. Thank You for Your patience with me. And
thank You for Your love.*

One thing I ask from the LORD . . . that I may dwell in the house of the LORD all the days of my life. [PSALM 27:4]

LET ME STAY!

As they made their way towards their car, Zander escaped his mother's arms and made a mad dash back towards the church doors. He didn't want to leave! His mum ran after him and tried to lovingly wrangle her son so they could depart. When his mother finally scooped four-year-old Zander back into her embrace, he sobbed and reached longingly over her shoulder towards the church as they walked away.

Zander may merely have enjoyed playing with friends at church, but his enthusiasm is a picture of David's desire to worship God. Though he might have asked God to thwart his enemies for his own comfort and security, David wanted peace to prevail so that he could instead "gaze on the beauty of the LORD and to seek him in his temple" (PSALM 27:4). His heart's desire was to be with God—wherever He was—and to enjoy His presence. Israel's greatest king and military hero intended to use peacetime to "sing and make music to the LORD" (V. 6).

We can freely worship God anywhere, for He now dwells within us through faith in the person of the Holy Spirit (1 CORINTHIANS 3:16; EPHESIANS 3:17). May we yearn to spend our days in His presence and to gather corporately to worship Him with other believers. In God—not the walls of a building—we find our safety and our greatest joy.   *KIRSTEN HOLMBERG*

When have you experienced a passionate yearning to worship God? What keeps you from experiencing that more frequently?

Father, You're my delight and my joy. I long to worship You without distraction or interruption.

Jesus said . . . , "Don't be afraid; from now on
you will fish for people." [LUKE 5:10]

OUR TRUE IDENTITY

First, the man selected a tackle box. Standing in his town's small bait shop, he then filled a shopping basket with hooks, lures, bobbers, line and weights. Finally, he added live bait and selected a new rod and reel. "Ever fished before?" the shop owner asked. The man said no. "Better add this," said the owner. It was a first-aid kit. The man agreed and paid, then headed off to a day of not catching a thing—except snags on his fingers from his hooks and gear.

That wasn't Simon Peter's problem. An experienced fisherman, he was surprised one dawn when Jesus told him to push his boat into deep water and "let down the nets for a catch" (LUKE 5:4). Despite a long night of catching nothing, Simon and his crew let down their nets and "caught such a large number of fish that their nets began to break." In fact, his two boats started to sink from the haul (V. 6).

Seeing this, Simon Peter "fell at Jesus' knees," urging Him to "go away from me, Lord; I am a sinful man!" (V. 8). Jesus, however, knew Simon's true identity. He told His disciple, "From now on you will fish for people." Hearing that, Simon "left everything and followed" Christ (VV. 10–11). When we follow Him, He helps us learn who we are and what we're called to do as His own.   *PATRICIA RAYBON*

> **Outside of Christ, what's your identity or role in life? When you follow Him, how does your identity change?**
>
> *Father, when I struggle to know my true identity, remind me to follow You to discover in You my true self.*

You are precious and honoured in my sight
. . . I love you. [ISAIAH 43:4]

ACCEPTED AND APPROVED

As a child, Tenny felt insecure. He sought approval from his father, but he never received it. It seemed that whatever he did, whether in school or at home, it was never good enough. Even when he entered adulthood, the insecurity remained. He continually wondered, *Am I good enough?*

Only when Tenny received Jesus as his Saviour did he find the security and approval he'd long yearned for. He learned that God—having created him—loved and cherished him as His son. Tenny finally could live with the confidence that he was truly valued and appreciated.

In Isaiah 43:1–4, God told His chosen people that, having formed them, He would use His power and love to redeem them. "You are precious and honoured in my sight," He proclaimed. He would act on their behalf because He loved them (v. 4).

The value God places on those He loves doesn't come from anything we do, but from the simple and powerful truth that He's chosen us to be His own.

These words in Isaiah 43 not only gave Tenny great security, but also empowered him with the confidence to do his best for God in whatever task he was called to do. Today he's a pastor who does all he can to encourage others with this life-giving truth: we're accepted and approved in Jesus. May we confidently live out this truth today.

LESLIE KOH

How do you think God sees you? What does John 1:12 tell you about your relationship with Him? What comfort do you find in that knowledge?

Heavenly Father, I know You love me, accept me and cherish me. Thank You for adopting me as Your child and loving me without conditions.

By grace you have been saved, through faith.
[EPHESIANS 2:8]

GOD HEALS OUR BROKENNESS

Collin and his wife, Kate, wandered through the shop, looking for a picture to hang in their home. Collin thought he'd found just the right piece and called Kate over to see it. On the right side of the ceramic artwork was the word *grace*. But the left side held two long cracks. "Well, it's broken!" Kate said as she started looking for an unbroken one on the shelf. But then Collin said, "No. That's the point. We're broken and then grace comes in." They decided to purchase the one with the cracks. When they got to the checkout, the clerk exclaimed, "Oh, no, it's broken!" "Yes, so are we," Kate whispered.

What does it mean to be a broken person? Someone defined it this way: a growing awareness that no matter how hard we try, our ability to make life work gets worse instead of better. It's a recognition of our need for God and His intervention in our lives.

The apostle Paul talked about our brokenness in terms of being "dead in [our] transgressions and sins" (EPHESIANS 2:1). The answer to our need to be forgiven and changed comes in verses 4 and 5: "Because of his great love for us, God, who is rich in mercy, made us alive . . . [it] is by grace [we] have been saved."

God is willing to heal our brokenness with His grace when we admit, "I'm broken."   *ANNE CETAS*

What brought you to your need to ask God to heal your brokenness? How do you need Him today?

God, thank You for being rich in mercy towards me! May I boast in You and Your gift of salvation through grace by faith.

Because of the LORD's great love we are not
consumed . . . great is [His] faithfulness.
[LAMENTATIONS 3:22–23]

WHEN YOU CAN'T GO ON

In 2006, my dad was diagnosed with a neurological disease that robbed him of his memory, speech and control over body movements. He became bedridden in 2011 and continues to be cared for by my mum at home. The beginning of his illness was a dark time. I was fearful: I knew nothing about caring for a sick person, and I was anxious about finances and my mum's health.

The words of Lamentations 3:22 helped me get up many mornings when the light was as grey as the state of my heart: "Because of the LORD's great love we are not consumed." The Hebrew word for "consumed" means "to be used up completely" or "to come to an end."

God's great love enables us to go on, to get up to face the day. Our trials may feel overwhelming, but we won't be destroyed by them because God's love is far greater!

There are many times I can recount when God has shown His faithful, loving ways to my family. I saw His provision in the kindness of relatives and friends, the wise counsel of doctors, financial provision and the reminder in our hearts that—one day—my dad will be whole again in heaven.

If you're going through a dark time, don't lose hope. You will not be consumed by what you face. Keep trusting in God's faithful love and provision for you.   *KAREN HUANG*

In the midst of difficulty, where do you go for strength?
How can you remind yourself to trust in God's great love?

Father, help me to keep trusting You. Open my eyes so I can
see Your love and faithfulness.

The thief comes only to steal and kill and
destroy; I have come that they may have life,
and have it to the full. [JOHN 10:10]

HE FILLS THE EMPTY

Psychologist Madeline Levine noticed the fifteen-year-old girl's
'cutter disguise'—a long sleeve T-shirt pulled halfway over her
hand commonly used by people who engage in self-harm.
When the young girl pulled back her sleeve, Levine was startled to
find that the girl had used a razor to carve "empty" on her forearm.
She was saddened, but also grateful the teen was open to receiving
the serious help she desperately needed.

The teen in some way represents many people who've carved
"empty" on their hearts. John wrote that Jesus came to fill the
empty and to offer life "to the full" (JOHN 10:10). God placed the
desire for a full life in every human being, and He longs for people
to experience a loving relationship with Him. But He also warned
them that the "thief" would use people, things and circumstances
to attempt to ravage their lives (VV. 1, 10). The claims each made to
give life would be counterfeit and an imitation. In contrast, Jesus
offers what's true—"eternal life" and the promise that "no one will
snatch [us] out of [His] hand" (V. 28).

Only Jesus can fill the empty spaces in our hearts with life. If
you're feeling empty, call out to Him today. And if you're experiencing serious struggles, seek out godly counsel. Christ alone
provides life that's abundant and full—life full of meaning found
in Him.　　　　　　　　　　　　　　　　*MARVIN WILLIAMS*

> *In your search for significance and excitement, what
> kinds of things have left you disappointed? How has
> Jesus made your life full?*
>
> *Jesus, as I consider the full and abundant life You've
> provided for me, please help me resist turning from
> You to things I think will satisfy me.*

BIBLE IN A YEAR | EZEKIEL 14–15; JAMES 2

Let the morning bring me word of your unfailing love.
[PSALM 143:8]

LABRADOR ANGEL

I n 2019, Cap Dashwood and his sweet black Labrador companion, Chaela ("Chae" in memory of his Labrador who died; "la," Dashwood's abbreviation for "Labrador angel"), accomplished something remarkable: reaching a mountain summit each day for 365 consecutive days.

Dashwood has a moving story to tell. He left home at sixteen, explaining simply, "Bad family life." But these past wounds led him to find healing elsewhere. He explains, "Sometimes when you're disappointed by people, you turn to something else. You know?" For Dashwood, mountain climbing and the unconditional love of his black Labrador companion has been a big part of that "something else."

For those of us, like myself, who deeply love our animal companions, a big piece of why we do is the sweet, utterly unconditional love they pour out—a kind of love that's rare. But I like to think the love they effortlessly give points to a much greater and deeper reality than the failures of others—God's unshakable, boundless love upholding the universe.

In Psalm 143, as in many of his prayers, it's only David's faith in that unshakable, "unfailing love" (V. 12) that tethers him to hope in a time when he feels utterly alone. But a lifetime of walking with God gives him just enough strength to trust that the morning will "bring me word of your unfailing love" (V. 8).

Just enough hope to trust again and to let God lead the way to paths unknown (V. 8).   *MONICA LA ROSE*

What signs of God's unfailing, unending love do you see in the world around you? How have your experiences of the love of God through others or even animal companions given you renewed hope and courage?

Loving God, thank You for showing me how to believe in love and joy again. Help me to be a channel of that hope for others.

True worshippers will worship the Father in
the Spirit and in truth. [JOHN 4:23]

TRUE WORSHIPPERS

She finally had the chance to visit the church. Inside, in the deepest part of the basement, she reached the small cave or grotto. Candles filled the narrow space and hanging lamps illuminated a corner of the floor. There it was—a fourteen-pointed silver star, covering a raised bit of the marble floor. She was in Bethlehem's Grotto of the Nativity—the place marking the spot where according to tradition Christ was born. Yet the writer Annie Dillard felt less than impressed, realising God was much bigger than that spot.

Still, such places have always held great significance in our faith stories. Another such place is mentioned in the conversation between Jesus and the woman at the well—the mountain where her "ancestors worshipped" (JOHN 4:20), referring to Mount Gerizim (SEE DEUTERONOMY 11:29). It was sacred to the Samaritans, who contrasted it to the Jewish insistence that Jerusalem was where true worship occurred (V. 20). However, Jesus declared the time had arrived when worship was no longer specific to a place, but a Person: "the true worshippers will worship the Father in the Spirit and in truth" (V. 23). The woman declared her faith in the Messiah, but she didn't realise she was talking to Him. "Then Jesus declared, 'I, the one speaking to you—I am he'" (V. 26).

God isn't limited to any mountain or physical space. He's present with us everywhere. The true pilgrimage we make each day is to approach His throne as we boldly say, "Our Father," and He is there.

JOHN BLASE

***What difference does it make to you knowing that
God is spirit, always and ever present? What will
you praise Him for in this moment?***

*Father, thank You for Your constant presence no
matter where I am.*

I have hidden your word in my heart that I
might not sin against you. [PSALM 119:11]

SHARING HOPE

A s Emma shared how God helped her embrace her identity as
His beloved child, she weaved Scripture into our conversation.
I could barely figure out where the school student stopped
speaking *her* words and began quoting the words of *God*. When I
commended her for being like a walking Bible, her brow furrowed.
She hadn't been intentionally reciting Scripture verses. Through daily
reading of the Bible, the wisdom found in it had become a part of
Emma's everyday vocabulary. She rejoiced in God's constant presence
and enjoyed every opportunity He provided to share His truth with
others. But Emma isn't the first young person God has used to inspire
others to prayerfully read, memorise and apply Scripture.

When the apostle Paul encouraged Timothy to step into leadership,
he demonstrated confidence in this young man (1 TIMOTHY 4:11–16).
Paul acknowledged that Timothy was rooted in Scripture from infancy
(2 TIMOTHY 3:15). Like Paul, Timothy faced doubters. Still, both men lived
as if they believed all Scripture was "God-breathed." They recognised
Scripture was "useful for teaching, rebuking, correcting and training in
righteousness, so that the servant of God may be thoroughly equipped
for every good work" (VV. 16–17).

When we hide God's wisdom in our hearts, His truth and love can
pour into our conversations naturally. We can be like walking Bibles
sharing God's eternal hope wherever we go.   *XOCHITL DIXON*

> **How do you hide Scripture in your heart and mind?**
> **How has God's wisdom helped you share His truth**
> **with others?**
>
> *Father, saturate my heart with Your wisdom so I can*
> *share You with others naturally and courageously.*

Yes, my soul, find rest in God; my hope comes from him. [PSALM 62:5]

THE WILL OF GOD

God's will is sometimes hard to follow. He asks us to do the right things. He calls us to endure hardship without complaining; to love awkward people; to heed the voice inside us that says, *You mustn't*; to take steps we'd rather not take. So, we must tell our souls all day long: "Hey soul, listen up. Be silent: Do what Jesus is asking you to do."

"My soul waits in silence for God alone" (PSALM 62:1 NASB). "My soul, wait in silence for God alone" (62:5 NASB). The verses are similar, but different. David says something *about* his soul; then says something *to* his soul. "Waits in silence" addresses a decision, a settled state of mind. "Wait in silence" is David stirring his soul to remember that decision.

David determines to live in silence—quiet submission to God's will. This is our calling as well, the thing for which we were created. We'll be at peace when we've agreed: "Not my will, but yours be done" (LUKE 22:42). This is our first and highest calling when we make Him Lord and the source of our deepest pleasure. "I desire to do your will," the psalmist said (PSALM 40:8).

We must always ask for God's help, of course, for our "hope comes from him" (62:5). When we ask for His help, He delivers it. God never asks us to do anything He won't or can't do.   *DAVID H. ROPER*

When have you thought God's will for you was difficult? How can you live in quiet submission?

I may not always understand Your will, Father, but I ask for help to submit to it. Teach me to trust Your good and faithful character. Give me a submissive heart.

Devote yourselves to prayer, being watchful
and thankful. [COLOSSIANS 4:2]

A THANKFUL HEART

Seneca, the great philosopher of ancient Rome (4 BC–AD 65), was once accused by the empress Messalina of adultery. After the Senate sentenced Seneca to death, the emperor Claudius instead exiled him to Corsica, perhaps because he suspected the charge was false. This reprieve may have shaped Seneca's view of thankfulness when he wrote: "homicides, tyrants, thieves, adulterers, robbers, sacrilegious men and traitors there always will be, but worse than all these is the crime of ingratitude."

A contemporary of Seneca's, the apostle Paul, may have agreed. In Romans 1:21, he wrote that one of the triggers for the downward collapse of humankind was that they refused to give thanks to God. Writing to the church at Colossae, three times Paul challenged his fellow believers in Christ to gratitude. He said we should be "overflowing with thankfulness" (COLOSSIANS 2:7). As we let God's peace "rule in [our] hearts," we're to respond with thankfulness (3:15). In fact, gratitude ought to characterise our prayers (4:2).

God's great kindnesses to us remind us of one of life's great realities. He not only deserves our love and worship, He also deserves our thankful hearts. Everything that's good in life comes from Him (JAMES 1:17).

With all we've been given in Christ, gratitude should be as natural as breathing. May we respond to God's gracious gifts by expressing our gratitude to Him.   *BILL CROWDER*

> **What are some of the biggest, most enduring blessings you've received in life? What everyday blessings have you experienced that are often easy to forget?**

> *Loving Father, forgive me for the times I've taken You and Your blessings for granted. Create in me a thankful heart, so I'll honour and praise You for all You've done and are doing.*

The LORD is with you, mighty warrior.
[JUDGES 6:12]

MIGHTY WARRIOR

Diet Eman was an ordinary, shy young woman in the Netherlands—in love, working and enjoying time with family and friends—when the Germans invaded in 1940. As Diet (pronounced *Deet*) later wrote, "When there is danger on your doorstep, you want to act almost like an ostrich burying its head in the sand." Yet Diet felt God calling her to resist the German oppressors, which included risking her life to find hiding places for Jews and other pursued people. This unassuming young woman became a warrior for God.

We find many stories in the Bible similar to Diet's, stories of God using seemingly unlikely characters to serve Him. For instance, when the angel of the Lord approached Gideon, he proclaimed, "The LORD is with you, mighty warrior" (JUDGES 6:12). Yet Gideon seemed anything but mighty. He'd been secretly threshing wheat away from the prying eyes of the Midianites, who oppressively controlled Israel at the time (VV. 1–6, 11). He was from the weakest clan of Israel (Manasseh) and the "least" in his family (V. 15). He didn't feel up to God's calling and even requested *several* signs. Yet God used him to defeat the cruel Midianites (SEE CH. 7).

God saw Gideon as "mighty". And just as God was with and equipped Gideon, so God is with us, His "dearly loved children" (EPHESIANS 5:1)—supplying all we need to live for and serve Him in little and big ways.   *ALYSON KIEDA*

Who are some other Bible characters God used despite their weakness to accomplish much for Him? How has God moved you outside your comfort zone to serve Him?

God, I'm so thankful You don't see me as I see myself. Help me to see myself as Your dearly loved child capable of doing big and small things in service to You.

BIBLE IN A YEAR | EZEKIEL 27–29; 1 PETER 3

Salvation is found in no one else.
[ACTS 4:12]

BOLD FAITH

After Prem Pradhan's (1924–1998) plane was shot down during World War II, he was wounded while parachuting to safety. As a result, he walked with a limp for the rest of his life. He once noted, "I have a lame leg. Isn't it strange of God that He called [me] to preach the gospel in the Himalaya Mountains?" And preach in Nepal he did—but not without opposition that included imprisonment in "dungeons of death" where prisoners faced extreme conditions. In a span of fifteen years, Prem spent ten years in fourteen different prisons. His bold witness, however, bore the fruit of changed lives for Christ that included guards and prisoners who took the message of Jesus to their own people.

The apostle Peter faced opposition due to his faith in Jesus and for being used by God to heal a "man who was lame" (ACTS 4:9). But he used the opportunity to boldly speak for Christ (VV. 8–13).

Today, like Peter, we too may face opposition (V. 3), yet we have family members, co-workers, fellow students and others we know who desperately need to hear about the One in whom "salvation is found" (V. 12), who died as payment for our sins and was raised from the dead as proof of His power to forgive (V. 10). May they hear as we prayerfully and boldly proclaim this good news of salvation found in Jesus.   *ARTHUR JACKSON*

> **How will you boldly share Jesus today? What keeps you from telling others about Him? How can you be better prepared to do so?**
>
> *Father, thank You for what You've done for me. Help me, in Jesus' name, to boldly share my faith with others.*

Man is born to trouble as surely as sparks
fly upward. [JOB 5:7]

INSULT TO INJURY

During the Golden Age of radio, Fred Allen (1894–1956) used
comedic pessimism to bring smiles to a generation living in
the shadows of economic depression and a world at war.
His sense of humour was born out of personal pain. Having lost his
mother before he was three, he was later estranged from his father
who struggled with addictions. He once rescued a young boy from
the traffic of a busy street with a memorable, "What's the matter
with you, kid? Don't you want to grow up and have troubles?"

The life of Job unfolds in such troubled realism. When his early
expressions of faith eventually gave way to despair, his friends
multiplied his pain by adding insult to injury. With good sounding
arguments they insisted that if he could admit his wrongs (4:7–8) and
learn from God's correction, he would find strength to laugh in the
face of his problems (5:22).

Job's 'comforters' meant well while being so wrong (1:6–12). Never
could they have imagined that they would one day be invoked as
examples of "With friends like that, who needs enemies?" Never
could they have imagined the relief of Job praying for them, or why
they would need prayer at all (42:7–9). Never could they have imagined
how they foreshadowed the accusers of the One who suffered so
much misunderstanding to become the source of our greatest joys.

MART DEHAAN

**How have others misjudged you, and how did you feel?
When have you been critical of others whose pain you
didn't understand?**

*Father, like Job's friends, I'm inclined to assume that the
troubles of others are somehow deserved. Please help me live
this day in the Spirit of Your Son rather than in the words and
thoughts of the accuser.*

BIBLE IN A YEAR | EZEKIEL 33–34; 1 PETER 5

But even if he does not . . . we will not serve
your gods or worship the image of gold you
have set up. [DANIEL 3:18]

TRUSTING GOD IN OPPOSITION

Raised in a tribe in the Philippines opposed to belief in Christ,
Esther received salvation through Jesus after an aunt prayed
for her during Esther's battle with a life-threatening illness.
Today, Esther leads Bible studies in her local community in spite of
threats of violence and even death. She serves joyfully, saying, "I
can't stop telling people about Jesus because I've experienced the
power, love, goodness and faithfulness of God in my life."

Serving God in the face of opposition is a reality for many today
just as it was for Shadrach, Meshach and Abednego, three young
Israelites living in captivity in Babylon. In the book of Daniel, we
learn that they refused to pray to a large golden image of King Nebuchadnezzar even when threatened with death. The men testified
that God was capable of protecting them, but they chose to serve
Him "even if" He didn't rescue them (DANIEL 3:18). When they were
thrown into the fire, God actually joined them in their suffering
(V. 25). To everyone's amazement, they survived without even "a
hair of their heads singed" (V. 27).

If we face suffering or persecution for an act of faith, ancient and
modern examples remind us that God's Spirit is present with us to
strengthen and sustain us when we choose to obey Him, "even if"
things turn out differently than we hope.   *LISA M. SAMRA*

> ***What are some ways you've chosen to follow God
> "even if"? What are ways He's been with you?***
>
> *God, thank You for loving me so generously. Help me to
> follow You with joy even in the face of opposition.*

The people walking in darkness have seen
a great light. [ISAIAH 9:2]

A GREAT LIGHT

In 2018, twelve Thai boys and their football coach descended into a maze-like cave, intending to enjoy an afternoon adventure. Due to unexpected rising water that forced them deeper and deeper into the cavern, it was two-and-a-half weeks before rescuers led them out. Dive teams, thwarted by rising water, attempted the rescue as the boys sat on a small rock shelf with only six flickering flashlights. They spent hours in darkness, hoping that somehow light—and help—would break through.

The prophet Isaiah described a world of brooding darkness, one overrun by violence and greed, shattered by rebellion and anguish (ISAIAH 8:22). Nothing but ruin; hope's candle flickering and fading, sputtering before succumbing to dark nothingness. And yet, Isaiah insisted, this dim despair was not the end. Because of God's mercy, soon "there will be no more gloom for those who were in distress" (9:1). God would never abandon His people in shadowy ruin. The prophet announced hope for his people then and pointed to the time when Jesus would come to dispel the darkness sin has caused.

Jesus *has* come. And now we hear Isaiah's words with renewed meaning: "The people walking in darkness have a seen a great light," Isaiah says. "On those living in the land of deep darkness a light has dawned" (V. 2).

No matter how dark the night, no matter how despairing our circumstances, we're never forsaken in the dark. Jesus is here. A great Light shines.   *WINN COLLIER*

How are you prone to experience darkness and despair?
Consider this image of Jesus as the great light—how does
this light renew you with hope?

God, there's so much darkness. I fear sometimes that the
darkness will overwhelm me. Be my great light. Shine on me
with radiant love.

WARM HEARTS AND OPEN ARMS

The night air in Caracas, Venezuela, was warm and thick. The jammed streets smelled of *panaderies* (local bakeries), street food and petrol fumes. My friend and I arrived at the block of flats where we'd been invited for dinner, and a large, gregarious man with a smile as wide as a sunrise opened the door and embraced us.

We sat with his family at a long wooden table holding massive platters of beef, rice and plantain. My friend knew Spanish, but I could only listen as the others swapped stories and laughed. Sometimes they made gestures for me so I could try to follow along. Occasionally, my friend paused to offer a summary or to translate a question they'd posed. Though for hours I understood almost nothing, I never felt like an outsider. Just the opposite; their loving welcome enveloped me. I was in a city I'd never visited before, meeting people with a completely different history and ethnicity—and I couldn't even communicate. And yet, because they offered me warm hearts and open arms, I belonged.

Paul reminds us that if we believe in Jesus, we're called to always live out this kind of radical welcome. We're to "accept one another . . . just as Christ accepted [us]" (ROMANS 15:7). We're to welcome one another, to open our hearts wide and gather others in; this should be our posture *especially* towards those who are different from us. Paul addressed conflict between Jews and gentiles, but it's the same for any differences in ethnicity, social class or any supposed barrier. Cultural differences aren't primarily obstacles but rather opportunities to demonstrate the same radical welcome Jesus has already extended to us.

Winn Collier, Our Daily Bread *author*

★ The devotions for **December 1, 9, 16** and **23** address the topic of **LIVING IN A MULTICULTURAL WORLD**. We trust these articles will help and encourage you as you interact with those who you find to be 'different' in any way.

How good and pleasant it is when God's
people live together in unity! [PSALM 133:1]

CELEBRATING DIVERSITY

A
t the 2019 graduation ceremony at a university, 608 students prepared to receive their degrees. The principal began by asking students to stand when he read the name of the country where they were born: Afghanistan, Bolivia, Bosnia . . . . The principal kept going until he'd named sixty countries and every student was standing and cheering together. Sixty countries; one university.

The beauty of unity amid diversity was a powerful image that celebrated something near to God's heart—people living together in unity.

We read an encouragement for unity among God's people in Psalm 133, a psalm of ascent—a song sung as people entered Jerusalem for annual celebrations. The psalm reminded the people of the benefits of living harmoniously (V. 1) despite differences that could cause division. In vivid imagery, unity is described as refreshing dew (V. 3) and oil—used to anoint priests (EXODUS 29:7)—"running down" the head, beard and clothing of a priest (V. 2). Together, these images point to the reality that in unity God's blessings flow so lavishly they can't be contained.

For believers in Jesus, despite differences such as ethnicity, nationality or age, there's a deeper unity in the Spirit (EPHESIANS 4:3). When we stand together and celebrate that common bond as Jesus leads us, we can embrace our God-given differences and celebrate the source of true unity.   *LISA M. SAMRA*

**When have you experienced the goodness of unity in Christ?
How has it brought blessing?**

*Heavenly Father, help me to do my part to live in unity
with all of God's people.*

BIBLE IN A YEAR | EZEKIEL 40–41; 2 PETER 3   349

[Let us] not [give] up meeting together,
as some are in the habit of doing, but
[encourage] one another. [HEBREWS 10:25]

WE NEED OUR CHURCH COMMUNITY

I grew up the eldest son of a preacher. Every Sunday the expectation was clear: I was to be in church. Possible exceptions? Maybe if I had a significant fever. But the truth is, I absolutely loved going, and I even went a few times feverish. But the world has changed, and the numbers for regular church attendance are not what they used to be. Of course, the quick question is *why*? The answers are many and varied. Author Kathleen Norris counters those answers with a response she received from a pastor to the question, "Why do we go to church?" He said, "We go to church for other people. Because someone may need you there."

Now by no means is that the only reason we go to church, but his response does resonate with the heartbeat of the writer to the Hebrews. He urged the believers to persevere in the faith, and to achieve that goal he stressed "not giving up meeting together" (HEBREWS 10:25). Why? Because something vital would be missed in our absence: "encouraging one another" (V. 25). We need that mutual encouragement to "spur one another on towards love and good deeds" (V. 24).

Brothers and sisters, keep meeting together, because someone may need you there. And the corresponding truth is that you may need them as well.   *JOHN BLASE*

What are the top four reasons you either go to church or don't go? How does knowing "someone may need you there" make you feel about meeting together?

Heavenly Father, as I meet with others to worship and praise Your name, help me to also encourage others in Your name. Forgive me when I overlook the latter because I'm too preoccupied with myself.

See what great love the Father has lavished on
us, that we should be called children of God!
[1 JOHN 3:1]

TRUE IDENTITY

As my friend reviewed the pictures I took of her, she pointed out the physical characteristics she saw as imperfections. I asked her to look closer. "I see a beautiful and beloved daughter of the Almighty King of Kings," I said. "I see a compassionate lover of God and others, whose genuine kindness, generosity and faithfulness have made a difference in so many lives." When I noticed the tears brimming her eyes, I said, "I think you need a tiara!" Later that afternoon, we picked out the perfect crown for my friend so she would never forget her true identity.

When we come to know Jesus personally, He crowns us with love and calls us His children (1 JOHN 3:1). He gives us the power to persevere in faith so that "we may be confident and unashamed before him at his coming" (2:28). Though He accepts us as we are, His love purifies us and transforms us into His likeness (3:2–3). He helps us recognise our need for Him and repent as we rejoice in the power to turn away from sin (VV. 7–9). We can live in faithful obedience and love (V. 10), with His truth hidden in our hearts and His Spirit present in our lives.

My friend didn't really *need* a tiara or any other trinket that day. But we both needed the reminder of our worth as God's beloved children.

XOCHITL DIXON

**What personal faults and past failings have you allowed to
determine your identity? How can knowing you're loved,
chosen and crowned as God's child help you live in
righteousness and love?**

*Loving God, thank You for reminding me that who I am is
based on whose I am—Yours, simply Yours.*

Hezekiah turned his face to the wall and prayed to the LORD. [2 KINGS 20:2]

GENERATION NOW

"**N**ever trust anyone over thirty," said young environmentalist Jack Weinberg in 1964. His comment stereotyped an entire generation—something Weinberg later regretted. Looking back, he said, "Something I said off the top of my head . . . became completely distorted and misunderstood."

Have you heard disparaging comments aimed at millennials? Or vice versa? Ill thoughts directed from one generation towards another can cut both ways. Surely there's a better way.

Although he was an excellent king, Hezekiah showed a lack of concern for another generation. When, as a young man, Hezekiah was struck with a terminal illness (2 KINGS 20:1), he cried out to God for his life (VV. 2–3). God gave him fifteen more years (V. 6).

But when Hezekiah received the terrible news that his children would one day be taken captive, the royal tears were conspicuously absent (VV. 16–18). He thought, "Will there not be peace and security in my lifetime?" (V. 19). It may have been that Hezekiah didn't apply the passion he had for his own wellbeing to the next generation.

God calls us to a love that dares to cross the lines dividing us. The older generation needs the fresh idealism and creativity of the younger, who in turn can benefit from the wisdom and experience of their predecessors. This is no time for snarky comments and slogans but for a thoughtful exchange of ideas. We're in this together.

TIM GUSTAFSON

In what ways do you think you may have ignored or disrespected others from a different age group? How might you use the gifts God has given you to serve them?

Forgive me, Father, for not appreciating others in a stage of life different from mine.

We will tell the next generation the
praiseworthy deeds of the LORD, his power,
and the wonders he has done. [PSALM 78:4]

ILLUSTRATING SCRIPTURE

Decorative blue and white ceramic tiles commonly found in Dutch households were originally made in the city of Delft. They often depict familiar scenes of the Netherlands: beautiful landscapes, ubiquitous windmills, and people working and playing.

In the nineteenth century, Charles Dickens wrote in his book *A Christmas Carol* how these tiles were used to illustrate the Scriptures. He described an old fireplace built by a Dutchman paved with these quaint Delft tiles: "There were Cains and Abels, Pharaohs' daughters; Queens of Sheba, . . . [and] Apostles putting off to sea." Many households used these tiles as a teaching tool as the family gathered around the warmth of a fire and shared the stories of the Bible. They learned about God's character—His justice, compassion and mercy.

The truths of the Bible continue to be relevant today. Psalm 78 encourages us to teach the "hidden lessons from our past—stories we've heard and known, stories our ancestors handed down to us" (VV. 2–3 NLT). It goes on to instruct us to "tell the next generation the praiseworthy deeds of the LORD, his power, and the wonders he has done" and "they in turn [can] tell their children" (VV. 4, 6).

With God's help, we can find creative and effective ways to illustrate the truths of Scripture to each generation as we strive to give God the full honour and praise He deserves. *CINDY HESS KASPER*

In what ways can you illustrate the truths of the Bible to someone who's new to Scripture? Who needs to know about the "praiseworthy deeds of the LORD"?

Loving God, show me ways to illustrate what I've learned from Scripture so others may know of Your wonders.

Each of you should give what you have decided in your heart to give, not reluctantly or under compulsion, for God loves a cheerful giver. [2 CORINTHIANS 9:7]

CHEERFUL GIVER

Nicholas, who was born in the third century, had no idea that centuries after his death he would be known as Santa Claus. He was just a man who loved God and genuinely cared for people and who was known for giving cheerfully of his own possessions and doing kind deeds. The story is told that after learning of a family who was in great financial distress, Nicholas came to their home at night and threw a bag of gold through an open window, which landed in a shoe or stocking warming by the fireplace.

Long before Nicholas, the apostle Paul urged the believers in Corinth to be cheerful givers. He wrote to them about the great financial needs of their brothers and sisters in Jerusalem and encouraged them to give generously. Paul explained to them the benefits and blessings that come to those who give of their possessions. He reminded them that "whoever sows sparingly will also reap sparingly, and whoever sows generously will also reap generously" (2 CORINTHIANS 9:6). As a result of their cheerful generosity, they would be "enriched in every way" (V. 11), and God would be honoured.

Father, would You help us to be cheerful givers not only during this Christmas season but all year long? Thank You for Your incredible generosity in giving us Your "indescribable gift," Your Son, Jesus (V. 15).   *ESTERA PIROSCA ESCOBAR*

> ***Where do you see a need you could help with this week?***
> ***How could you give generously of your time or resources?***
>
> *Thank You, giving God, for encouraging me to be generous because in Your economy, generosity will bring the giver and the receiver abundant blessings.*

The Lord himself will give you a sign: The
virgin will conceive and give birth to a son,
and will call him Immanuel. [ISAIAH 7:14]

THE PERFECT NAME

On a hot and humid day one August, my wife gave birth to our second son. But he remained nameless as we struggled to settle on a given name. After spending many hours in ice cream shops and taking long car rides, we still couldn't decide. He was simply "Baby Williams" for three days before finally being named Micah.

Choosing the right name can be a little frustrating. Well, unless you're God, who came up with the perfect name for the One who would change things forever. Through the prophet Isaiah, God directed King Ahaz to ask Him "for a sign" to strengthen his faith (ISAIAH 7:10–11). Though the king refused to ask for a sign, God gave him one anyway: "The virgin will conceive and give birth to a son, and will call him Immanuel" (V. 14). God named the child, and He would be a sign of hope to people going through despair. The name stuck and Matthew breathed new meaning into it when he wrote the narrative of Jesus' birth (MATTHEW 1:23). Jesus would be "Immanuel." He wouldn't just be a representative of God, but He would be God in the flesh, coming to rescue His people from the despair of sin.

God gave us a sign. The sign is a Son. The Son's name is Immanuel—*God with us*. It's a name that reflects His presence and love. Today, He invites us to embrace Immanuel and know that He's with us.

MARVIN WILLIAMS

**What keeps you from believing that God can breathe new
life into your dark times and desperate circumstances?
How will you embrace Jesus as Immanuel this week?**

*Heavenly Father, thank You for Immanuel—Jesus, Your Son.
May I rejoice in His presence and love today.*

BIBLE IN A YEAR | DANIEL 5–7; 2 JOHN

Keep the unity of the Spirit through the bond
of peace. [EPHESIANS 4:3]

STAY TOGETHER

Dewberry Baptist Church split in the 1800s over a chicken leg. Various versions of the story exist, but the account told by a current member was that two men fought over the last drumstick at a church lunch. One man said God wanted him to have it. The other replied God didn't care, and he really wanted it. The men became so furious that one moved a couple kilometres down the road and started Dewberry Baptist Church #2. Thankfully, the churches have settled their differences, and everyone concedes the reason for their split was ridiculous.

Jesus agrees. The night before His death Jesus prayed for His followers. May they "be one, Father, just as you are in me and I am in you." May they "be brought to complete unity. Then the world will know that you sent me" (JOHN 17:21–23).

Paul agrees. He urges us to "make every effort to keep the unity of the Spirit through the bond of peace. There is one body and one Spirit" (EPHESIANS 4:3–4), and these cannot be divided.

We who weep for Christ's body broken for our sin must not tear apart His body, the church, with our anger, gossip and cliques. Better to let ourselves be wronged than be guilty of the scandal of church division. Give the other guy the chicken leg—and some pie too!

MIKE WITTMER

What have you done to contribute to the unity of your church? What else might you do?

Heavenly Father, help me do the best I can to be at peace with others. May I never separate what You've joined.

Before me was a great multitude that no one
could count, from every nation, tribe, people
and language. [REVELATION 7:9]

A GREAT MULTITUDE

We came together for our Sunday morning church service
with joy and anticipation. Although we were spatially
distanced because of the coronavirus pandemic, we welcomed the opportunity to celebrate Gavin and Tijana's wedding.
Our technologically-gifted Iranian friends broadcast the service to
friends and family spread out geographically—including in Spain,
Poland and Serbia. This creative approach helped us overcome the
constraints as we rejoiced in the covenant of marriage. God's Spirit
united us and gave us joy.

That Sunday morning with our wonderfully multinational congregation was a small taste of the glory to come when people from "every
nation, tribe, people and language" will stand before God in heaven
(REVELATION 7:9). The beloved disciple John glimpsed this "great multitude" in a vision he recounts in the book of Revelation. There those
gathered will worship God together along with the angels and elders:
"Praise and glory and wisdom and thanks and honour and power and
strength be to our God for ever and ever" (V. 12).

The union and marriage of Jesus and His international bride in
the "wedding supper of the Lamb" (19:9) will be an amazing time
of worship and celebration. Our experience at our Sunday church
service with people from many nations points to this celebration
that one day we'll enjoy.

While we wait in hope for that joyful event, we can embrace the
practice of feasting and rejoicing among God's people. *AMY BOUCHER PYE*

**How do you picture the wedding supper of the Lamb? How does
being invited to this celebration affect you in your daily life?**

*Lamb of God, You take away the sin of the world—and my sin.
Thank You for the invitation to the heavenly wedding.*

I will bring Judah and Israel back from captivity and will rebuild them as they were before. [JEREMIAH 33:7]

RESTORED

ears filled her eyes as Rose retold her late husband's story. As a child in 1938, Jim had needed to flee his home country and move to England, leaving his family behind. He'd kept a battered box for what he called his family's "treasures". The box looked beyond repair. Yet the team at the BBC's The Repair Shop spent hours cleaning, fixing and restoring it back to its original state. When they showed it to her, Rose gasped, "I don't believe it. While I've got that, I've always got Jim."

Restoration was also an important part of God's message to His people in Jerusalem when they continued ignoring His Law and refusing His love. Babylon's army was approaching as an act of God against their wickedness (JEREMIAH 33:5). Yet that wasn't the end of the story. Through His faithful prophet Jeremiah, God promised: "I will bring Judah and Israel back from captivity and will rebuild them as they were before" (V. 7).

As they were before. Forgiven. At peace. Restored. That's still God's desire for His people. We may feel in a state of disrepair, like Jim's box, but that's not the end of our story. God is at work restoring us, drawing us closer into His loving care and transforming our hearts. As we see "all the good things he has done" for us, we can keep bringing Him the "joy, praise and honour" He deserves (V. 9).

CHRIS WALE

Where have you seen God restore and rebuild parts of your life? In what areas do you still need to seek His restorative touch?

Heavenly Father, thank You that I am a masterpiece of Your patience and grace. Please bring Your restoration to every part of my life and my heart so that I might give You praise!

I command you to be openhanded towards your fellow Israelites who are poor and needy in your land. [DEUTERONOMY 15:11]

CARING FOR THOSE IN NEED

Evan Summers answered the door to find Sally, a frail woman who stopped by regularly to ask for empty cans to return for cash. This money was her primary source of income. Evan got an idea. "Could you show me where you sleep?" he asked. Sally led him to a narrow patch of dirt about two feet wide next to a house. Moved by compassion, Summers built her a small house—a simple shelter that provided space for her to sleep safely. Summers ran with the idea. He started a GoFundMe page and teamed with local churches to provide land to build more shelters for others who were homeless.

Throughout the Bible, God's people are reminded to care for those in need. When God spoke through Moses to prepare the Israelites to enter the promised land, He encouraged them to "be openhearted and freely lend [to the poor] whatever they need" (DEUTERONOMY 15:8). This passage also noted that "there will always be poor people in the land" (V. 11). We don't have to go far to see this is true. As God compassionately called the Israelites "to be openhanded towards your fellow Israelites" (V. 11), we too can find ways to help those in need.

Everyone needs food, shelter, and water. Even if we don't have much, may God guide us to use what we do have to help others. Whether it's sharing a sandwich or a warm winter coat, small things can make a big difference!   *JULIE SCHWAB*

Who do you know who needs help today?
What can you do to help?

Jesus, please help me to find ways I can help those around me. Please give me a generous heart.

I resolved to know nothing while I was with
you except Jesus Christ and him crucified.
[1 CORINTHIANS 2:2]

HEROES, TYRANTS AND JESUS

Beethoven was angry. He'd intended to name his Third Symphony
"The Bonaparte." In an age of religious and political tyranny,
he saw Napoleon as a hero of the people and champion of
freedom. But when the French general declared himself emperor,
the celebrated composer changed his mind. Denouncing his former
hero as a rascal and tyrant, he rubbed so hard to erase Bonaparte's
name that he left a hole in the original score.

Early believers in Jesus must have been disappointed when their
hopes of political reform were dashed. He'd stirred hopes of life
without the tyranny of Caesar's heavy-handed taxes and military
presence. Yet, decades later, Rome still ruled the world. Jesus'
messengers were left with fears and weakness. His disciples were
marked by immaturity and infighting (1 CORINTHIANS 1:11–12; 3:1–3.)

But there was a difference. Paul saw beyond what remained
unchanged. His letters began, ended, and overflowed with the
name of Christ. Christ resurrected. Christ with a promise to return
in power. Christ in judgement of everything and everyone. First and
foremost, however, Paul wanted believers in Jesus to be grounded
in the meaning and implications of Him crucified (2:2; 13:1–13).

The love expressed in Jesus' sacrifice made Him a different kind
of leader. As Lord and Saviour of the world, His cross changes
everything. The name of Jesus will forever be known and praised
above every name.   *MART DEHAAN*

How is Jesus different from other leaders?
Can you identify with Paul's weakness and fear?
How does Jesus help you with that?

Father, please help me to see Your heart in the
sacrifice of Your Son.

The LORD longs to be gracious to you
. . . . Blessed are all who wait for him!
[ISAIAH 30:18]

A WORTHWHILE WAIT

Stuck in a stressful job with long hours and an unreasonable boss, James wished he could quit. But he had a mortgage, a wife and a young child to take care of. He was tempted to resign anyway, but his wife reminded him: "Let's hang on and see what God will give us."

Many months later, their prayers were answered. James found a new job that he enjoyed and gave him more time with the family. "Those months were long," he told me, "but I'm glad I waited for God's plan to unfold in His time."

Waiting for God's help in the midst of trouble is hard; it can be tempting to try to find our own solution first. The Israelites did just that: under threat from their enemies, they sought help from Egypt instead of turning to God (ISAIAH 30:2). But God told them that if they would repent and put their trust in Him, they would find strength and salvation (V. 15). In fact, He added, "the LORD longs to be gracious to you" (V. 18).

Waiting for God takes faith and patience. But when we see His answer at the end of it all, we'll realise it was worth it: "Blessed are all who wait for him!" (V. 18). And what's even more amazing, God is waiting for us to come to Him!

LESLIE KOH

> **What prayer request has you waiting on God?
> How can you meditate on His faithfulness as you
> seek His answer?**
>
> *Father, give me the patience to wait for Your
> answer. I know You're a good and loving God
> whose timing and will are always perfect.*

I prayed to the God of heaven, and I
answered the king. [NEHEMIAH 2:4–5]

WHAT SHOULD I SAY?

When I stopped to browse through a box of books marked
"C. S. Lewis" at a second-hand bookshop, the shop owner appeared. As we chatted about the available titles, I
wondered if he might be interested in the faith that inspired much
of Lewis' writing. I prayed silently for guidance. Information from a
biography came to mind, and we began to discuss how C. S. Lewis'
character pointed to God. In the end, I was thankful that a quick
prayer had reoriented our conversation to spiritual matters.

Nehemiah paused to pray before a pivotal moment in a conversation
with King Artaxerxes in Persia. The king had asked how he could help
Nehemiah, who was distraught over Jerusalem's destruction. Nehemiah
was the king's servant and therefore in no position to ask for favours,
but he needed one—a big one. He wanted to restore Jerusalem. So,
he "prayed to the God of heaven" before asking to leave his job so
he could re-establish the city (NEHEMIAH 2:4–5). The king consented
and even agreed to help Nehemiah make travel arrangements and
procure timber for the project.

The Bible encourages us to pray "on all occasions with all kinds
of prayers and requests" (EPHESIANS 6:18). This includes moments
when we need courage, self-control or sensitivity. Praying before
we speak helps us give God control of our attitude and our words.

How might He want to direct your words today? Ask Him and find
out!

JENNIFER BENSON SCHULDT

> ***What patterns of speech do you need God's help to
> change? What situations in your life could benefit
> most from prayer?***

> *Dear God, I surrender my words to You. Use them for Your
> glory. Help them to inspire and encourage others.*

The eye cannot say to the hand, "I don't need you!" [1 CORINTHIANS 12:21]

I AM HIS HANDS

Jia Haixia lost his sight in the year 2000. His friend Jia Wenqi lost his arms as a child. But they've found a way around their disabilities. "I am his hands and he is my eyes," Haixia says. Together, they're transforming their village in China.

Since 2002 the friends have been on a mission to regenerate a wasteland near their home. Each day Haixia climbs on Wenqi's back to cross a river to the site. Wenqi then 'hands' Haixia a shovel with his foot, before Haixia places a pail on a pole between Wenqi's cheek and shoulder. And as one digs and the other waters, the two plant trees—more than 10,000 so far. "Working together, we don't feel disabled at all," Haixia says. "We're a team."

The apostle Paul likens the church to a body, each part needing the other to function. If the church were all eyes, there'd be no hearing; if all ears, there'd be no sense of smell (1 CORINTHIANS 12:14–17). "The eye cannot say to the hand, 'I don't need you!' " Paul says (V. 21). Each of us plays a role in the church based on our spiritual gifts (VV. 7–11, 18). Like Jia Haixia and Jia Wenqi, when we combine our strengths, we can bring change to the world.

Two men combining their abilities to regenerate a wasteland. What a picture of the church in action!   *SHERIDAN VOYSEY*

Based on your spiritual gifts, what part do you play in the body of Christ? How are you joining with others to fulfil His mission?

Holy Spirit, thank You for giving me spiritual gifts and arranging me in a body where I'm needed.

In Christ Jesus you are all children of God
through faith. [GALATIANS 3:26]

WHAT ARE YOU?

When I walked into the ice cream shop with my five-year-old
biracial son, the man behind the counter glanced at me
and stared at my child. "What are you?"

His question and harsh tone triggered the all-too-familiar anger
and heartache I'd experienced growing up as a mixed-race person
who didn't fit stereotypes. Pulling Xavier closer, I turned towards
my black husband as he entered the store. With eyes narrowed, the
shop assistant completed our order in silence.

I prayed silently for the man as my son listed the flavours of ice
cream he wanted to try. Repenting of my bitterness, I asked God to
give me a spirit of forgiveness. With my light-but-not-white complex-
ion, I'd been the target of similar glares accompanying that same
question over the years. I'd struggled with insecurities and feelings
of worthlessness until I began learning how to embrace my identity
as God's beloved daughter.

The apostle Paul declares that believers in Jesus are "all children
of God through faith," equally valued and beautifully diverse. We're
intimately connected and intentionally designed to work together
(GALATIANS 3:26–29). When God sent His Son to redeem us, we became
family through His blood shed on the cross for the forgiveness of our
sins (4:4–7). As God's image-bearers, our worth cannot be determined
by the opinions, expectations or biases of others.

What are we? We're children of God.　　　　　　*XOCHITL DIXON*

> **When have you doubted your value as a person due to
> the opinions, expectations or biases of others? How does
> knowing all God's children are His image-bearers help you
> love those who are different from you?**

> *Father God, please help me to see myself and others through
> Your eyes. Help me love with Your heart as I come into
> contact with people who are different from me.*

　　BIBLE IN A YEAR | AMOS 4–6; REVELATION 7

I am forgotten as though I were dead; I have
become like broken pottery. [PSALM 31:12]

BEAUTIFULLY BROKEN

Our bus finally arrived at our much-anticipated destination—an
archaeological dig in Israel where we would actually do some
excavation work of our own. The site's director explained that
anything we might unearth had been untouched for thousands of
years. Digging up broken shards of pottery, we felt as though we
were touching history. After an extended time, we were led to a
workstation where those broken pieces—from huge vases shattered
long, long ago—were being put back together.

The picture was crystal clear. Those artisans reconstructing cen-
turies-old broken pottery were a beautiful representation of the
God who loves to fix broken things. In Psalm 31:12, David wrote,
"I am forgotten as though I were dead; I have become like broken
pottery." Though no occasion is given for the writing of this psalm,
David's life difficulties often found voice in his laments—just like
this one. The song describes him as being broken down by danger,
enemies and despair.

So, where did he turn for help? In verse 16, David cries out to God,
"Let your face shine on your servant; save me in your unfailing love."

The God who was the object of David's trust is the same One who
still fixes broken things today. All He asks is that we call out to Him
and trust in His unfailing love.   *BILL CROWDER*

What areas of brokenness have you experienced?
How has God helped you through those difficult times?

God of my help, I thank You for all the times I've fallen and
been broken—times when You've put me back together.

I have fought the good fight, I have
finished the race, I have kept the faith.
[2 TIMOTHY 4:7]

WELL DONE!

The school where my son Brian teaches football lost a key game
in a hard-fought battle. Their opponent was undefeated over
the past two years. I sent Brian a text to commiserate with
him and received a terse reply: "Kids battled!"

None of the teachers shamed the players after the game. No one
shouted at them for their mishaps or bad decisions along the way.
No, the teachers showered the young players with praise for what
could be praised.

Along the same vein, it's good to know that believers in Jesus will
not hear harsh words of condemnation from Him. When Christ comes
and we stand before Him, He won't shame us. He'll see what we've
done as we've followed Him (2 CORINTHIANS 5:10; EPHESIANS 6:8). I think
He'll say something like, "You battled! Well done!" The apostle Paul
testified that he had "fought the good fight" and looked forward to
being welcomed by God (2 TIMOTHY 4:7–8).

Life is a relentless struggle with a fierce, unyielding foe devoted
to our destruction. He will resist every effort we make to be like
Jesus and to love others. There'll be a few good wins and some
heart-breaking losses—God knows—but there will be no eternal
condemnation for those in Jesus (ROMANS 8:1). If we stand before
Him in the merits of God's Son, each one will "receive [his] praise"
from God (1 CORINTHIANS 4:5).　　　　　　　　　*DAVID H. ROPER*

> **Does the thought of standing before God fill you with
> dread or delight? What would make the difference?**
>
> *Thank You, God, for the promise that because I have
> Jesus as my Saviour, I'll never be condemned.*

Then God remembered Rachel; he listened to her. [GENESIS 30:22]

REMEMBERED IN PRAYER

I n the church the pastor fell to his knees, praying to God, "Remember us!" As the pastor pleaded, the congregation responded, crying, "Remember us, Lord!" Watching this moment on YouTube, I was surprised that I shed tears too. The prayer was recorded months earlier. Yet it recalled childhood times when I heard our family's pastor make the same plea to God. "Remember us, Lord!"

Hearing that prayer as a child, I'd wrongly assumed that God sometimes forgets about us. But God is all-knowing (PSALM 147:5; 1 JOHN 3:20), He always sees us (PSALM 33:13–15), and He loves us beyond measure (EPHESIANS 3:17–19).

Even more, as we see in the Hebrew word *zakar,* meaning "remember," when God "remembers" us, He acts for us. *Zakar* also means to act on a person's behalf. Thus, when God "remembered" Noah and "all the wild animals and the livestock that were with him in the ark," He then "sent a wind over the earth, and the waters receded" (GENESIS 8:1). When God "remembered" barren Rachel, He "listened to her and enabled her to conceive. She became pregnant and gave birth to a son" (30:22–23).

What a great plea of trust to ask God in prayer to remember us! He'll decide how He answers. We can pray knowing, however, that our humble request asks God to move.   *PATRICIA RAYBON*

> *In what area of your life do you need God to remember you? How willing are you to pray with such intent and purpose?*
>
> *Dear heavenly Father, grow my understanding of Your remembrance of me. Then, where I need You to act, please remember me.*

Do not be afraid . . . a Saviour has been
born to you. [LUKE 2:10–11]

FEAR NOT

Linus, in the *Peanuts* comic strip, is best known for his blue security blanket. He carries it everywhere and isn't embarrassed at needing it for comfort. His sister Lucy especially dislikes the blanket and often tries to get rid of it. She buries it, makes it into a kite and uses it for a science fair project. Linus too knows he should be less dependent on his blanket and lets it go from time to time, always to take it back.

In the movie *A Charlie Brown Christmas,* when a frustrated Charlie Brown asks, "Isn't there anyone who knows what Christmas is all about?" Linus, with his security blanket in hand, steps centre stage and quotes Luke 2:8–14. In the middle of his recitation, as he says, "Fear not," he drops his blanket—the thing he clung to when afraid.

What is it about Christmas that reminds us we don't need to fear? The angels that appeared to the shepherds said, "Do not be afraid . . . a Saviour has been born to you" (LUKE 2:10–11).

Jesus is "God with us" (MATTHEW 1:23). We have His very presence through His Holy Spirit, the true Comforter (JOHN 14:16), so we don't need to fear. We can let go of our 'security blankets' and trust in Him.   *ANNE CETAS*

> **What are you afraid of? How can the Holy Spirit's
> presence help you with what troubles you?**
>
> *I'm still learning, God, that You're the greatest
> Comforter. Help me to let go of the things that give me
> false security, and please guide me to cling to You.*

Your word is a lamp for my feet, a light on my path. [PSALM 119:105]

GOD'S COMPASS

During World War II, Waldemar Semenov was serving as a junior engineer aboard the SS *Alcoa Guide* when a German submarine surfaced and opened fire on the ship. The ship was hit, caught fire and began to sink. Semenov and his crew lowered a lifeboat into the water and used the vessel's compass to sail towards the shipping lanes. After three days, a patrol plane spotted their lifeboat and the USS *Broome* rescued the men the next day. Thanks to that compass, Semenov and twenty-six other crewmembers were saved.

The psalmist reminded God's people that they were equipped with a compass for life—the Bible. He compared Scripture to "a lamp" (PSALM 119:105) that provides light to illuminate the path of life for those pursuing God. When the psalmist was adrift in the chaotic waters of life, he knew God could use Scripture to provide spiritual longitude and latitude and help him survive. Thus, he prayed that God would send out His light to direct him in life and bring him safely to the port of His holy presence (43:3).

As believers in Jesus, when we lose our way, God can guide us by the Holy Spirit and by the direction found in the Scriptures. May God transform our hearts and minds as we read the Bible, study it, and follow its wisdom.   *MARVIN WILLIAMS*

> *How have you experienced a particular verse or*
> *passage as a compass for your life in recent days?*
> *When are you tempted not to follow the directions*
> *the compass of Scripture gives?*

> *Jesus, thank You that when I'm tempted to drift away,*
> *the wisdom of Scripture helps bring me back.*

Though I am absent from you in body, I am present with you in spirit. [COLOSSIANS 2:5]

VIRTUAL PRESENCE

As the novel coronavirus marched across the globe, health experts advised increased physical distance between people as a means to slow the spread. Many countries asked their citizens to self-quarantine. Organisations sent employees home to work remotely if they could, while others suffered a financially debilitating loss of employment. Like others, I participated in church and small-group meetings through digital platforms. As a world, we practised new forms of togetherness despite being physically disconnected.

It isn't just the internet that lets us maintain a sense of connection. We connect to one another as members of the body of Christ through the Spirit. Paul expressed this notion centuries ago in his letter to the Colossians. Though he hadn't personally founded their church, he cared deeply for them and their faith. And even though Paul couldn't be with them in person, he reminded them that he was "present with [them] in spirit" (COLOSSIANS 2:5).

We can't always be with those we love for financial, health or other practical reasons, and technology can help fill that gap. Yet any form of virtual connection pales in comparison to the togetherness we can experience as fellow members of the body of Christ (1 CORINTHIANS 12:27). In such moments, we can, like Paul, rejoice in one another's firmness of faith and, through prayer, encourage each other to fully "know the mystery of God, namely, Christ" (COLOSSIANS 2:2).

KIRSTEN HOLMBERG

How have you experienced a sense of connection with other members of the body of Christ? Who needs your prayers of encouragement today?

Jesus, thank You for being with me even when no other person can be physically present. Thank You for the connection You give me to others through the Holy Spirit.

The disciples were called Christians first at
Antioch. [ACTS 11:26]

HOW THEY'LL KNOW

"The Gathering" in northern Thailand is an interdenominational, international church. On a recent Sunday, believers in Jesus from Korea, Ghana, Pakistan, China, Bangladesh, the US, the Philippines and other countries came together in a humble, thread-worn hotel conference room. They sang "In Christ Alone" and "I Am a Child of God," lyrics that were especially poignant in that setting.

No one brings people together like Jesus does. He's been doing it from the start. In the first century, Antioch contained eighteen different ethnic groups, each living in its own part of the city. When believers first came to Antioch, they spread the word about Jesus "only among Jews" (ACTS 11:19). That wasn't God's plan for the church, however. Others soon came who "began to speak to Greeks [gentiles] also, telling them the good news about the Lord Jesus," and "a great number of people believed and turned to the Lord" (VV. 20–21). People in the city noticed that Jesus was healing centuries of animosity between Jews and Greeks, and they declared this multi-ethnic church should be called "Christians," or "little Christs" (V. 26).

It can be challenging for us to reach across ethnic, social and economic boundaries to embrace those different from us. But this difficulty is our opportunity. If it wasn't hard, we wouldn't need Jesus to do it. And few would notice we're following Him.　*MIKE WITTMER*

> *Why is it so challenging for you to reach out to those*
> *who are different from you? What has Jesus provided*
> *to help you do so?*
>
> *Jesus, may they know I'm a Christian by Your love.*

And he will be called Wonderful Counsellor,
Mighty God, Everlasting Father, Prince of
Peace. [ISAIAH 9:6]

THE PRINCE OF PEACE

When John's cold turned into pneumonia, he ended up in the hospital. At the same time, his mother was being treated for cancer a few floors above him, and he felt overwhelmed with worries about her and about his own health. Then on Christmas Eve, when the radio played the carol "O Holy Night," John was flooded with a deep sense of God's peace. He listened to the words about it being the night of the dear Saviour's birth: "A thrill of hope the weary soul rejoices, for yonder breaks a new and glorious morn!" In that moment, his worries about himself and his mother vanished.

This "dear Saviour" born to us, Jesus, is the "Prince of Peace," as Isaiah prophesied (ISAIAH 9:6). Jesus fulfilled this prophecy when He came to earth as a baby, bringing light and salvation to "those living in the land of the shadow of death" (MATTHEW 4:16; SEE ISAIAH 9:2). He embodies and gives peace to those He loves, even when they face hardship and death.

There in the hospital, John experienced the peace that passes all understanding (PHILIPPIANS 4:7) as he pondered the birth of Jesus. This encounter with God strengthened his faith and sense of gratitude as he lay in that sterile room away from his family at Christmas. May we too receive God's gift of peace and hope.   AMY BOUCHER PYE

> **How have you experienced God's peace in the midst of a
> difficult situation? Which aspect of God in Isaiah 9:6 do
> you most need today? Why?**
>
> *God of peace, when I'm anxious and fretting about many
> things, help me to turn to You and receive Your gift of peace.*

*He made himself nothing by taking the very
nature of a servant, being made in human
likeness.* [PHILIPPIANS 2:7]

CHRISTMAS CHILD

Imagine the One who made cedars spring from seeds starting
life over as an embryo; the One who made the stars submitting
Himself to a womb; the One who fills the heavens becoming
what would be in our day a mere dot on an ultrasound. Jesus, in
very nature God, making Himself nothing (PHILIPPIANS 2:6–7). What
an astonishing thought!

Imagine the scene as He's born in a plain peasant village,
among shepherds and angels and bright lights in the sky, with the
bleating of animals His first lullabies. Watch as He grows in favour
and stature: as a youngster, astounding teachers with answers to
grand questions; as a young man at the Jordan, getting His Father's
approval from heaven; and in the wilderness, as He wrestles in
hunger and prayer.

Watch next as He launches His world-changing mission—healing
the sick, touching lepers, forgiving the impure. Watch as He kneels in
a garden in anguish and as they arrest Him while His closest friends
flee. Watch as He is spat on and nailed to two wooden posts, the
world's sins on His shoulders. But watch, yes watch, as the stone
rolls away, an empty tomb ringing hollow, because He is alive!

Watch as He is lifted to the highest place (V. 9). Watch as His name
fills heaven and earth (VV. 10–11).

This Maker of the stars who became a dot on an ultrasound. This,
our Christmas Child.   *SHERIDAN VOYSEY*

**What would life and history be like had Jesus
never been born? What prayer or poem can you
offer God to thank Him?**

*Jesus, thank You for making Yourself nothing
so I could be forgiven.*

BIBLE IN A YEAR | ZEPHANIAH 1–3; REVELATION 16

Settle matters quickly with your adversary.
[MATTHEW 5:25]

TIMELY RESOLUTION

The unresolved hurt between Simon and Geoffrey had persisted for years, and Simon's attempts to re-enter the friendship had been resisted. Upon hearing the news of the death of Geoffrey's mother, Simon travelled "up country" in Kenya to attend her funeral service. Simon reflected on their encounter: "I had no expectations at all in terms of how the whole thing would turn out, [but] after the service, we opened up and had a fruitful talk. We hugged, shared the moment, prayed together and planned to meet again." If only Simon and Geoffrey had been able to reconcile earlier, so much ongoing pain could have been avoided.

The words of Jesus in Matthew 5:21–26 help to put unresolved relational tensions in perspective. The anger that can lead to such rifts is a serious matter (V. 22). Furthermore, getting things in order relationally is a fitting prelude to worshipping God (VV. 23–24). The wise words of Jesus to "settle matters quickly with your adversary" (V. 25) remind us that the sooner we do what we can to work towards reconciliation the better for all.

Relationships are risky; they demand work—in our families, in the workplace, in educational settings, and among people who share our faith in Christ. But as those who represent Him, the "Prince of Peace" (ISAIAH 9:6), may we find ourselves going out of our way to extend our hearts and hands to those with whom we have unresolved conflict.   *ARTHUR JACKSON*

*Who comes to mind when you think of someone you need
to reach out to so that relational healing might begin?
What's keeping you from doing so?*

*Father, You know where the relational fissures are in my life.
Forgive me for my slowness to attempt resolution. Give me
the strength to take the next steps.*

I am the LORD your God who takes hold of
your right hand and says to you, Do not
fear; I will help you. [ISAIAH 41:13]

GOD'S RIGHT HAND

helped my elderly dog, Wilson, out to the grass and in the process,
I released the leash of our younger dog, Coach, for just a minute.
As I bent to pick up Coach's lead, he spied a bunny. Off he went,
ripping the leash from my right hand and corkscrewing my ring finger
in the process. I fell to the grass and cried out in pain.

After returning from hospital and learning I'd need surgery, I begged
God for help. "I'm a writer! How will I type? What about my daily
duties?" As God sometimes does, He spoke to me from my daily
Bible reading. "For I am the LORD your God who takes hold of your
right hand and says to you, Do not fear; I will help you" (ISAIAH 41:13).
I scanned the context, which indicated that God's people in Judah,
to whom Isaiah was communicating His message, enjoyed a special
relationship with Him. He promised His presence, strength and help
through His own righteous standing, symbolised by His right hand
(V. 10). Elsewhere in Scripture, God's right hand is used to secure
victories for His people (PSALM 17:7; 98:1).

During my weeks of recovery, I experienced encouragement from
God as I learned to dictate on my computer and trained my left
hand in household and grooming functions. From God's righteous
right hand to our broken and needy right hands, God promises to
be with us and to help us.   *ELISA MORGAN*

**How do you need God's help today? How have
you experienced His help in the past?**

*Healing God, I need Your help! Please use Your
righteous right hand to take hold of my broken,
weary hands and help me, I pray.*

Always [give] thanks to God the Father
for everything. [EPHESIANS 5:20]

"THANK YOU!"

As I hand the items I'm buying to the cashier I say, "Thank you." She takes them and replies, "Thank you." As she tells me the total she says, "Thank you." I tap my card and mumble another, "Thank you." Receipts, bags of shopping and exiting require two or three more "thank yous" before we're done.

This repeated thanking of one another is an endearing part of British culture. But it's also a mark of the culture of God's kingdom. The Apostle Paul wrote, "always [give] thanks to God the Father for everything" (EPHESIANS 5:20).

Most of us probably thank God for His blessings—the extraordinary and maybe even the mundane. But what about when life is hard and the blessings seem to have dried up? The word "everything" means that we can adopt an attitude of thankfulness towards God even in difficult times.

Christian thankfulness isn't just about being polite; it comes from being "filled with the Spirit" and joyfully united with other believers (VV. 18–19). Our thankfulness shows we draw close to our Father in all circumstances, living, "not as unwise, but as wise people" (V. 15).

We may not always feel thankful for every circumstance we encounter in this dark world (VV. 8–11), but we can thank God that He is always with us—through His Spirit and His church. When we do, joyful songs will flow out of our hearts. *DEBBI FRALICK*

In what ways have you experienced the joyful and transformative power of being thankful towards God? How can you incorporate a spirit of gratitude into your life, even when you don't feel particularly thankful?

Heavenly Father, please teach me the joy of being thankful. May I experience the wisdom of a life lived in gratitude for all You have done for me.

Whoever lives in love lives in God, and God in them. This is how love is made complete among us. [1 JOHN 4:16–17]

LEARNING TO LOVE

C olin, brought up apart from his family, didn't know what love was. He said, "I knew what rejection was. I knew what bitterness was. I think from that early age I learned how to hate."

Colin left school, bought a motorbike and joined various gangs. "I was doing the things they did: the drinking, the drugs, the violence . . . I had an edge over everyone else, because I hated."

At that dark time in his life, Colin embodied John's words: "Whoever does not love does not know God, because God is love" (1 JOHN 4:8). Only after Colin gave his life to Jesus did he begin to understand love.

Of course, not everyone will feel as unable to love as Colin. Yet the true extent of love can only be experienced when we live in union with God (V. 16). As Colin learned, love shows itself in sacrificial action for the good of others (V. 9); it's defined by Jesus who became "an atoning sacrifice for our sins" (V. 10).

Transformed by Jesus' sacrificial love, Colin has dedicated his life to serving others, sharing his faith in maximum security prisons and helping launch the Biker's Church in the UK. He's discovered one of the greatest joys of God's love: it's not just something we receive, but something we live. That's when God's love is "made complete among us" (V. 17). *CHRIS WALE*

> **How has your understanding and experience of love deepened since you gave your life to Christ? Who can you show His sacrificial love to today?**

> *Heavenly Father, thank You that You are love. All You are and all that You do reveal love's true nature. Reveal Your love through me today I pray.*

He guides me along the right paths.
[PSALM 23:3]

THE RIGHT PATHS

Six ducks waddled up the hill into the woods behind our home in the Lake District. Moments later, a ruckus of squawking and quacking brought five ducks scrambling back down the hill. They'd met a hungry fox. To my amazement, just a few hours later I saw the five ducks waddling back up that hill. Dashing outside, I rounded them up and led them to safety.

Psalm 23 shows that we have a similar relationship with God; He is our Shepherd and we are His sheep. Sheep, like ducks, are not famous for their wisdom or clear sense of direction. As with them, left to ourselves, we are prone to wander to places that seem good to us, but may actually hold hungry foxes.

The psalmist writes that the Good Shepherd always "guides me along the right paths" (PSALM 23:3). As we listen to His voice and follow where He leads, He provides our souls with good, nourishing refreshment (V. 3). Even when He takes us "through the darkest valley", His presence is the comfort and reassurance we need (V. 4).

Ducks, sheep, people—they all can find it hard to stick to the right paths. Just as I had to steer those ducks, Jesus takes the responsibility to guide us. We don't have to figure everything out for ourselves; we need only to stay close to our Good Shepherd.   *DEBBI FRALICK*

What decisions do you face at the moment? How can you keep putting your trust in your Good Shepherd to lead you, rather than trying to figure things out for yourself?

Lord, thank you for being the Good Shepherd who leads me in goodness and love all the days of my life. Please help me to trust You to take me along the right paths and to stay close to me.

Our citizenship is in heaven. And we
eagerly await a Saviour from there,
the Lord Jesus Christ. [PHILIPPIANS 3:20]

ONE DAY CLOSER TO CHRISTMAS

"I can't believe Christmas is over," my dejected daughter said.
I know how she feels: The aftermath of Christmas can
feel dreary. Presents have been opened. The tree and lights
must come down. Listless January—and, for many, the need to shed
holiday pounds—awaits. Christmas—and the breathless anticipation
that comes with it—suddenly feels eons away.

A few years ago, as we were putting Christmas stuff away, I realised:
*no matter what the calendar says, we're always one day closer to
the next Christmas.* It's become something I say frequently.

But far more important than our temporal celebration of Christmas
is the spiritual reality behind it: the salvation Jesus brought into our
world and our hope for His return. Scripture talks repeatedly about
watching, waiting and longing for Christ's second coming. I love what
Paul says in Philippians 3:15–21. He contrasts the world's way of
living—with "mind[s] set on earthly things" (V. 19)—with a lifestyle
shaped by hope in Jesus' return: "Our citizenship is in heaven. And
we eagerly await a Saviour from there, the Lord Jesus Christ" (V. 20).

The reality that our "citizenship is in heaven" changes everything,
including what we hope for and how we live. That hope is fortified
by the knowledge that with every passing day, we're indeed one
day closer to Jesus' return.   *ADAM R. HOLZ*

> *What are some of the things you hope for in this world?*
> *How do you think your hope in Jesus influences and affects*
> *the earthly things you long and hope for?*

> *Father, thank You for the hope that I have in Jesus and in His*
> *return. When lesser hopes compete for my heart's affection*
> *and attention, help me to lift my eyes to You.*

Our Daily Bread Ministries

In 1938, our ministry started with a radio programme called the Detroit Bible Class. Since then, our audience has grown from a small group of dedicated radio listeners to millions of people around the world who use our Bible-based resources. Over the years, our focus has remained the same: reaching out to people all around the world with the message of God's love.

Our Daily Bread Ministries is a non-denominational, non-profit organisation with staff and volunteers in over 37 offices working together to distribute more than 60 million resources annually in 150 countries. Regardless of whether it's a radio broadcast, DVD, podcast, book, mobile app or website, we provide materials to help people grow in their relationship with God.

Our Daily Bread Publishing

Our Daily Bread Publishing was founded in 1988 as an extension of Our Daily Bread Ministries. Our goal is to produce resources that feed the soul with the Word of God, and we do this through books, music, video, audio, software, greeting cards and downloadable content. All our materials focus on the never-changing truths of Scripture, so everything we produce shows reverence for God and His wisdom, demonstrates the relevance of vibrant faith, and equips and encourages people in their everyday lives.

❀ OUR DAILY BREAD MINISTRIES OFFICES

Europe Offices

For information on our resources, visit **odb.org**. Alternatively, please contact the office nearest you from the list below, or go to **ourdailybread.org/locations** for the complete list of offices.

BELARUS

Our Daily Bread Ministries, PO Box 82, Minsk, Belarus 220107
belarus@odb.org, (375-17) 2854657, (375-29) 9168799

GERMANY

Our Daily Bread Ministries e.V., Schulstraße 42, 79540 Lörrach
deutsch@odb.org, +49 (0) 7621 9511135

IRELAND

Our Daily Bread Ministries, 64 Baggot Street Lower, Dublin 2, D02 XC62
ireland@odb.org, +353 (0) 1676 7315

RUSSIA

MISSION Our Daily Bread, PO Box "Our Daily Bread",
str.Vokzalnaya 2, Smolensk, Russia 214961
russia@odb.org, +8(4812)660849, +7(951)7028049

UKRAINE

Christian Mission Our Daily Bread, PO Box 533, Kiev, Ukraine 01004
ukraine@odb.org, +380964407374, +380632112446

UNITED KINGDOM (EUROPE REGIONAL OFFICE)

Our Daily Bread Ministries, PO Box 1, Millhead, Carnforth, LA5 9ES
europe@odb.org, +44 (0) 15395 64149

ourdailybread.org

TOPIC INDEX

JANUARY – DECEMBER 2023

Abuse .... Jan. 12

Addiction .... June 18; Sept. 16

Ageing .... Feb. 18

Apologetics .... May 1,9,16,23

Bible, authority .... Mar. 2,8,15,22;
Aug. 17; Sept. 11,13; Dec. 21

Bible, inspiration .... Mar. 15

Bible, study .. Feb. 11; June 16; July 10;
Sept. 1; Oct. 21; Nov. 23; Dec. 5

Caregiving .... Feb. 18; June 5

Christ, birth .... Dec. 6,7,24,25

Christ, death .. Feb. 14; Apr. 7; Dec. 12

Christ, deity .... Mar. 4

Christ, life and teaching .... Feb. 8;
Mar. 27

Christ, names .... Dec. 7,24

Christ, resurrection .. Jan. 22; Feb. 14;
Apr. 9; Nov. 11

Christ, return .... Mar. 26; June 6;
Aug. 28; Oct. 3; Dec. 31

Christ, Saviour/Messiah .. Jan. 14,15;
Mar. 25; Apr. 2; Aug. 29;
Dec. 12,18,24,25

Christian celebrations .... Aug. 19

Christianity & culture . Dec. 1,9,16,23

Church life & unity .... Apr. 6; June 12;
July 23,29; Sept. 10;
Dec. 2,4,8,15,22,23

Conflict & Confrontation ..... Jan. 10;
Mar. 20; Apr. 1, 21; June 12; Dec. 26

Contentment .... June 30; July 30

Creation ..... Jan. 20; Mar. 9,16; May 9

Death .... Oct. 5,31

Depression .... Mar. 14,16; May 6

Despair .... Sept. 25

Discipleship .... Aug. 10; Nov 1,9,16,23

Encouragement ...... Apr. 22; Aug. 13;
Sept. 18; Oct. 6; Nov. 3; Dec. 2

Enemies .... Apr. 23

Eternal life .... Feb. 12; Mar. 26;
May 14,22; Sept. 12; Oct. 31;
Nov. 20; Dec. 18

Evangelism .... Jan. 4,22; Feb. 6,23;
Mar. 24; Apr. 17,30; June 13,24;
July 5; Aug. 11,31; Sept. 16; Oct. 26;
Nov. 1,27; Dec. 14

Faith ... Apr. 16; May 1,9,16,23; July 31;
Aug. 26; Oct. 10,14; Nov. 18

False teachers .... Mar. 25

Family of God .... August 1,9,16,23

Fear .... Jan. 17,30; Apr. 19;
May 21,26; June 28; Dec. 20

Fellowship with God .... July 8, 13;
Dec. 9

Forgiveness of sin .... Jan. 27; Feb. 12;
Mar. 13,21; April 1,9,16; May 16,18;
July 13; Sept. 12; Oct. 20; Nov. 18